35

Nixon, Ford
and the Abandonment
of South Vietnam

D1713628

Nixon, Ford and the Abandonment of South Vietnam

by J. EDWARD LEE
and H.C. "TOBY" HAYNSWORTH

McFarland & Company, Inc., Publishers
Jefferson, North Carolina, and London

Library of Congress Cataloguing-in-Publication Data

Lee, J. Edward, 1953–
    Nixon, Ford, and the abandonment of South Vietnam / by
J. Edward Lee and H.C. "Toby" Haynsworth.
      p.   cm.
    Includes bibliographical references and index.
    ISBN 0-7864-1302-6 (softcover : 50# alkaline paper) ∞
    1. Vietnamese Conflict, 1961–1975 — United States.   2. Ford,
Gerald R., 1913–   3. Nixon, Richard M. (Richard Milhous), 1913–
I. Haynsworth, Toby. II. Title.
DS558.L394   2002
959.704'31— dc21   2002003341

British Library cataloguing data are available

©2002 J. Edward Lee and H.C. "Toby" Haynsworth. All rights reserved

*No part of this book may be reproduced or transmitted in any form
or by any means, electronic or mechanical, including photocopying
or recording, or by any information storage and retrieval system,
without permission in writing from the publisher.*

On the cover: Refugees at the United States embassy, Saigon, April 29,
1975

Manufactured in the United States of America

McFarland & Company, Inc., Publishers
  Box 611, Jefferson, North Carolina 28640
   www.mcfarlandpub.com

For Lea, Elizabeth, and Mary Beth —J.E.L.

To the members of the Saigon Mission Association and all of the others, military and civilian, American and Vietnamese, who risked their lives to help save hundreds of thousands of refugees from imprisonment or death.—H.C.H.

Acknowledgments

This fresh look at America's presence in Southeast Asia would have been impossible without the assistance and encouragement of many people. The Saigon Mission Association, an organization composed of the last Americans to leave Vietnam and their Vietnamese colleagues and friends, provided invaluable help beginning in 1994. This group wanted a fresh study of the war and its members fully shared their thoughts and documents with us. They opened many doors for us, and we ventured forth.

The last two American commanders, General John Murray and General Homer Smith, who witnessed the death throes of South Vietnam, spoke candidly with us on several occasions. Also helpful in providing a military perspective was General Smith's executive officer, General James Piner, and several other members of the Defense Attaché Office staff. Adding civilian views were Sally Vinyard, John Guffey, and Rosalie Redmond. They — and the others listed in the bibliography — believed in the objectivity of our project, and we thank them.

Students enrolled in "America at War," a graduate history course at Winthrop University, reacted to our research and offered the enthusiasm of students who have only read about the war. One of these graduate students, Jacqueline Lukich, shared her Marine father's memories of the war in 1967 and 1968, as America's involvement reached its apogee. We commend these students, especially Jackie, for their assistance.

As always, our spouses, Ann Lee and Martha Haynsworth, allowed us to immerse ourselves in topics like Watergate, détente, and Operation Frequent Wind. Ann and Martha are acknowledged for their unwavering support of our research.

Contents

Introduction

"It sets the example, which will enable all future Presidents to bring about a state of things, in which Congress shall be forced without deliberation or reflection, to declare war, however opposed to its convictions of justice and expediency."

Senator John C. Calhoun, upon President James K. Polk's
request for war with Mexico, 1846.

War and politics are violently symbiotic, ripping each other apart in a frenzy. Some presidents, as commander in chief, can find themselves wounded by unpopular wars that erode public confidence. Other presidents, more fortunate, earn for themselves places of honor, respect, and the adulation of a grateful nation. Since the founding of the Republic, presidents have ordered troops into battle on more than 250 separate occasions, in locations as widespread as Tripoli, the Halls of Montezuma, Inchon, and the Caribbean island of Grenada. War has been formally declared on only five of these occasions: the 1812 conflict with our former mother country, the 1846 clash with Mexico when President James K. Polk announced "American blood was spilled on American soil," the "splendid little war" with Spain, World War I, and World War II. These uses of military force were, for the most part, widely supported by the American people, and those men in the White House — James Madison (1812), James K. Polk (1846), William McKinley (1898), Woodrow Wilson (1917), and Franklin D. Roosevelt (1941) — escaped with their reputations relatively unscathed. Historians have been kind to these chief executives. The Mexican War's Polk continues to rise in the rankings compiled by the historians. He accomplished what he set out to do: avenge the soldiers who, he

1

argued, had been attacked in the disputed area between the Nueces and
Rio Grande rivers. FDR has a fitting tribute on the corridor of monuments
in the nation's capital. He mastered the economic demons of his era, and
subdued Adolph Hitler, Benito Mussolini, and the brutal Japanese. While
he did not live to see the end of World War II, he earned the laurels of
presidential greatness and a permanent place in the hearts of a grateful people.[1]

Despite the fact that America's Civil War was never formally declared,
the Union's commander in chief, Abraham Lincoln, settled for all time the
questions of liberty in America and secession. His four-year search for the
right generals to defeat the South ultimately ended in success. Generals
William T. Sherman and Ulysses S. Grant saw to that. Under Lincoln's tute-
lage, the Civil War became more than an effort to mend "a house divided";
it became a crusade to bestow freedom upon those Americans held in
bondage by the Confederacy. Therefore, Lincoln sits majestically in his
marble temple, acknowledged worldwide as the champion of basic human
dignity. His administration reminded us that we were a nation, indeed,
"conceived in liberty," and that no state dare attempt to leave the Union.[2]

On the last day of April 2000, the twenty-fifth anniversary of another
conflict that ended quite differently, war and politics intertwined at the
site of the Vietnam Memorial. In the distance, granite tributes to great
presidents remind us of some of these earlier wars and earlier commanders. The warning of George Washington's farewell address is especially
poignant: "It is our true policy to steer clear of permanent alliances with
any portion of the foreign world." Washington, whom Virginia's Henry
Lee eulogized as "first in war, first in peace, first in the hearts of his coun-
trymen," advised us to carefully steer clear of permanent forays into costly
foreign conflicts. Washington, in his time, was speaking of the war between
Great Britain and France, a clash that he deemed to be of no strategic
importance, and full of pitfalls, for the young nation that he had led to
independence.[3]

As the sun rose on April 30, 2000, Thomas Jefferson stood majestically
in his memorial. Jefferson, who sent the U.S.S. *Constitution* to do battle
with the Barbary pirates in 1803, spoke often of the things worth fighting
for: "life, liberty, and the pursuit of happiness." These were simple values
but they were (and are) cherished by the American people. We have fought
for them in the past, and we will again in the future, if the need arises.
Middle Eastern pirates simply could not be permitted to harass our citizens. While his administration was plagued by political battles with the
Congress and the media, Jefferson could take solace in the fact that he left
office without seeing the country embroiled in the foreign conflict between

On the 25th anniversary of the end of the Vietnam War, a rose has been placed at the memorial in Washington, D.C., April 30, 2000. *Courtesy of J. Edward Lee.*

Great Britain and France. He was inclined to favor all things French, but he had the good judgment to avoid sending American troops to faraway places to aid our former ally in its clash with England. By and large, he heeded George Washington's advice.[4]

The dark granite memorial to those 58,200 Americans who lost their lives in Southeast Asia stands in stark contrast to the monuments honoring Washington, Jefferson, and Lincoln. America's longest war, which was being commemorated on that spring morning, summons forth images of failed presidencies. Lyndon Johnson, assuming office under such sad circumstances in 1963, saw his dreams of a Great Society turned to nightmares. Vietnam would quickly become "Johnson's War." He would fail, with a troop commitment of more than 500,000 military personnel and billions of dollars spent, both in Asia and in the impoverished neighborhoods within our own borders. Unlike Lincoln, LBJ would not be able to outwit his political foes. Richard Nixon, who was elected in 1968 to "bring us together," saw his goal of "peace with honor" in Vietnam swept away by the torrents of Watergate, the 1973 war in the Middle East, a preoccupation with China and the Soviet Union, a weakened economy, and his ultimate disgraceful exit from the White House. The unelected Gerald Ford was tainted almost immediately by his pardon of Nixon. A war-weary and economically threatened American public accepted Ford's assessment that Vietnam was "finished." Congress squeezed the life from our ally. Before it was pronounced dead, South Vietnam was interred, buried alive, abandoned.[5]

There will be no magnificent monuments to the manipulative Johnson, the distracted Nixon, or the impotent Ford. Their presidencies will be judged by an unpopular war governed by domestic political forces that they could not conquer. Cynicism replaced idealism. Partisanship eclipsed what Lincoln called "the better angels of our nature." Those people assembled at the Vietnam Memorial on April 30, 2000, recalled the fury of a war, and its politics, that will deny those three presidents the admiration of a grateful populace — an undeclared war that ripped the United States apart and led to the abandonment of South Vietnam.

Chapter 1

The Worst Day

"In times of war, it is the women who pay the supreme price. The women and the children."
— U.S. Representative Jeanette Rankin,
voting against World Wars I and II, 1917 and 1941.

Standing in an early morning dew, on the twenty-fifth anniversary of the evacuation of Americans from Saigon, Major General Homer E. Smith, the last defense attaché, spoke of the events of April 1975. Smith, a logistician, commanded the small contingent of uniformed military and civilian personnel that made up the staff of the Defense Attaché Office in South Vietnam that April. His role, unlike the role of earlier generals such as William Westmoreland and Creighton Abrams, was to preside over the bitter end of America's presence in Southeast Asia. Where Westmoreland had asked for — and received — from Lyndon Johnson more troops and supplies until in excess of 500,000 military personnel were "in country," Smith was limited to fifty uniformed servicemen, 1,200 American civilians, and several thousand Vietnamese employees.[1] Additionally, the political mood in the United States had changed radically. Johnson had been driven from office, and his Democratic Party had imploded in the streets of Chicago at the 1968 convention. His successor, Richard Nixon, had likewise forfeited the presidency. His August 1974 resignation, the result of a series of domestic scandals known collectively as Watergate, produced a volatile political situation in Washington. Gerald Ford, an unelected replacement, was no match for a hostile U.S. Congress, tired of America's longest war, and reeling from an economic malaise with winding gas lines and spiraling inflation.

Homer Smith's mission was doomed. The die had been cast two years earlier when the North Vietnamese and their Viet Cong allies reached a favorable peace settlement. The Paris Peace Accords, with their champagne toasts by National Security Advisor Henry Kissinger and Communist Foreign Secretary Le Duc Tho, allowed the North Vietnamese to remain south of the demilitarized zone, poised to strike the South Vietnamese when they judged the time right. South Vietnamese President Nguyen Van Thieu had resisted the treaty because of the obvious military advantages that it gave to his enemies to the north. He caught a glimpse of his nation's ultimate demise. By this time, however, January 1973, the American public and the Congress had turned against the war that, in fact, had been supported until 1968. Policymakers like Nixon and Kissinger were determined to rid themselves of what Nixon called the "irritant" of Vietnam. Safely re-elected, Nixon wished to concentrate on other wars, such as his overtures to the Soviet Union and the People's Republic of China. He wished to triumph in the grand Cold War — not just the sideshow of Vietnam. While Nixon pledged to Thieu that we would supply the south with material, the American President did not grasp that the political landscape in the U.S. was about to shift dramatically. In slightly more that eighteen months, Nixon would be driven from office and the Communists would begin their final offensive. An unstable American economy, weakened by an oil boycott from petroleum-producing countries, further accelerated an end to General Smith's doomed mission. We were being punished for our support of Israel in the 1973 Yom Kippur War. As a result, Vietnam was not of primary concern as our country's other crises— political and economic — engulfed us.[2-3]

On April 30, 2000, at the Vietnam Memorial, Smith spoke of the sadness of a generation ago. Those uniformed Americans in Vietnam in 1975 had been handpicked for their Saigon mission. The civilians serving in support roles were also exceptional professionals. Many of these people had been in Vietnam before 1975. For example, Sally Vinyard, the housing director, had lived there for seven years, since the Tet Offensive of 1968. Disbursing Officer Ann Hazard had been there one year longer. Smith's executive officer, Lieutenant Colonel James Piner, had completed three tours of duty and had ably assisted Smith's predecessor, Major General John Murray. Intelligence Officer Captain Stuart Herrington, married to a Vietnamese woman, spoke the language fluently. Army Division Chief Colonel Edwin Pelosky had seen combat not only in Vietnam, but had been wounded in that earlier Asian war on the Korean peninsula. Air Force secretary Rosalie Redmond, a single parent, had come to Vietnam in 1974 for adventure and the hazardous duty pay. She was a tenacious survivor.

These people formed strong bonds and developed strong opinions about why, in 1975, it had become necessary to flee a dying ally.[3]

In his remarks that spring morning, General Smith focused on the tragic April 5, 1975, crash of a C-5 aircraft, part of "Operation Babylift." The plane carried more than 300 orphans, civilian Defense Attaché Office employees, Air Force personnel, and third-country nurses. While the flight was humanitarian, it was also a veiled effort to evacuate Americans from South Vietnam. By April 5, the Communists, sensing the weakness of President Thieu's military, had swept down the peninsula, overrunning Da Nang and assaulting retreating South Vietnamese troops in the Central Highlands. Not wanting to panic the Thieu government, United States Ambassador Graham Martin and General Smith had authorized American personnel to quietly leave on the orphan flights. These Americans would be the logical escorts for the babies, most of whom were Amerasians. No one, Martin and Smith reasoned, would piece together the fact that the adult escorts would not be returning to Vietnam. The escorts were instructed to tell the media that, after the children had been delivered to their adoptive parents, the adults would return to their duties in Vietnam. Those Americans crowded into the ill-fated C-5 were exiting a collapsing country. They had one-way tickets and would not be returning to Saigon.[4]

The C-5 transport had brought in a load of reconditioned 105 mm howitzers from Taiwan for the Armed Forces of the Republic of [South] Vietnam (AFRVN). Filled with babies and adult escorts, the plane headed out to the South China Sea at 4:30 P.M. on April 5. A malfunction in the aft loading ramp caused it to pop open at 23,000 feet triggering massive damage to the tail section. The flight crew, struggling to maintain control, turned the plane and headed back to Saigon. In an unparalleled feat of airmanship, using only ailerons and engine power for control, Captain Dennis Traynor, the pilot, was able to nurse the plane back over land. He was, however, forced to crash-land in rice paddies some five miles short of the runway. The aircraft touched down initially on the east side of the Saigon river, bounced over the water, and came to rest having broken into four major sections. The lower section with its human cargo was destroyed. Ambulances raced to the crash scene. Babies cried and adults screamed. The death toll was staggering: seventy-six children, thirty-four Defense Attaché Office employees, five civilian dependents, eleven Air Force personnel, and eight third-country nurses. Only the superior piloting skills of Captain Traynor permitted 175 of the passengers and crew to survive.[5]

As dark clouds of billowing smoke engulfed the crash site, Executive Officer James Piner rushed to General Smith shouting, "Boss, you aren't going to believe this!" Smith remembers Piner adding, "They are killing our women." In the confusion, there was some belief that the plane might have been sabotaged. The truth was that it was no more than a terrible accident. Small bodies were placed in pillowcases. Survivors were treated as best they could be. Air Force secretary Rosalie Redmond, whose name was on the passenger list, recalls that people, when they saw her, seemed to react as if they had seen a ghost. She, on the afternoon of the flight, had decided to remain at her post; her life was perhaps saved by that decision.[6]

Unlike Redmond, Defense Intelligence Agency employee Vivienne Clark took the flight. Clark brought with her her eighteen-year-old daughter, Linda. When the plane's cargo door blew away, the two Clarks were separated. On the ground, Linda found herself knee-deep in mud. Frantically searching for her mother, she roamed the crash site. Finally, Vivienne was found by Linda, lying on the bank with her neck broken.[7]

Reflecting on the disastrous C-5 flight and its large number of casualties, Smith told the people at the Vietnam Memorial twenty-five years after the fact that April 5, 1975, was "the saddest day of my life. It was then. And it is now."[8]

The entire history of the Vietnam War is characterized by days such as that one. Death, confusion, heroism and luck — bad and good — were in the air. Good intentions went awry. Events sped out of control. Body bags and memorial services were too plentiful. There would be no light at the end of the tunnel, only a mad scramble to exit a country abandoned by Washington policymakers who had other wars to fight, domestically and internationally. The wreckage left behind was composed of human beings, military and political careers, and jagged metal. By April 1975, the war had long been this way. Politics and war had intertwined for nearly a decade to produce such days as April 5, and the somber audience at the Vietnam Memorial on April 30, 2000, knew that only too well.

Chapter 2

Turning Point

"So we have been repeatedly faced with the cruel irony of watching Negro and white boys on TV screens as they kill and die together for a nation that has been unable to seat them together in the same schools."
Martin Luther King, Jr., 1967.

By 1967, Dr. Martin Luther King, Jr., had been on the front lines of the modern civil rights battle for over a decade and had the arrest record to prove it. As a young minister, with the ink still moist on his doctorate from Boston University, he had steered the Montgomery, Alabama, bus boycott to victory in 1955 and 1956. The following year, he and his followers had created the Southern Christian Leadership Conference, targeting racial discrimination in America's Deep South.[1]

King pleaded for nonviolent civil disobedience. Skillfully using the media, he gained the respect of such politicians as John F. Kennedy, who phoned Coretta Scott King with concern when her husband was jailed during the 1960 presidential campaign and when King was incarcerated two years later. Thus, there took place a noticeable shift in African-American support from the party of Lincoln to the New Frontier of JFK. With Kennedy in the White House, King constantly lobbied for substantive governmental action to combat racism. King was unafraid to embarrass the Kennedy Administration in an attempt to prod the hesitant president further along the civil rights pathway.[2]

When King was imprisoned in Birmingham, Alabama, in April 1963, he gained national headlines with his public response to the town's sympathetic — but timid — white clergy who urged him to refrain from directly challenging segregation in that city. King's "Letter From Birmingham Jail" was aimed not at just weak ministers but also at vacillating politicians. He lambasted "moderates" who, while understanding the injustices of discrimination could not — would not — speak out against the system of separate schools, restaurants, rest rooms, ball parks, libraries, and taxis. He maintained that those "moderates" must take bold risks if such widespread prejudices were to be eradicated.

That summer, King's massive march on Washington, with its soaring rhetoric and racially mixed crowd, became legendary. His impassioned "I have a dream" speech rallied whites and blacks to his banner. His dream was of a color-blind America where citizens would be judged by the content of their character and not by their skin color. His influence grew dramatically after Lyndon B. Johnson, the artful master of legislative procedure, succeeded the assassinated John Kennedy. After November 1963, King's troops now armed themselves with the Civil Rights Act of 1964, that year's Economic Opportunity Act, the Voting Rights Act of 1965, Johnson's Great Society initiatives, favorable court rulings, an increasing African-American presence in high governmental offices, and sympathetic media coverage. No one could defend snarling police chiefs, growling dogs, and the use of water cannons on peaceful demonstrators. With Johnson as president, King had a skillful and strong ally who aided his efforts to break through racial barriers; LBJ's war on poverty was a masterful effort to work in tandem with King in a way that John Kennedy could never achieve. Johnson, who as a young congressman had been tutored by FDR, envisioned himself to be Roosevelt's heir, the champion of liberal causes much like those espoused by King.[3]

While nonviolent in his tone, King was unafraid to expose the ugly sides of discrimination in the United States. For his part, Johnson, always obsessed with stepping out from under the glitter of Camelot left behind by the slain Kennedy, shrewdly used the powers of his office to help King's cause. A Federal Housing and Urban Development Department was established in 1966, and Johnson appointed Thurgood Marshall to the United States Supreme Court the following year. Marshall, the first African-American to be elevated to the highest court in the land, had brilliantly argued civil rights cases before the court as Solicitor General. All of these things were accomplished with the president's assent.[4]

Until 1967, King had remained silent concerning the war in Southeast Asia. He had refrained from criticizing the commander in chief who had been such a dependable ally on the civil rights front. In an eloquent speech that year, however, King turned his attention to the war. He argued that the Vietnam conflict was taking African-American men "8,000 miles away to guarantee liberties in Southeast Asia which they had not found in

Southwest Georgia and East Harlem." Tracing decades of the tragic history of Vietnam, he suggested that the civilians, having been abused by Japanese and French overlords, "must see Americans as strange liberators" since we could be viewed as just another outside force attempting to inflict our will upon the bewildered Vietnamese people. Were we, really, soldiers of freedom, King might ask, or just another colonial power?[5]

King's speech, with its five-point blueprint for peace in the area, documented a major turning point in the war. Questions about the direction of the war would dramatically increase from this day onward. Johnson's presidency itself became a casualty of the public reappraisal begun by Martin Luther King. Johnson, who wished to fight — and win — wars against poverty and Communists found himself by 1968 increasingly lonely and frustrated by the war in Asia. Victory on both fronts would elude him. His last year in office was one of chaotic on-and-off peace negotiations with the Communists, bombing halts, bombing resumptions, the Tet Offensive which was incorrectly interpreted in America as a humiliating defeat for our troops, his bitter decision in March not to seek re-election, the assassinations of King (April 1968) and Robert Kennedy (June 1968), evaporating public support for the war among Americans, generational estrangement within families of all socioeconomic groups, the political implosion of the Democratic Party at its national convention in Chicago that August, and a daily barrage of television images from a faraway war that had no clear end in sight despite constant positive assessments from Johnson and General Westmoreland. In his 1967 remarks, King had observed, "The image of America will never again be the image of revolution, freedom and democracy; but the image of violence and militarism." It was among those strained images that the turning point of the Vietnam War occurred in 1968.[6]

When General Creighton Abrams formally succeeded General William Westmoreland as chief of the Military Assistance Command Vietnam (MACV) in June 1968, a fundamental shift took place in the conduct of the Vietnam War. Abrams, having closely observed the conflict for a year and correctly sensing the changing mood back home in the United States, abandoned Westmoreland's "search and destroy" strategy. Both men had graduated from West Point in 1936 and participated in the liberation of France in 1944, but the two soldiers radically diverged in their approach to the increasingly unpopular war at hand. Abrams believed that his classmate's three year long war of attrition had cost too many lives on all sides, wasted valuable resources and time, and dangerously fueled the fires of domestic dissent in the United States.[7]

The enemy's January-February 1968 Tet Offensive (with televised news reports of our Saigon embassy under attack), followed by that spring's mini–Tet, and a third assault that summer, (while military failures for the Communists) illustrated the flaws in Westmoreland's strategy, as did the ninety-day siege of 6,000 U.S. Marines at Khe Sanh. In addition, atrocities such as the one at My Lai that March documented the frustration that ate away at discipline in the field. Who, exactly, were the enemy and could they ever be subdued without turning our soldiers into demons every bit as evil as the Communists who butchered at least 3,000 civilians, hands tied behind their backs, during the 1968 occupation of Hue? What had Martin Luther King and CBS's Walter Cronkite, who spoke out against the war following the January Tet Offensive, been trying to tell us? Would Hanoi ever yield on the battlefield and at the Paris negotiating table? Was it an opportune time to alter strategy?[8]

Abrams stepped back from the abyss and adopted a "one war" approach. "Search and destroy" was destroying us—and the Vietnamese country-side—as we futilely sought an opportunity to lure the Communists into a major winner-take-all battle. The Central Highlands were not Nor-mandy; there would be no Asian Battle of the Bulge at Khe Sanh. Abrams' philosophy would be to "clear and hold" territory and population centers. It developed into a "pacification program" designed to calm the fright-ened South Vietnamese populace, neutering the enemy's ability to roam into hamlets to terrorize civilians. It was a strategy that consisted of shov-ing the Communists out of villages and away from Saigon, judiciously using military force (including relentless B-52 missions), minimizing American casualties, interdicting enemy supplies along the Ho Chi Minh Trail, and boosting the confidence of the South Vietnamese military.[9]

With the help of Ambassador Ellsworth Bunker and counterinsur-gency director William Colby, Abrams moved quickly to place his imprint on the war. Out of his control, however, were factors and personalities that would eventually lead to America's defeat in Southeast Asia. Political turmoil in our nation, tensions in the Middle East and in Eastern Europe, and media coverage of the violence along the Golan Heights and in the streets of Chicago, Prague, and Saigon converged to prevent the realiza-tion of Abrams' goals. Time, economics, politics, and the war intertwined in late 1968 to create a fateful turning point in the history of the Ameri-can Vietnam experience.

Chapter 3
Nixon's Doctrine

"In the previous administration, we Americanized the war in Vietnam.
In this administration, we are Vietnamizing the search for peace."
Richard Nixon, 1969.

Richard Nixon feared losing as much as John Kennedy feared being perceived as soft and as much as Lyndon Johnson feared being alone. In his more than two decades in the political arena, Nixon had won elections (hard fought victories for the U.S. House of Representatives in 1946 and the U.S. Senate in 1950 and as Dwight Eisenhower's running mate in 1952 and 1956), and he had felt the sting of defeat in the close and questionable 1960 presidential loss to Kennedy and in the humiliating outcome of the 1962 California gubernatorial race. He often explained his views on defeat succinctly: "You show me a good loser and I'll show you a loser." He was determined not to lose in the 1968 presidential campaign against Democrat Hubert Humphrey, Johnson's scarred vice president, and the Independent, George Wallace (with his efforts to turn the civil rights clock backward). Richard Nixon's triumph, however, was just a razor-thin one, and was due largely to the voters' support of an ill-defined plan to extricate the United States from Southeast Asia. The electorate, weary of the nightly scenes of carnage broadcast on television and the bloody domestic political landscape, endorsed Nixon's secret plan — despite suspicions that the "new Nixon" might not be too different from the "old Nixon" who bludgeoned Jerry Voorhis in 1946 and Helen Gahagan Douglas in 1950. "Tricky Dick" was a moniker that Nixon could never discard despite numerous attempts throughout his career to appear statesmanlike. In 1968, though, Nixon's pledge to "bring us together" kept him from being a loser.[1]

Nixon was determined that he not inherit "Johnson's War." While he supported the Eisenhower Administration's explanation of the domino theory, with its frightening images of Communist takeovers of the Philippines and Japan if we failed to challenge the aggressions in Indochina, he also saw the wisdom of Ike's reluctance to commit large numbers of American ground forces in Southeast Asia. By the time Nixon took office in January 1969, the American presence in Vietnam was nearly 540,000 personnel. To Nixon and his foreign-policy advisors, the war seemed to be a bottomless pit where the political risks for the new president were enormous.[2]

Henry Kissinger, the Harvard University professor who would serve as Nixon's national security advisor and later Secretary of State, published an article in *Foreign Affairs* in January 1969 analyzing the situation facing the new administration regarding the conflict in Vietnam. In the journal, Kissinger sifted through the wreckage of the Johnson Administration's futile efforts to reach an accord with the Communists during the negotiations in Paris. If the diplomats had been successful, Humphrey — not Nixon — might have been victorious in the 1968 election. Hopes for peace fell victim, Kissinger explained, to "the classic Vietnamese syndrome: optimism alternating with bewilderment; euphoria giving way to frustration." Interestingly, the professor omitted the role played by the Nixon campaign advisors, such as Anna Chenault and himself, to sabotage the 1968 peace negotiations so as to deny Johnson and Humphrey a last-minute chance to secure a peace agreement. They had sent President Thieu a clandestine message that he should wait; help (and a better friend in the White House) was on the way.[3]

Kissinger reviewed the events of 1967 and 1968. General Westmoreland had assured a joint session of Congress in November of 1967 that the war was being won. President Johnson, in his January 1968 State of the Union address, told the Congress and the nation the same thing. A week later, the Tet Offensive raised questions about strategy and credibility. Kissinger suggested that the nature of guerrilla warfare, where "Guerrillas rarely seek to hold real estate; their tactic is to use terror and intimidation to discourage cooperation with constitutional authority," made Westmoreland's approach a flawed one.[4]

In Kissinger's judgment, the Tet Offensive, while a military failure for the Communists, "made a point that far transcended military considerations in importance: there are no secure areas for Vietnamese civilians." Thus, South Vietnamese troops could be in control of much of the countryside in daylight, but Communists could roam about in the darkness and could, as they did throughout 1968, launch offensives. It was this freedom of movement that General Abrams' pacification effort was designed to eliminate.[5]

Units of the 1st Battalion, 77th Armor crossing over Highway 9, west of Con Thien, April 1969. *Courtesy of John Moore.*

Kissinger addressed the question of President Nguyen Van Thieu's reluctance to negotiate with the Communist National Liberation Front (NLF). (Later in 1969, this body was to change its name to Provisional Revolutionary Government, PRG.) A desperate Lyndon Johnson, seeking to extricate himself from the Vietnamese quagmire, had pressured Thieu to consent to four-party negotiations: Washington, Hanoi, Saigon, and the Vietcong's National Liberation Front. Thieu saw such negotiations as taking his government perilously close to de facto recognition of the Communist presence in South Vietnam. The public friction between Thieu and Johnson over the role of the NLF weakened the non–Communist alliance. Kissinger observed, "To split Washington and Saigon had been a constant objective of Hanoi...."[6]

As the Nixon Administration assumed power, Kissinger considered global events that might have bearing on the conflict in Southeast Asia and the stalled Paris Peace negotiations. The Soviet Union and the People's Republic of China were rattling sabers at each other. Israel had soundly defeated its Arab neighbors in 1967. The Soviets had invaded Czechoslovakia and jerked their satellite back into orbit. Would China, Kissinger asked, feel justified to similarly venture into North Vietnam? All of these occurrences "may have convinced Hanoi that time is not necessarily on its side."[7]

With Nixon — and Kissinger — installed in the White House, the American policy should be one that stressed the withdrawal of "external forces." Nixon's murky "secret plan" was unveiled. The Nixon Doctrine, as outlined by Kissinger in the *Foreign Affairs* analysis and by the President himself on several occasions in 1969 (including the June announcement at Midway of forthcoming reductions in U.S. troops in South Vietnam), was now clear. America would withdraw its forces, pressure North Vietnam to do the same, supply the Thieu government with materiel, and allow the South Vietnamese to map their own future. Kissinger cautioned against immersing "ourselves deeply in the issue of South Vietnam's internal arrangements...."[8] The word he used was "morass." Nixon would reverse the previous course, speeding withdrawal, stepping clear of the "morass" that had gnawed away at Lyndon Johnson's presidency. While Nixon would prefer not to "lose" South Vietnam, he was willing, from the beginning of his own presidency, to accept a permanent Communist presence south of the 38th parallel if such an outcome was necessary to avoid the "morass" which had ruined Johnson's legacy.

While the withdrawal of Americans would be gradual, there was no mistaking the fact that the sand in the hourglass was filtering downward. As the grains of sand flowed, hopes of victory evaporated. America still had a commitment to Thieu, but it was increasingly a commitment backed by fewer troops who were to be replaced by materiel with which the South Vietnamese could defend themselves. Early in 1969, Nixon sent Secretary of Defense Melvin Laird to Vietnam to make this new policy, which now was defined as "Vietnamization," clear to Abrams. The general later confided to someone that Laird "certainly had not come to help us win the war."[9] Nixon hoped that, ideally, with American aid, Thieu could negotiate a favorable accommodation with the Provisional Revolutionary Government. The abandonment of South Vietnam was under way.

Chapter 4

The Widening Morass

"I know all Americans are tired of the war in Southeast Asia. I know the Congress and the administration are tired of the war. I am tired of the war."

Senator John Tower, 1970.

Secretary of Defense Laird, National Security Advisor Kissinger, and President Nixon agreed that the only route for the United States to follow was Vietnamization. Disengagement could only come from supplying Thieu with weaponry, bringing American troops home, promoting dialogue at the Paris peace conference, persuading the North Vietnamese that good faith negotiations were the only solution to the war, and stepping clear of any action that would create unrest in America. Politically, there needed to be clear signs that America's grand presence in this conflict was diminishing. Within a few days of Laird's March 1969 meeting with Abrams, however, the military challenges facing the South Vietnamese became evident.[1]

When Communist forces struck Saigon with a rocket attack in March, Nixon gave the green light for Operation Menu, the secret bombing of Cambodia, to begin on the 18th of that same month. What was originally projected to be a "short-duration" operation, continued for the next fifteen months and resulted in 3,630 secret B-52 raids against suspected Communist positions in Cambodia. In a purely military sense, the secret bombing had a positive impact in the long run because it reduced the outside support available to the Communist forces in South Vietnam. Nonetheless even as Nixon was putting the finishing touches on Vietnamization, he realized that time was at a premium. His hope was that the secret bombing would weaken the Communist forces in the south and provide more time for his new policy to work.[2]

Similarly, Abrams ordered U.S. forces to keep the North Vietnamese and Viet Cong off balance so that the Communists would not be able to mount any prolonged actions that would interfere with the upgrading of the Republic of Vietnam Armed Forces (RVNAF) by Vietnamization. To this end, Abrams broke his forces into small platoon-sized task forces and ordered them to concentrate on extensive patrolling and night operations. He described this tactic as "getting into [the enemy's] system."[3]

Not all of the efforts to throw the Communists off balance were of the small-force variety, however. In the A Shau Valley, a rugged mountain area near the Laotian border and some sixty miles south of the demilitarized zone (DMZ) separating the two Vietnams, the northerners had established a large logistics complex, which served as a staging area for possible attacks on Hue and the northernmost provinces of South Vietnam. It was a terminus of the Ho Chi Minh Trail and was referred to as Base 611. This network of roads and storage areas that used as many as 1,000 trucks to keep the supplies moving had been uncovered by the U.S. 9th Marine Regiment in an earlier operation code-named Dewey Canyon.[4]

The effort to neutralize Base 611 began with a helicopter assault into the area by a battalion from the 101st Airborne Division on May 10, 1969. A primary objective of the attack was a strongly fortified position located on the crest of a 3,000-foot peak, denoted as Hill 937 on the maps, which came to be known as Hamburger Hill. For the next week, the paratroopers struggled to attain their objective, but it became clear that reinforcements would be needed to complete the job. A battalion from the 502nd Infantry was brought in from the northeast and the Army of the Republic of Vietnam (ARVN) 2nd Battalion attacked from the southeast. Also, two companies of infantry reinforced the initial attacking force of airborne troops. Hamburger Hill was finally taken on May 20, 1969, after a protracted and brutal struggle. The American casualties from this battle were forty-six killed and some 400 wounded. However, the enemy suffered 630 dead and an unknown number of wounded.[5]

The logistics complex had been destroyed and the North Vietnamese Army (NVA) had suffered heavy casualties. The threat to Hue and to allied forces in Military Region I (MR I) had been significantly reduced, at least for the short run. Operation Apache Snow, as it was called, had been a success, militarily speaking, but as it turned out, a disaster in the minds of many at home. Vietnam, of course, was a television war and the carnage atop Hamburger Hill disturbed viewers who, by and large, had never before seen such scenes of the reality of war.[6]

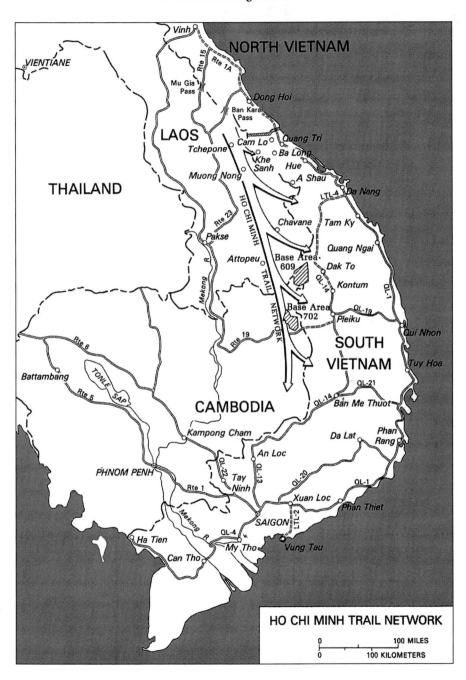

Ho Chi Minh Trail.

As was called for in the operation plans, the American and ARVN troops pulled back to their base camps and abandoned Hamburger Hill once the battle had been won. The action was widely reported in the American press, including an article in the June 27, 1969, issue of *Life Magazine*. The story included photographs of 241 servicemen killed throughout Vietnam over a week's time. Many readers mistakenly believed that these men had all died in the taking of Hamburger Hill. A portion of the story quoted from a letter sent home by one of the soldiers who had participated in Operation Apache Snow. It read, "You may not be able to read this. I am writing in a hurry. I see death coming up the hill." Images of approaching death flashed across the pages of publications such as *Life*.[7]

The opponents of the war leapt at the opportunity to accentuate the negative. Massachusetts Senator Edward Kennedy shrieked that the battle had been "senseless and irresponsible." Ignoring that the mission had succeeded in achieving General Abrams' goal of knocking the enemy off balance while the Vietnamization effort was in progress, the last remaining Kennedy brother went on to ask, "How can we justify sending our boys against a hill a dozen times, finally taking it, and then withdrawing a week later?" The *New York Times* declared, "The public is certainly entitled to raise questions about the aggressive posture of the United States military in South Vietnam."[8]

As the result of the generally negative press coverage of the battle for Hamburger Hill and the outcries from those who opposed the effort to defend South Vietnam, doubts were raised as to whether Nixon had changed the strategy to end the war. It became clear that if the President was going to be able to achieve his 1968 campaign goal of "peace with honor," there could be no more Hamburger Hills. Accordingly, Nixon sent word to General Abrams that he was to do what was necessary to hold down casualties.[9]

Even as American units battled the enemy at Hamburger Hill and at many other locations around South Vietnam, Nixon heralded his Vietnamization policy and associated plans to reduce the number of American combat troops in Vietnam.[10] Now, Abrams would have to fight the war with less manpower while at the same time dealing with the sensitive issue of preparing the RVNAF to assume primary responsibility for combat against the North Vietnamese and Viet Cong. He had to carry out these assignments even as Nixon and Laird continued to push for more — and faster — troop reductions.

While General Abrams was in the process of turning over the war to the South Vietnamese and allied efforts intensified in the pacification process, Nixon and Kissinger were attempting to devise a way to bring the war to a negotiated end. Although these actions were far removed from the battlefield in South Vietnam, they, the reactions of the North Vietnamese, and the ongoing controversies at home all had a significant impact on the Vietnamization program and U.S. policies throughout Indochina. On May 14, 1969, in a televised speech, the President offered a peace plan that proposed that all foreign troops, both American and North Vietnamese, withdraw from South Vietnam within one year after an agreement was signed. It further called for an international body that would monitor the withdrawals and supervise free elections in South Vietnam. Nixon warned the Communists not to mistake a willingness to talk for weakness. He said, "Reports from Hanoi indicate that the enemy has given up hope for a military victory in South Vietnam, but is counting on a collapse of will in the United States. There could be no greater error in judgment." There was no response from Hanoi. According to Kissinger, the North Vietnamese refused even to discuss the president's proposals.[11]

Discussions about U.S. troop withdrawals had begun shortly after President Nixon's inauguration. On his way to Midway for a June meeting with President Thieu, where he planned to announce the initiation of his Vietnamization program, a conference was held in Honolulu to draw up a withdrawal strategy. Those in attendance included Nixon, Kissinger, Laird, Secretary of State William Rogers, Ambassadors Ellsworth Bunker and Henry Cabot Lodge, and Generals Earle Wheeler and Abrams. Kissinger reports that the "military approached the subject [of troop withdrawals] with a heavy heart ... it would make victory impossible and even an honorable outcome problematical."[12] Prior to this meeting, Abrams had questioned the size and pace of any contemplated withdrawals. According to Abrams' biographer, Professor Lewis Sorley, the U.S. commander believed his forces were beginning to enjoy more American success in combating the Communists and naturally wanted to retain as many troops as possible to press the advantage. Sorley maintains that Abrams "also had the sensitivity to understand the political realities in the United States and what they portended in terms of continued support for the war." In addition, General Wheeler had assured him on two separate occasions that any American redeployment would take into consideration the situation on the battlefield. Nevertheless, Abrams still had reservations about the wisdom of withdrawing troops when the enemy's strength appeared to be waning. Despite the concerns of the operational commander, the President made the decision to announce the first withdrawal increment at Midway and get on with the disengagement of U.S. forces. Further reductions were to be based on three criteria: the level of enemy activity, progress in the Paris peace talks, and the strengthening of the Republic of Vietnam Armed

Forces. Kissinger wrote, "Henceforth we [the United States] would be in a race between the decline in our combat capabilities and the improvement of South Vietnam forces—a race whose outcome was at best uncertain."[13]

On June 8, 1969, with a stoic President Thieu standing at his side on the barren little island of Midway located some 1,150 miles northwest of Honolulu, Nixon declared that the first increment in the withdrawal of American forces from South Vietnam would number 25,000 and would commence immediately. After the meeting was over, Nixon was "jubilant" and considered the announcement a "political triumph." He thought that it would accomplish several significant things. First, the initial withdrawal would buy the administration time to develop its strategy. Second, it would send a signal to the North Vietnamese that the United States was serious about seeking peace in Southeast Asia. Finally, Nixon hoped that it would quiet the domestic war critics. Its effect on Thieu was of minor importance.[14]

Later in June, after returning to Washington from the Midway conference, Nixon told a group gathered on the White House south lawn to welcome him and his party home that the May peace plan and the Midway troop withdrawal announcement left the door to peace wide open. He declared, "And now we invite the leaders of North Vietnam to walk with us through that door." According to Kissinger aid Alexander M. Haig, Nixon hoped that Hanoi and the antiwar elements in the U.S. would see his actions as a sign of his "flexibility."[15]

In the weeks following the Midway meeting with the South Vietnamese President, there were continuing discussions concerning size and rate of future reductions in U.S. forces in Vietnam. Laird developed plans that included options of from 50,000 to 100,000 men. However, in a memorandum to President Nixon, Secretary Laird warned him to be careful and not bring home too many of the troops too quickly as this could impede General Abrams' pacification program already in progress. Nixon and Laird were given new motivation to expand their troop withdrawal plans by former Secretary of Defense Clark Clifford, a confidant of former President Johnson. In June 1969, Clifford published an article in *Foreign Affairs* that urged the unilateral withdrawal of 100,000 troops by the end of the year, and all other personnel by the end of 1970, leaving only logistics and Air Force personnel. Nixon stated at a press conference that he could improve on Clifford's schedule. This rather impulsive and unwise statement was to have serious consequences for the peace negotiations and the ultimate effectiveness of the eventual cease-fire agreement. It effectively committed the United States to unilateral withdrawal from South Vietnam and removed the promise of troop reductions as a bargaining chip in Kissinger's dealings with the North Vietnamese in Paris.[16]

On July 7, 1969, the President met with Kissinger, Laird, Rogers, Wheeler, Attorney General John Mitchell, and Deputy CIA Director Marine General Robert E. Cushman, Jr. aboard the presidential yacht *Sequoia*. The purpose of the meeting was to discuss an apparent lull in the fighting in South Vietnam. The number of enemy attacks had diminished after the battle for Hamburger Hill and American casualties had fallen to their lowest level in a year. Gone were the 1,000 per week killed in action statistics of the previous year. According to Kissinger, the discussion centered on ascertaining why the level of fighting had decreased. Was it due to Hanoi's exhaustion?; was it a new negotiating strategy?; or was it an attempt by Hanoi to achieve de-escalation by tacit understanding? Kissinger later wrote, "It was symptomatic of the intellectual confusion of the period that in the relief felt when a military lull eased both casualties and domestic pressures, no one asked the question whether the lull might not reflect the fact that our strategy was succeeding and should therefore be continued." Instead, there was "unanimity" that the situation provide an excellent opportunity to reciprocate and de-escalate U.S. operations in South Vietnam, while at the same time bring MACV efforts more in line with the Vietnamization effort. Nixon agreed and authorized Laird to issue new guidelines to Creighton Abrams.[17]

The result was a new mission statement for MACV that emphasized the desire of the United States "to assist the Republic of Vietnam Armed Forces to take over an increasing share of combat operations." The new mission statement, effective August 15, 1969, directed Abrams and his command to focus first, on providing "maximum assistance" to the South Vietnamese to strengthen their military forces; second, on supporting the pacification effort; and third, on reducing the flow of supplies to the enemy. Abrams was once again told to minimize American casualties. Henry Kissinger later reported that Nixon changed his mind about these orders and attempted to rescind them. However, Laird said that they had already been sent so they were allowed to stand. Nixon never revealed why he had second thoughts about the official mission change for MACV. Perhaps he was worried about interfering in military matters, or perhaps he did not want to send the signal to the North Vietnamese that the U.S. was beginning to sharply reduce its commitment to the war. Regardless, the President let the orders stand and he reiterated the new guidelines in person when he made a surprise visit to Vietnam later that month. In country, he stressed the new focus for U.S. forces, saying that "the primary mission of American troops is to enable the South Vietnamese forces to assume full responsibility for the security of South Vietnam." Notably, the President did not make this new guidance public until a nationally televised speech on November 3, 1969.[18]

Abrams, who had previously expressed misgivings about the accelerated U.S. troop withdrawals, understood his marching orders and stepped up measures to improve the combat capabilities of the South Vietnamese units. This was not a new problem for Abrams. He had been concerned since his assumption of command in 1968 with what were essentially two separate wars being fought by the U.S. and South Vietnamese forces. Abrams had sought to end the division of roles between American and South Vietnamese combat forces by the adoption of a single combined allied strategy, thus eliminating "the tacit existence of two separate strategies, attrition and pacification." Abrams described this "one war" concept as "a strategy focused upon protecting the population so that the civil government can establish its authority as opposed to an earlier conception of the purpose of the war — destruction of the enemy's forces." The "one war" concept was formalized in the MACV Objectives Plan approved in March 1969.[19]

Abrams and Ambassador Bunker convinced President Thieu that Abrams' approach was the right way to proceed and succeeded in getting Thieu to agree that the MACV Objective Plan should be the basis for the efforts of all allied forces in South Vietnam. The decision was made official when Abrams and General Cao Van Vien, chairman of the South Vietnamese Joint General Staff, signed the Combined Strategic Objectives Plan, which specified that the "RVNAF must participate fully within its capabilities in all types of operations ... to prepare for the time when it must assume the entire responsibility." The plan further established the prime objective of the American and South Vietnamese forces to be population security and support of pacification.[20]

As soon as the new plan was signed, Abrams set out to make sure that MACV forces fully accepted this "one war" concept, forever eliminating the division of labor that often had fragmented allied efforts. Abrams was already shifting focus of MACV when he received the official change of mission from President Nixon. Armed with the new "one war" combined strategy and urged by his commander in chief to Vietnamize the war, Abrams hoped to bring the combat situation under control while at the same time shifting the preponderance of the responsibility for the war effort to the South Vietnamese as American troop withdrawals increased in size and frequency.

On July 15, 1969, President Nixon sent a letter to North Vietnam's leader, Ho Chi Minh, who was near death. The time had come, he wrote, "to move forward ... toward an early resolution of this tragic war," and promised to be "forthcoming and open-minded" in negotiations. While the President did not offer Ho any specific concessions or proposals, he alluded to the offer he had made in a speech delivered on May 14, 1969. He concluded, "Let history record that at this juncture, both sides turned their face toward peace rather that toward conflict and war." The letter was to be hand-carried by French businessman and intermediary Jean Saintenay. Nixon told him to impress upon Ho Chi Minh that the U.S. President was serious about peace, but he also instructed Saintenay to warn the North Vietnamese that if there was no breakthrough in the peace negotiations by November 1, the anniversary of the pre-election 1968 bombing halt, the President would feel obliged to resort to "measures of great consequence and force."[21] In the process of making a peace overture, Nixon had essentially issued an ultimatum to Hanoi.

While the North Vietnamese considered Nixon's letter, the President came to the conclusion that he had to do something to break the deadlock and back up his ultimatum. Historian George Herring maintains that Nixon was fearful that rising domestic protests might doom his efforts to pressure the North Vietnamese into a settlement. Regardless of his innermost motivations, Nixon later wrote that he had decided to "...'go for broke' in the sense that I would attempt to end the war one way or the other — either by negotiated agreement or by increased use of force." Accordingly, Kissinger instructed his staff to complete a new war plan "designed for maximum impact upon the enemy's military capability." The result was a plan devised by the Joint Chiefs of Staff code-named Duck Hook. It called for a massive four-day bombing campaign of Hanoi, Haiphong, and other key areas in North Vietnam. The mining of harbors and rivers and the destruction of the Red River dike system to bring on extensive flooding were also part of this plan. The target date for Duck Hook, should Hanoi continue to avoid serious negotiations, was November 1, 1969.[22]

While this planning was going on, the North Vietnamese agreed to secret talks in Paris between Kissinger and their representatives Xuan Thuy and Mai Van Bo. Nixon told Kissinger to be firm with the North Vietnamese. He was to remind the Communists that U.S. troop withdrawals had begun and that the United States was prepared to accept the results of free elections. If Hanoi was not prepared to reciprocate, Kissinger was to reiterate the previously issued ultimatum and tell them "that if by November 1 no major progress had been made toward a solution, we will be compelled — with great reluctance — to take measures of great consequences." The secret negotiations began on August 4, 1969. Kissinger made no headway with Xuan Thuy, who demanded the complete withdrawal of all American forces from South Vietnam, the removal of President Thieu, and the establishment of a coalition government composed of the Communist Provisional Revolutionary Government and the remnants of the Saigon administration. As Kissinger later wrote, he and Xuan Thuy "had achieved little except to restate established positions."[23]

The North Vietnamese provided a sterner response to Nixon's peace overtures when, on August 6, 1969, the Communists initiated attacks on the huge American base at Cam Ranh Bay. This was followed only five days later with assaults on more than 100 cities, towns, and military installations across South Vietnam. An official North Vietnamese history of the war revealed that the Politburo in Hanoi had concluded that the United States had "lost its will to fight in Vietnam."[24] This assessment had been based upon the not unreasonable inference that the Communists were in a position of strength and could take this kind of offensive action.

When making his announcement at Midway Island that U.S. troops would begin their withdrawal from Vietnam, Nixon had added the caveat that any future reduction in forces would depend upon the willingness of the Communists to respond by reducing, not increasing, their belligerence. As Kissinger later wrote, "The most generous interpretation [of the new attacks] could not avoid the conclusion that Hanoi did not believe in gestures, negotiations, goodwill, or reciprocity." So, when the enemy reacted to Nixon's peace overtures by attacking a large variety of targets across South Vietnam, Nixon declared that he would delay any further troop reductions pending a more cooperative response by the North Vietnamese. When he made the announcement of this break in bringing the American forces home on August 23, many in the Congress and the media considered this delay to be a form of backsliding by the President and a huge uproar on Capitol Hill and in the press ensued.[25]

On August 25, Ho's reply to the President's July letter arrived. It was, in Nixon's word, a "cold rebuff." Ho demanded that "...the United States must cease the war of aggression and withdraw their troops from South Vietnam, [and] respect the right of the population of the South and the Vietnamese nation to dispose of themselves without foreign influence." Hanoi's answer was unequivocal. It was becoming increasingly clear, as Kissinger put it, that the "North Vietnamese were less interested in stopping the fighting than in winning it."[26] It appeared that any attempts at a negotiated settlement would be rejected out of hand.

Then, the situation became even more uncertain when Ho died on September 4, 1969. How would this effect the war? Many in Congress and the media urged Nixon to declare a cease-fire as a gesture to the Communists, but he was not prepared to go that far. He did decide to suspend military operations for the day of Ho Chi Minh's funeral, an act that led to more speculation about an armistice.[27]

While trying to figure out what the implications of Ho's death were for his peace initiatives, Nixon also had to deal with an increasingly volatile domestic situation. The antiwar protestors had been quieted somewhat by the Midway announcement of troop reductions and its subsequent implementation through the withdrawal of the 9th Infantry Division from the Mekong Delta. In early September, however, Laird had warned the President, "I believe this may be a illusory phenomenon. The actual and potential antipathy for the war is, in my judgment, significant and increasing." Laird was proved correct. The death of Ho Chi Minh and the possibility of an armistice gave those who wanted the U.S. out of Vietnam renewed vigor. Antiwar sentiment grew in the press, in Congress, and in the streets of America. There was a rush by congressmen to introduce resolutions designed to disengage the U.S. from the war, and the Senate Foreign Relations Committee, which had tormented LBJ, called a new round of hearings on the war. Antiwar activists called for a "moratorium" on October 15, November 15, and monthly thereafter until America was completely out of Vietnam.[28]

On September 12, the National Security Council met to discuss the situation. Kissinger sent Nixon a memorandum two days before the meeting in which he expressed his concern about the administration's "current course" in South Vietnam. He warned that "Withdrawals of U.S. troops will become like salted peanuts to the American public; the more U.S. troops come home, the more will be demanded." This could eventually result, in effect, in demands for a unilateral withdrawal. The more troops were withdrawn, the more Hanoi would be encouraged. While Kissinger would be proved right, he was the only one at the NSC meeting to dissent in the decision to continue the scheduled troop reductions. He later commented that it would have been "a very natural response for us to stop bringing soldiers home, but by [then] withdrawal had gained its own momentum." On September 16, Nixon ordered a second increment of 35,000 Americans to be brought home by that Christmas. He pointed out that this withdrawal was a significant step and that "the time for meaningful negotiations has therefore arrived." Three days later, he said that because of this drawdown, draft calls for November and December would be canceled, and on December 1 the first draft lottery would be held. By these actions, Nixon was trying to influence both the North Vietnamese and the antiwar movement. According to Kissinger, the repatriation of U.S. troops had become "inexorable ... [and] the president never again permitted the end of a withdrawal period to pass without announcing a new increment for the next."[29]

Nixon found himself in a very difficult position. He knew that he could not simply withdraw all U.S. troops without reneging on the American commitment to the South Vietnamese people and delivering the country to the Communists. Therefore, he had to continue the war in the field while trying to find a way to convince the North Vietnamese that it would be in their best interests to arrive at a negotiated end to the conflict. Somehow, he also had to get the support of the American people for continuing the war while he pursued a negotiated settlement. As Nixon biographer Stephen Ambrose has pointed out, however, "The war had always been a hard sell; once Nixon began to withdraw, it was a nearly impossible one."[30] While Nixon knew that he had to get the American military forces out of Vietnam, he was not prepared to show his enemies, both foreign and domestic, any weakness. "Weakness" was not in Nixon's vocabulary. Moreover, given his antipathy toward the dissidents, he was loath to risk even giving the appearance of kowtowing to them.

At a press conference on September 16, 1969, President Nixon again reignited the fury of the dissenters. When asked his view of the upcoming moratorium, he replied, "As far as that kind of activity is concerned, we expect it. However, under no circumstances will I be affected by it." Despite his denials that the protesters would have any affect upon his decision making, it appears that they did, but in a way that they did not anticipate. The more vocal and violent the protests, the more bellicose Nixon seemed to become.[31]

On September 30, in a meeting with Republican congressional leaders, the President made reference to Duck Hook and his ultimatum to the North Vietnamese. He said that the next sixty days would be crucial and went on to declare that "I can't tell you everything that will be going on, because if there is any chance of success, it will have to be done in secret. All I can tell you is this: I am doing my damnedest to end the war ... I won't make it hard for the North Vietnamese if they genuinely want a settlement, but I will not be the first President of the United States to lose a war." In a second meeting with nine Republican senators, he let out the Duck Hook secret, admitting that blockading Haiphong and invading North Vietnam were options being considered. The next day, the story appeared in a Roland Evans and Robert Novak newspaper column. Nixon had leaked the story himself in an attempt to get the attention of the new leadership in Hanoi.[32]

Secretary of Defense Laird and Secretary of State William Rogers were shocked by this news. They urged the President not to implement the plan.

They pointed out that over the previous few months the American casualty rates had been relatively low and they noted the improved performance by the South Vietnamese as result of the stepped-up pace of the Vietnamization efforts. They urged Nixon not to escalate the war. Undeterred by their pleas, the President responded by sending Kissinger a memo that said, "It would be helpful if a propaganda offensive could be launched, constantly repeating what we have done in offering peace in Vietnam in preparation for what we may have to do later." Nixon was preparing to increase the stakes if his call for a negotiated settlement failed to work.[33]

Nixon's actions had the predictable effects on the antiwar dissidents both in the government and outside it. Senator J. William Fulbright, the antiwar chair of the Foreign Relations Committee, announced new hearings on the war and said that Nixon had been in office nine months, but had not made any "progress in delivering on his campaign promises to give birth to his plans to end the war." Other senators, such as Edward Kennedy, Eugene McCarthy, John Sherman Cooper, Gaylord Nelson, and Mike Mansfield, joined in the chorus severely criticizing Nixon and his policies. The President also came under fire from the public, especially from the world of academia. The presidents of seventy-nine colleges signed a letter to Nixon urging him to step up the troop withdrawals. There were angry protests at Berkeley, the University of Pennsylvania, Cornell, Duke and other campuses around the country. Picketers carried signs in front of the White House that denounced President Nixon and the war.[34] Rapidly, "Lyndon's War" was becoming "Nixon's War."

Nixon provided his response to the unrest in a public reply to a letter he received from Randy Dicks, a Georgetown University student, who questioned the President's refusal to be swayed by the moratorium's appeal to conscience and urged him to "take note of the will of the people." Nixon said that there was little to be learned from the student demonstrations. He went on to say that, "Whatever the issue, to allow government policy to be made in the streets would destroy the democratic process ... [by giving] the decision, not to the majority ... but to those with the loudest voices. Others can say of Vietnam, 'get out now,' when asked how, they can give the flip answer, 'By sea.' They can ignore the consequences ... [but] history would rightly condemn a president who took such a course."[35]

On October 15, the moratorium came off as scheduled. Thousands of protestors marched all across the country. More than 100,000 gathered on the Boston Common, 200,000 in New York City, and more than 250,000 marched in Washington, D.C. Some of Nixon's advisors were disturbed by the fact that the moratorium had brought out members of the middle class and the middle-aged in great numbers. Nonetheless, the President put out the word that he was unmoved by the display and that he had spent the afternoon watching a football game on television. Privately, Nixon brooded that the protests might have "destroyed whatever small possibility may have still existed of ending the war in 1969."[36]

As 1969 ended, the President saw "Lyndon Johnson's War" evolving into "Richard Nixon's War." Vietnamization was now in place but congressional critics sniped at the policy's pace. Nixon was at a disadvantage here that President Johnson never had to face: the Republican Party was in the minority in both houses of Congress. Thus, it was frustrating for Nixon to have to deal with powerful foes such as Senate Foreign Relations Committee Chairman J. William Fulbright, Senate Majority Leader Mike Mansfield and the last remaining Kennedy brother, Senator Edward Kennedy. It seemed that doves flew throughout the halls of Congress. "Peace with honor" was assailed as an empty campaign phrase. The country was, by 1970, as Texas' Republican Senator John Tower remarked, "tired of the war."[37]

The reduction in American armed forces in Vietnam soon accelerated. In mid December a reduction of 50,000 men was ordered. On April 20, 1970, President Nixon announced that even though only 110,000 soldiers had been scheduled to return home by that time, 115,000 had, in fact, been redeployed. Over the next twelve months, an additional 150,000-man reduction in troop strength was carried out. Between the Midway Island June 8, 1969, disclosure of Nixon's policy of Vietnamizing the war and November 1972, the U.S. reduced its force size from a gargantuan 549,000 down to only 27,000. As this downsizing was taking place, the Republic of Vietnam Armed Forces were given the responsibility for operational areas vacated by the departing Americans. Could they adjust to the changes occurring as a result of Vietnamization? Would Nixon be able to outwit his congressional and academic foes?

Chapter 5

Incursion

"I would rather be a one-term President and do what I believe is right than to be a two-term President at the cost of seeing America become a second-rate power and to see this nation accept its first defeat in its proud 190 year history."

Richard Nixon, 1970.

The decade of the 1960s had been a roller-coaster ride for the United States. The decade commenced with John Kennedy's close victory in the presidential election. At JFK's inauguration, he pledged to "go anywhere, bear any burden, pay any price in the cause of freedom." The aging Dwight Eisenhower, the hero of Normandy, seemed to wince when the youthful Kennedy spoke of "the torch of leadership being passed to a new generation." Within 1,000 days, Kennedy was dead and 14,000 American troops had gone to Southeast Asia. The total would rise steadily, until Lyndon Johnson committed half a million military personnel, making a mockery of his 1964 promise not to send America's sons 10,000 miles away to do what Asian sons should do.[1]

Social unrest, as we have seen, climaxed with Martin Luther King's crusade. When he spoke out against the Vietnam War in 1967, Johnson felt abandoned. Had he not toiled in the vineyards beside King, turning mere dreams into tangible legislation? King's assassination in the spring of 1968 raised the slain minister to martyrdom. Johnson was the tarnished warrior; King was the prince of peace, gone but revered. He had sacrificed his own life to save lives half a world away.

The 1968 presidential battle, with Johnson's forfeiture of a second term, New York Senator Robert Kennedy's murder, tear gas in the streets of Chicago, and the rise of a "new Nixon," proved that America was desperately searching for something just beyond its grasp.[2]

When Neil Armstrong set foot on the moon in July 1969 it seemed that, for a moment, stability and accomplishment were returning. Nixon's congratulatory long-distance telephone call to the lunar astronauts was almost surreal. But there would be no relief from the decade's horrors. In a drug-induced rage, Charles Manson ordered the murder of pretty Sharon Tate, the pregnant Hollywood actress, in a bizarre scheme to start a race war. Senator Edward Kennedy, the sole heir to Camelot, drove his Oldsmobile off of a narrow bridge on Chappaquiddick Island, drowning a female passenger. Homosexuals rioted when police attempted to arrest them at the Stonewall Inn in the Greenwich Village section of New York City. Women across America asserted themselves politically; their loose fashions and their even looser morals made the older generation nervous. In addition, the nation's college campuses continued to simmer with hostility toward Nixon's Vietnamization policy, despite the fact that he had reduced the American troop commitment from 540,000 to 400,000 military personnel. That August's Woodstock Festival had an obvious antiwar tone as musicians and a crowd of 500,000 sang, "Give peace a chance."[3] As 1970 dawned, there would be no respite in these societal tensions.

After the 1968 Tet Offensive, the Communists evaluated their efforts. They correctly acknowledged that the assaults in South Vietnam had failed militarily. Large-scale attacks, such as those on Saigon and provincial capitals, grabbed headlines and unnerved the Americans but failed to yield long-term results. Thus, the Communists passed the word among themselves that, "We secure victory not through a one-blow offensive, and not through a phase of attack, not even through a series of attacks culminating in a final hill...." They asserted, "Success would come in a complicated and torturous way." The strategy would return to guerrilla tactics and a stance of protraction at the Paris peace talks. The Communists, surveying the growing antiwar mood in the United States and fully aware that time could be their ally, were prepared to wait as long as it took to see the disheartened Americans withdraw from Southeast Asia. Kissinger alerted Nixon in a January 7, 1970, memorandum that "Hanoi would play for time until enough American forces had left to allow it to challenge Saigon's forces on a more equal basis."[4]

By April 1970, Nixon had become frustrated with the lack of progress in South Vietnam. In an attempt to "drop a bombshell on the gathering storm of antiwar protests," he announced on April 20 a phased withdrawal of another 150,000 U.S. troops to take place over the next year. In his speech, Nixon was upbeat. He said that gains in training and equipping the South Vietnamese had "substantially exceeded our expectations" and he could announce this major withdrawal because Vietnamization was working so well. He reviewed American offers for negotiations and stressed that by April 1971 he would have cut in half the number of American soldiers in Vietnam. He warned Hanoi, "If I conclude increased enemy action jeopardizes our remaining forces in Vietnam, I shall not hesitate to take strong and effective measures to deal with the situation."[5]

By this announcement of new troop reductions, Nixon hoped to satisfy the growing demand in the U.S. for an end to American involvement in Southeast Asia. He also hoped that the time span for the reductions would allay any fears in Saigon about accelerated withdrawals. Nevertheless, General Abrams was not pleased with this announcement, because he thought it made U.S. forces in South Vietnam vulnerable to new attacks by the Communists and might affect the progress of Vietnamization.[6] While this may have been true from a military perspective, Nixon was in a political bind and he had to do something to quiet the protestors and answer the growing number of questions being raised by the American public.

Nixon still wanted to achieve a negotiated settlement in Vietnam which would give the Thieu regime a fighting chance to stand on its own two feet as it mapped its future relationship with the Provisional Revolutionary Government. The Communists, taking note of the U.S. withdrawals, concluded correctly that the pressure on Nixon to get out of Vietnam would only increase. The Communists could then achieve their objectives by simply continuing their policy of "fighting and talking" and waiting out the American President until he had finally withdrawn all of U.S. forces from Vietnam. They would then be able to take over South Vietnam without worrying about American interference. The Communists saw the conflict in broad historical terms: the Japanese had been ousted in 1945, the French in 1954, and the Americans would soon exit because Nixon feared the domestic political consequences of staying. He would, the Communists understood, have to face re-election in two years and, they believed, would not want a smoldering war igniting as a campaign issue.

Angry that the North Vietnamese had not taken his warnings seriously and come to the negotiating table in good faith, Nixon decided that he needed a demonstration of force "to show the enemy that we were still serious about our commitment in Vietnam." Events in Cambodia gave him the opportunity for which he yearned.[7]

While Communist activity in South Vietnam had declined in early 1970, it had, if anything, increased in Cambodia and Laos. Prince Norodom

Sihanouk of Cambodia had previously maintained his country's neutrality while permitting the North Vietnamese and Viet Cong to use Cambodian territory along the entire Cambodian-Vietnamese border for the resupply routes and staging areas used to support their operations in South Vietnam. Moreover, Sihanouk had permitted supplies to land at the port of Sihanoukville and cross overland to the Communist border bases. By this point in the war, an estimated 85 percent of all supplies to the Communist forces in the south arrived by this route.[8]

On March 18, 1970, while Sihanouk was vacationing in Paris, his Premier, General Lon Nol, engineered a bloodless coup and promptly asked the North Vietnamese and Viet Cong to leave Cambodia. The Vietnamese Communists refused to give up their sanctuary areas and with their Cambodian allies, the Khmer Rouge, launched a wave of attacks to secure a strip of Cambodian territory ten to fifteen kilometers wide along the South Vietnamese frontier. The inexperienced Cambodian army was no match for the Communist forces and it soon appeared that the North Vietnamese and Khmer Rouge were going to take all of Cambodia east of the Mekong River. Lon Nol requested assistance form the United States.[9]

The sanctuaries and Communist supply routes along the Vietnamese-Cambodian border had long been a thorn in the side of the allied war effort. A delegation of U.S. congressmen had traveled to Vietnam in 1968 and had reported that the North Vietnamese and Viet Cong were using the eastern provinces of Cambodia as troop-concentration areas, training centers, and logistics bases. This area also contained the southern portion of the Ho Chi Minh Trail, an intricate network of trails and roads that extended along the Cambodian and Laotian borders from North Vietnam to just west of Saigon. Intelligence reports in early 1970 estimated that a monthly average of 4,000 tons of war materiel moved down the Ho Chi Minh Trail to the Communist forces operating out of numerous bases in Cambodia.[10]

These bases were essentially safe havens for the enemy forces, who could conduct operations in South Vietnam and then withdraw into the relative safety of Cambodia where they could not be pursued by American ground forces. General Dave Richard Palmer, author of *Summons of the Trumpet*, best described the problem this way:

> Two-thirds of South Vietnam's population lived in the two southern military regions, both of which bordered Cambodia. Fourteen major North Vietnamese bases stood inside Cambodia, three neighboring the Fourth Corps area and seven by the Third Corps. Some were within thirty-five miles of Saigon. As long as they remained "off limits" to Allied forces, it

was [as] if a loaded and cocked pistol was being held to the head of South Vietnam.[11]

President Nixon had authorized the secret Menu bombings in 1969 to attack the Cambodian sanctuaries, but the trail and base area complex proved resistant to attack from the air. B-52 raids slowed down infiltration through the area, but did not stop Communist use of the trail complex or the staging areas. By the time of the Cambodian coup in 1970, there were an estimated 40,000–60,000 North Vietnamese Army in the area and they were expanding toward the central provinces of Kompong Cha, Prey Veng, and Svay Rieng, which put them within striking distance of the capital city of Phnom Penh. The United States could not allow the North Vietnamese to take Cambodia because then the whole of that country would become a sanctuary for the Communist forces and the overland route from Sihanoukville would be open to full-scale resupply efforts. The situation was critical, not only for the U.S. forces remaining in South Vietnam, but for the RVNAF as more American forces withdrew and the South Vietnamese were left to their own devices. As General Palmer wrote after the war, "So long as Hanoi persisted in aggression, so long as the North Vietnamese Army enjoyed sanctuaries within easy striking distance of Saigon … then so long would the war or the threat of imminent invasion cast a dark shadow across South Vietnam."[12]

In February 1970, Secretary of Defense Laird again visited Saigon. While briefing the secretary, General Abrams made a strong case for invasion of not only the Cambodian sanctuaries, but also others located in Laos. Hesitant to see an expansion of the war, Laird was unconvinced. That month, news of the secret bombing in Laos became public and the outcry in Congress was immediate. Laird was persuaded that neither Nixon's critics nor a growing sector of the American people would favorably receive any further widening of the war.[13]

Shortly after Laird's return to the United States, the situation in Cambodia took a turn for the worse. In a February message to the Joint Chiefs of Staff, Admiral John S. McCain, Commander in Chief, U.S. Pacific Forces (CINCPAC), warned that "the Cambodian sanctuary had become a primary base essential to the enemy if he is to accomplish his overall objectives against Vietnamization." Moreover, McCain warned that intelligence indicators pointed toward a major Communist offensive in Cambodia in April or May. His warning proved timely and accurate because on March 29 North Vietnamese troops began moving westward in the direction of Phnom Penh from their sanctuary bases in the "Fishhook," a strategic sliver of land that pushed into South Vietnam west of An Loc, and the

"Parrot's Beak," in Cambodia's Svay Rieng province, where the border comes within thirty-three miles of Saigon. The North Vietnamese Army launched major ground attacks against Cambodian strong points all along the Cambodian-South Vietnamese border and then turned into the Cambodian interior. Within a few days, the much stronger Communist forces had pushed Lon Nol's troops completely out of the Parrot's Beak area, which was abandoned to North Vietnamese control on April 10. By the middle of the month, it appeared that the Communists were preparing to encircle Phnom Penh, and the Lon Nol government was in imminent danger of falling.[14]

Nixon and his advisors had been anxiously watching the worsening situation in Cambodia very closely. On March 25, alarmed by the North Vietnamese assault on Lon Nol's forces, the President had charged the Joint Chiefs of Staff (JCS) with drafting a plan for an assault into Cambodia by either U.S. or South Vietnamese forces to relieve the pressure on Phnom Penh if the city came under direct attack by the Communists. The JCS passed the President's request on to General Abrams in Saigon on March 30. Abrams submitted a plan to Kissinger and the National Security Council for the President's consideration — it offered three potential courses of action. The first option was to encourage the South Vietnamese to increase their heretofore-limited cross-border raids into enemy sanctuaries. The second was to permit the South Vietnamese to launch larger and more effective forays into Cambodia by providing additional American artillery and air support. The last option was to launch a full-scale attack into the base areas and supply depots by South Vietnamese forces accompanied by U.S. advisors. The object would be to disrupt the enemy's command and control elements, demolish his logistical installations, and eliminate the elusive Central Office of South Vietnam (COSVN), headquarters for all enemy operations in the south. Nixon delayed a decision and Abrams was told to hold the plans in abeyance for the time being while the administration tried to determine what was going on inside Cambodia.[15] As the situation became clearer in early April, Nixon and his advisors realized that something had to be done.

On April 19, the President flew to Hawaii to greet the crew of Apollo 13, which had just returned from a near-disastrous mission to the moon. While in Honolulu, Nixon received a briefing from Admiral McCain, who stressed that the situation was becoming desperate. He told the President, "If you are going to withdraw another 150,000 from South Vietnam this year, you must protect Saigon's western flank by an invasion of the Cambodian sanctuaries." [16]

McCain's briefing was on Nixon's mind upon his return to Washington, where a heated debate ensued over what to do next. Kissinger and the Joint Chiefs of Staff believed that Cambodia was ready to fall and urged the President to do something to preclude that potential disaster from becoming reality. On the other hand, Secretary of State Rogers warned Nixon that U.S. intervention in Cambodia, on top of the breaking news of secret bombing in Laos, might prove to be a political nightmare for the President.

Despite the potential for a debacle in Cambodia, Nixon went ahead with his troop withdrawal announcement on April 20. Such a move in the face of the rapidly deteriorating situation on Vietnam's flank was fraught with danger, but the administration was confronted with a serious predicament that Kissinger later described in his memoirs:

> The dilemma was plain to see. Troop cuts poulticed public sores at home, but they were evaporating Hanoi's need to bargain about our disengagement. And if Vietnamization was not making good the defensive gaps created by our withdrawals, we hazarded not only the negotiating lever but also South Vietnam's independence and the entire basis for our sacrifices.17

Nixon was caught between the proverbial rock and hard place. He had to continue his force drawdowns or suffer a political disaster at home. On the other hand, he had to do something about Cambodia in order to protect the Vietnamization effort and buy time to continue the buildup of the RVNAF. The question raised by this last choice was how to do it without creating a firestorm of controversy here in the United States.

On Tuesday, April 21, the President met with Kissinger and Richard Helms, the director of the Central Intelligence Agency. Helms briefed the President on the attacks and emphatically warned him that the Cambodian Army faced almost certain destruction. Nixon authorized an immediate transfer of funds and military equipment to Lon Nol's army. He met later in the day with Kissinger and Laird to discuss strategic options. It was clear to all that something had to be done in Cambodia or it would soon fall to North Vietnamese and Khmer Rouge forces. The loss of Cambodia would have dire consequences for the Vietnamization program, and destroy Nixon's timetable for "peace with honor." South Vietnam would then be in serious jeopardy.[18]

Later that day, Nixon sent Kissinger a message that began, "I think we need a bold move in Cambodia ... to show that we stand with Lon Nol.... They [the Communists] are romping in there, and the only government in Cambodia in the last twenty-five years that had the guts to take a pro–Western and pro–American stand is ready to fall." The president called for a National Security Council (NSC) meeting the next day.[19]

Meanwhile, the White House received a long message from Ambassador Bunker and General Abrams. They emphasized the dire consequences for Vietnamization if Cambodia fell and recommended U.S.-South Vietnamese operations against the key Communist sanctuaries.[20]

During the meeting of the National Security Council the next day, Kissinger presented a detailed report on the military situation in Vietnam. He emphasized that the loss of Cambodia, or even the expansion of their sanctuary areas, would give the Communists the capacity to inflict increased casualties on U.S. forces in South Vietnam, and the resulting situation would almost certainly endanger the Vietnamization program. This would likely force a slowdown in the withdrawal of American forces. Kissinger enumerated three options. The first was to do nothing, which he said in his memoirs was the "preferred course of the State and Defense Departments." Kissinger's preferred option was to attack the sanctuaries only with South Vietnamese units. The last option was to use whatever force was necessary, including American troops, to neutralize all of the base areas, which was strongly supported by Bunker, Abrams, and the JCS.[21]

The consensus from the ensuing discussion was that the first option lacked viability. The U.S. could not afford to let the Communists take Cambodia, despite the potential political fallout from any American involvement. There was some discussion of the use of American troops, but generally it was felt that the U.S role should be limited to air and artillery support. According to Kissinger, Laird and Rogers even opposed this limited American participation. Vice President Spiro Agnew spoke up, saying that if the administration really wanted to protect Vietnamization, it should attack both sanctuaries and use whatever American troops were necessary to achieve success. Nixon agreed that something had to be done, but believed that the South Vietnamese should carry out the strike. He authorized the use of U.S. air support, but only "on the basis of demonstrated necessity." He did not commit himself to an attack of the Fishhook area. He later described his thought process in his memoirs. He wrote, "Giving the South Vietnamese an operation on their own would be a major boost to their morale as well as provide a practical demonstration of the success of Vietnamization." When the meeting adjourned, Wheeler sent Abrams a message advising him to begin planning for the Cambodian operation. He said, "Our objective is to maximize the use of ARVN assets, so as to minimize U.S. involvement, and to maintain lowest possible U.S. profile.... U.S. advisors in Cambodia will be restricted to those required to control U.S aircraft when and if introduced."[22]

The order to go into Cambodia was well received by Abrams and Ambassador Bunker. The Americans had long wanted the freedom to pursue the Communists into the Cambodian sanctuaries. As for the South Vietnamese, President Thieu had some reservations about sending his troops into the Communist strongholds in Cambodia, but the ARVN forces had already made limited forays into the border areas. On March 27–28, a South Vietnamese Ranger battalion, supported by artillery and tactical air support, had gone three kilometers into Kandal Province to destroy a Communist base camp. Four days later, ARVN troops penetrated sixteen kilometers into Cambodia in pursuit of the Communists. On April 20, 1970, South Vietnamese soldiers went into the Parrot's Beak area and killed 144 of the enemy. Now it appeared that Nixon was willing to give a green light to a much bigger push into Cambodia.

After the meeting on April 22, Kissinger received a telephone call from the President. According to Kissinger, Nixon hated to be shown up in a group as being less tough than his advisors and in this case the President appeared to be somewhat chagrinned that Agnew had been more forceful than he had been in the NSC meeting. Also, he had been considering what the intelligence briefers had told him about the Fishhook area. They had said that this area was even larger than the Parrot's Beak and reportedly contained the elusive COSVN, the supposed "nerve center" of the entire Communist effort in Southeast Asia. Nixon told Kissinger that he was thinking about widening his guidance to include attacks on all the sanctuaries along the Cambodian border, not just the Parrot's Beak as previously discussed at the NSC meeting, the Fishhook too. Kissinger took this to mean that he was contemplating the use of U.S. troops in a much broader Cambodian operation. In a memorandum to Kissinger on April 22, Nixon contended, "We need a bold move in Cambodia to show that we stand with Lon Nol." Laird urged restraint, but Nixon decided on "the big play" even though he expected "a hell of an uproar at home."[23]

In the days leading up to the incursion, Nixon retreated to Camp David where he repeatedly viewed the movie *Patton* starring George C. Scott. On the screen of the lodge's theater, Patton towered over Nixon, ordering troops across North Africa and into Italy as World War II reached its climax. Patton, Nixon reflected, was a commander of action and decision. A quarter of a century after the legendary tank commander fearlessly matched wits with Erwin Rommel, Nixon was determined to "go for broke" in Southeast Asia. It was a gamble that could secure Nixon's place in history — if it succeeded.

On April 29, South Vietnam announced that its military had advanced on the Parrot's Beak. Nixon's congressional foes urged the President to refrain from sending Americans into action in Cambodia. Nixon took his case to the American people the following evening in a televised address. He suggested that the military operation would be a temporary one, designed to expel Communist forces from staging areas along the Cambodian-South Vietnamese border. In fact, Nixon argued, the incursion would speed up the pace of America's exit from Vietnam. The action was necessary to protect the lives of American soldiers who were being struck by Communists who would then retreat into safe havens in Cambodia. Then, refreshed, they would strike our troops again. An "incursion," the President contended, was not an "invasion." By whatever name, the fighting was to continue for two months.

Nixon's speech had words of warning for antiwar protestors. While heroes in uniform were risking their lives 10,000 miles from our shores, "We live in an age of anarchy both abroad and at home...." He lambasted "mindless attacks on ... great universities...." The Vietnam War was a test of America's "will and character." Nixon, who knew much about tests and challenges, vowed, "we will not be humbled. We will not be defeated."[24]

On May 1, Nixon visited the Pentagon and urged the military to "blow the hell" out of the Communist staging areas. He told civilian employees, "you see those bums, you know, blowing up the campuses ... those boys that are on the college campuses are the luckiest people in the world...." He contrasted the protestors, enjoying the safety offered by a college environment, with the brave men in uniform "who are just doing their duty.... They stand tall and they are proud."

It was not just the students who were loud in their anger about what they perceived to be just another sleight of hand by Richard Nixon. Congress had not been consulted prior to the action; neither had Cambodia's Lon Nol. Editorialists criticized the incursion. The *New York Times* (which had published an article a week earlier predicting the invasion), the *Washington Post*, and the *Wall Street Journal* voiced their reservations. The last-mentioned publication, not known for its radical opinions, labeled the action "deeper entanglement" in the morass of a war that showed no sign of resolution. Even a sizeable number of State Department officials voiced their objections to the incursion, as did thirty-seven college presidents.[25]

It would be on the nation's college campuses that the rawness of dissent manifested itself most clearly. The University of South Carolina closed down amid protests. Similar student unrest took hold in California and in New England's Ivy League schools. Ohio Governor James Rhodes condemned protests at his state's universities, led by instigators, Rhodes asserted, who were "worse than the Brown Shirts and the Communist element...." The governor promised to "eradicate" the disloyal protestors. At

Kent State University, on May 4, Rhodes sent in the National Guard, which amid the confusion, fired upon the students, killing four and wounding fifteen. The photograph of that incident, with blood flowing down a campus walkway, illustrated the fracturing of our society. The guardsmen and the students were of the same generation, torn open by the war.[26]

At four o'clock on the morning of May 8, Nixon ventured from the White House to talk to a student encampment on the Ellipse, near the Washington Monument, near where the Vietnam Memorial now stands. He tried to explain that his goals, like theirs, were "to stop the killing and end the war." The young Americans were mourning the deaths at Kent State and another fatal encounter at predominantly black Jackson State University. Nixon told the students assembled in the shadow of the Washington monument, "Most of you think I'm an S.O.B., but ... I understand how you feel." He attempted to discuss football and clean water and shook hands with a "bearded fellow." There would be no rapprochement, however, and the contest of wills between the increasingly vocal opponents of the war and the man in the White House would continue unabated.[27]

The results of the incursion into the Cambodian regions of the Parrot's Beak and Fishhook were mixed. Large quantities of ammunition and supplies were captured and over 10,000 North Vietnamese and Viet Cong soldiers were killed while the allies lost less than 1,000 dead, including 338 Americans. The RVNAF fought well under the leadership of Lieutenant General Do Cao Tri, a soldier referred to as the "Patton of Parrot's Beak" by *Time* magazine. The operation gave the South Vietnamese a much-needed boost in morale and General Dave Palmer later called the Cambodian incursion "a benchmark in the maturing of the ARVN."[28] All of that having been said, however, the gains in these large battles in the Cambodian hinterlands were, like those of the victory on Hamburger Hill, short-lived. The Soviet Union and the People's Republic of China would replace the materiel lost by the Communists. The mothers of North Vietnam would supply replacements for the dead soldiers, heroes of the war against colonialism. And Richard Nixon would fail to gain hero status for himself.

Chapter 6
Irritants

"The question is: which danger does the People's Republic face? Is it the danger of American aggression, or Soviet aggression?"
Richard Nixon to Mao Zedong, 1972.

Before the Vietnam War divided America, the country was wrestling with the question of racial equality. The modern civil rights movement took form in the 1955–1956 Montgomery Bus Boycott that was led by the charismatic Martin Luther King, Jr. Strengthening the movement was the 1954 *Brown v. Board of Education* decision in which the U.S. Supreme Court exposed the farce of "separate but equal" schools. The court followed the next year with the second Brown ruling that ordered integration to take place "with all deliberate speed." Still, pockets of segregation held out, resisting change, throughout the decade of the 1960s. That is why King went to Memphis, Tennessee, in the spring of 1968, to lead sanitation workers as they argued for fairer wages and better working conditions. Despite more than a decade of protests, legislation, and court decisions, racism refused to die.[1]

The Supreme Court, in 1969, mandated the immediate integration of the South's schools. It would seem, after fifteen years, that such change should be orderly. However, in the era of Vietnam, nothing was orderly. Chaos—not order—flowed across America. Even with a long, unbroken line of court cases and legislation, some southern school districts prayed for an extension to be granted to segregation. In 1968, Richard Nixon had won the presidency with the help of South Carolina's Senator Strom Thurmond, a Republican who had sought the White House in 1948 as the Dixiecrat nominee, vowing, "There are not enough soldiers in the army" to force the South to integrate. Was there a tacit understanding that Thurmond's reward for backing Nixon — instead of the more conservative California Governor Ronald Reagan — would be weak enforcement of civil rights? For a few months, Nixon's Departments of Health, Education, and Welfare and Justice seemed sympathetic to Thurmond's wishes to see segregated schools allowed in the Deep South. Token integration sprinkled African-American pupils in some school districts, "freedom of choice" it was called, while many districts, believing that Nixon owed his election to Thurmond's "Southern Strategy," ignored court rulings and the law of the land. Finally, in the summer of 1970, Thurmond and his allies realized that the federal government would now put its authority solidly behind integration. Integration would come within weeks, and in some districts, violence occurred as black schools were hurriedly consolidated with white ones.[2] These violent displays, coming within the first few months of the clashes on college campuses, were yet more examples of how fractured the country had become. A decade of conflict had weakened the social fabric. Race and politics still divided people into factions, suspicious of each other's intentions and loyalties.

After the sharp reaction to his Cambodian incursion, Richard Nixon had suspicions of his own. He ordered Chief of Staff Bob Haldeman to restrict the flow of White House news to the *New York Times* and the *Washington Post* and to favor media outlets that had not criticized the Cambodian operation. Educational institutions that had seemed sympathetic to antiwar protesters were also to be punished by withholding grants and government contracts. Nixon's enemies were the country's enemies, the President reasoned. They were to be pursued, cornered, and silenced. At a June 5 meeting, Nixon urged the Central Intelligence Agency, the Federal Bureau of Investigation, the National Security Agency, and the Defense Intelligence Agency to work with White House staff member Tim Huston to spy on American civilians. Remarkably, the FBI Director, J. Edgar Hoover, rescinded the Huston Plan and Nixon shelved the alarming domestic surveillance effort, even though the seeds of Watergate had been sown.[3]

Nixon continued to believe that disloyal radical groups such as the Black Panthers and the antiwar Weathermen were undermining the country. He argued that Abraham Lincoln, trying to preserve the Union in 1861, had trampled upon citizens' liberties; the President believed that a similar course had to be followed in 1970. The nation was at war abroad and at home; Communists were masquerading in the guise of the Students for a Democratic Society and black militant groups. Thus, the Huston Plan's elements, including the use of the Internal Revenue Service, would slip into use with Nixon's endorsement. These abuses would in four years drive Nixon from office.[4]

A special commission, chaired by Pennsylvania's former governor William Scranton, sifted through the debris left behind by the 1970 campus demonstrations. The commission urged Nixon to end America's involvement in Southeast Asia. The long war, and that spring's Cambodian incursion, had radicalized the nation's college campuses. Scranton argued that students, seeing themselves perilously close to the military draft, did not trust Nixon. To eighteen-year-old males, unable to vote until 1971, Vietnamization was a failure, and they had to vocally express their displeasure. To them, the reality was that the United States was trapped in Vietnam. Women and African-Americans were also wary of the commander in chief. They saw him as out of touch with the grievances of the people who believed themselves to be excluded from political power. Scranton warned that other social confrontations, such as the one at Kent State University, were bound to happen if Nixon did not find a way out of the Asian morass.[5]

Nixon, however, had a visceral dislike for Ivy League college students and their eastern establishment allies in the media. Always sensitive about his humble origins and degree from California's small Whittier College, Nixon sought to align himself with "disaffected Democrats" who were troubled by antiwar disruptions. They were hard-working patriots, loyal beyond question to their anti–Communist commander in chief, regardless of his party affiliation. Many Americans, he suggested, believed that the civilian population should mute their criticism of the war while soldiers were under fire in the field. The "silent majority" of Americans, Democrats and Republicans, knew when to lower their voices. Vice President Spiro Agnew phrased the question this way: "Will America be led by a president elected by a majority of the American people, or will we be intimidated by a disruptive, radical, and militant minority—the pampered prodigies of the liberals in the United States Senate?" Loyal Americans, Nixon added, had had enough of the "creeping permissiveness" that had eroded the nation's unity. In a classic battle cry, the president rallied his supporters by asserting, "It's time for the great silent majority of Americans to stand up and be counted."[6]

An analysis of the 1970 elections certainly reveals the polarization occurring in the United States. In Tennessee, Republican William Brock defeated Senator Albert Gore, Sr., who had become a critic of Nixon on Vietnam. The GOP picked up another Senate seat but lost nine House of Representative seats as well as eleven governorships. Nixon, however, was jubilant. He controlled the White House and he focused on the pathway that he believed would lead him to re-election two years later. The "irritant" of Vietnam, as he labeled the war, would not stand in the way of bold foreign policy initiatives that would guarantee his victory in 1972.[7]

When he took office in January 1969, Nixon had spoken of the need for an "era of negotiation" that would create "a structure of peace." In Southeast Asia, he felt frustrated by unfruitful negotiations where the Communists seemed to be intent on just biding their time while Vietnamization progressed. Nixon was realistic about the Communist strategy and he was determined to achieve "peace with honor" in Vietnam in his own time frame, at his pace, in his own way. He would not buckle under to congressional critics; they could be defeated like Tennessee's Gore. He certainly would not cave in to pampered college students or militant minorities.

Henry Kissinger, a student of the Congress of Vienna's Prince Metternich, nurtured Nixon's realism. The world was a volatile, unpredictable place where order almost had to be forced upon warring parties. In January 1971, Nixon identified five great economic powers: the United States, the Soviet Union, Western Europe, Japan, and the People's Republic of China. Nixon, who had built his political résumé upon vigorous anti–Communism and pursuit of agents of totalitarianism such as Alger Hiss and the Rosenbergs, was about to take a starkly realistic position on China.[8]

Nixon's plan was to apply pressure on the Soviet Union, North Vietnam's most reliable ally, by reaching out to China. Mao's regime had clashed with Moscow and there had been bloodshed on the frozen frontier between China and the Soviet Union. The old belief, almost dogma to Nixon earlier in his career, that China and the Soviet Union were carbon copies of each other, was erroneous—unrealistic. The two nations were actually rivals with each other, and Nixon could capitalize on their rivalry.[9]

The first contacts between the United States and China were modest. Ping-pong teams would compete with each other. The real game was far more substantive. Kissinger was employed to covertly open a diplomatic door to Mao and premier Zhou Enlai. Aiding the Nixon Administration was Pakistani President Yahyn Khan, who retained the confidence of both Chinese and American leaders.[10]

Thus, in late 1970 and early 1971 the framework was laid for dialogue between the United States and China. There would be obstacles, however, such as the February 1971 incursion into Laos, which the Chinese criticized. Nixon provided air support for the Thieu government's troops, who were trying to locate enemy bases in Laos, but he was determined to look beyond Vietnam if he could. The real goal was diplomacy with China which would rearrange the dynamics of global power. In early July 1971, Kissinger, unbeknownst to Secretary of State William Rogers, traveled secretly from Pakistan to meet with authorities in Beijing. Remarkably, Rogers was continuing to espouse the traditional American policy of loyalty to Taiwan and criticism of Mao. Nixon and Kissinger had excluded the Secretary of State from their plans just as they would exclude Thieu time and time again from discussions concerning Vietnam.[11]

By July 11, Kissinger was able to cable Nixon with the codeword "Eureka!" China and the United States had had serious discussions about the future of Taiwan, the tensions between India and Pakistan, the war in Indochina, and the threat posed by the Soviet Union. Kissinger had shared with the Chinese satellite photographs of Soviet troop movements that proved the danger posed by Moscow. Four days later, Nixon announced to the world that he had accepted an invitation to visit the People's Republic of China the following year in an attempt "to build a lasting peace."[12] Skillfully, Nixon had played the China card. He hoped to prod the Soviets into reducing the world's supply of strategic weapons and into applying pressure on the North Vietnamese to seriously negotiate in Paris. Furthermore, the President hoped to rid himself of the "irritant" of the Vietnam conflict as he embarked on a new relationship with mainland China. In 1971 there would, however, be other irritants with which he must deal.

Chapter 7

Madman

"They're just a bunch of shits. Tawdry filthy shits."
Henry Kissinger, 1972.

Even as Richard Nixon stood on the brink of his greatest diplomatic achievement, he could not escape the clamor of the antiwar movement. It appeared to Nixon that a vocal minority, as opposed to the silent majority, was unwilling to endorse the commander in chief's Vietnamization policy. Thousands of Vietnam veterans banded together to form Vietnam Veterans Against the War. From January 31 through February 2, 1971, 116 veterans testified before sympathetic members of Congress in what is called the Winter Soldier Investigation. Veteran John Kerry, who would eventually become Senator Kerry, explained, "The My Lai massacre was not an aberration, the isolated act of a ne'er-do-well second lieutenant gone berserk.... It was symbolic of a war gone berserk." The veterans told of rapes, decapitations, severed limbs, murdered civilians and numerous other atrocities committed by Americans in Southeast Asia.[1]

While the public listened to Kerry and the other witnesses, Thieu's government launched its February 1971 invasion of Laos, code-named Lam Son 719. What followed was a monthlong debacle for the South Vietnamese. Not only did they fail to sever the Ho Chi Minh Trail, a primary objective of the operation, but the ARVN became mired in a muddy quagmire that symbolized the war itself. Without massive U.S. air cover, the South Vietnamese would not have been able to pull back from Laos without incurring even more losses than they suffered as it was. However, General Abrams announced that Lam Son 719 had been a success for Thieu's soldiers, estimating that the enemy had suffered 20,000 casualties. The

South Vietnamese, in turn, incurred 7,682 casualties, almost half of their force, including 1,764 killed. The United States lost 215 killed in action as well as 108 helicopters. In addition, 1,187 Americans were wounded in the operation. In Washington, Nixon announced during an April 7 speech, "Tonight, I can report that Vietnamization has succeeded."[2]

Actually, the failure of Lam Son 719 raised serious questions in the Pentagon about whether Vietnamization could ever succeed. The South Vietnamese had assembled a million-man army, backed by U.S. air power and equipped with modern technology. Still, they could not defeat the Communists who faded into the jungles and rice paddies, while continuing to move along the Ho Chi Minh Trail in spite of American air power and the persistent efforts of Thieu's forces.

Lam Son 719 exposed two of the biggest impediments to Vietnamization's success: the poor quality of leadership in the RVNAF, starting with South Vietnam's President himself, and the politicization of that leadership. In the first days of the action, from February 8 to February 10, 1971, the ARVN forces met little North Vietnamese resistance and they had reached their first objective, A Luoi, a village about twenty kilometers inside Laos at the crossroads of Routes 9 and 92. However, by that time, the weather had turned the main path of attack, Route 9, into a muddy track that inhibited the effective use of armor by the invaders. At that point, the advance stopped and the Communists began positioning reinforcements to block the attackers. General Hoang Xuan Lam, the operation's overall commander ,and his major subordinate commanders did nothing to restart the advance. On February 12, President Thieu, concerned about the potentially negative political consequences of large casualties, directed General Lam to hold down losses and to cancel the operation if their number should rise to as many as 3,000. From that point on, the minimization of casualties became a major concern of the leadership. As the situation in Laos continued to deteriorate, President Thieu became exasperated by the lack of progress being made. He ordered General Do Cao Tri of Parrot's Beak fame to relieve General Lam. But while on his way to the front, General Tri's helicopter crashed and he was killed. No change in leadership took place.[3]

The failure of the command structure was also reflected in the fact that at times the commanders of the Airborne and Marine divisions, who were supposedly under General Lam's command, simply ignored his orders. They themselves were both lieutenant generals and had become accustomed to answering directly to Saigon. Thieu refused to intercede in these counterproductive squabbles because these two generals were commanders of some of his most important anticoup forces. The North

Vietnamese, under the direction of General Vo Nguyen Giap, began to counterattack and, combined with the indecision at the top of the South Vietnamese leadership, the erstwhile invasion turned into a rout. The ARVN now had to fight its way back across the border and some simply ran or fought their way on to helicopters sent there to evacuate wounded. While many units maintained their cohesion and fought well during Lam Son 719, the overall impression of the ARVN performance was negative. James McCarney wrote in the *Philadelphia Inquirer*:

> The South Vietnamese have invented a new kind of warfare in Laos. They avoid fighting whenever they can, they flee an area when the communists start showing up on the battlefield, and they consistently claim "victory" or "success" when the operation is over.... Many U.S. military men used to criticize the South Vietnamese tendency to "cut and run" when a battle loomed.... Now, when the Vietnamese flee, the Pentagon spokesmen are inclined to praise their "mobility."[4]

While the *Philadelphia Bulletin* published a more balanced account of the Laotian campaign, it also provided an analysis that was an unwitting prophecy of things to come in 1975. "Without air cover and without 51 battalions of U.S. troops holding the fort ... [one] can only guess how much worse the situation might have been."[5]

Lam Son mobilized the antiwar protesters in the United States. John Kerry and 1,000 Vietnam Veterans Against the War sponsored a rally at the Tomb of the Unknown Soldier. The Nixon Administration secured a court order prohibiting the protesters from camping on the Mall. The crowd defied the order as the demonstrators, now numbering more than 200,000 and including mothers of men killed in the war, converged on Arlington Cemetery. On April 23, 2,000 veterans tossed medals that they had won in combat on the Capitol steps. Kerry described the dilemma that faced his fellow veterans—"whether to kill on military orders and be a criminal, or to refuse to kill and be a criminal."[6]

Agonizing over the war, Daniel Ellsberg, one of Kissinger's former Harvard students and a Pentagon researcher, had evolved from a loyal prowar Defense Department official into a man troubled by what his research into the origins of America's policy told him. Since early 1969, he had been photocopying secret documents from this research, which had been authorized when Robert McNamara was Defense Secretary. These documents came to be known as the Pentagon Papers. They told an embarrassing story of duplicity and manipulation by our government in Southeast Asia stretching back to the 1950s. While the time frame for the study concluded before Richard Nixon came to power. He was incensed when

Ellsberg passed the documents on to the *New York Times* (Ellsberg also shared them with Senator J. William Fulbright). Nixon secured an injunction against that publication, but it was too late to keep the story from the press. Throughout June 1971, the *Times*, the *Boston Globe* and the *Washington Post* published the tale of assassinations and lies under the protection of a favorable Supreme Court ruling. The First Amendment shielded the press, and so Nixon ordered his administration to search for any official who might be tempted to contribute to the sordid literature of American involvement in the war.[7]

In South Vietnam, President Thieu was seeking re-election. He had been humiliated in 1967 when he won with only thirty-five percent of the total vote. With CIA assistance, Thieu bribed his way to victory in the autumn 1971 presidential elections. He excluded his chief rival, former president Nguyen Cao Ky, from the ballot. Thus, Thieu received 94.3 percent of the vote, earning what he referred to as a "mandate from heaven," a term that he borrowed from Confucianism and the belief that the right to rule was granted to an individual by heaven alone.[8]

Henry Kissinger sought to achieve a breakthrough in his negotiations with North Vietnam's Le Duc Tho, but secret meetings and public sessions seemed to yield nothing for Kissinger. The Communists held fast to their demands that Thieu leave power and that the Provisional Revolutionary Government participate in creating a new South Vietnam. Four years in Paris had produced little change and the Communists seemed prepared to wait for the inevitable final exit of the American troops. Kissinger described Le Duc Tho and the Communists as "a bunch of shits" but his expletives could not force the Communists to accept terms favorable to the Americans. They were determined not to be victimized by a repeat of the 1954 agreement, which, despite the pledges from the Western powers, had never been fully implemented. The promised 1956 national elections had never occurred and the North Vietnamese would stubbornly resist Kissinger.[9]

As we have seen, Nixon considered Vietnam an "irritant," an impediment to his wish to reach out in a grand gesture to China. How could he pressure the North Vietnamese and their Soviet sponsors so that the "irritant" could be removed. By the spring of 1972, with visits to China and the Soviet Union upon him, Nixon shared with Kissinger his plan to bring the war to a close: "I'm going to show the bastards. Unless they deal with us, I'm going to bomb the hell out of them." True to the script, Kissinger informed Le Duc Tho that Nixon was behaving like a "madman"; the unbalanced American commander in chief might try anything to bolster Thieu.[10]

The North Vietnamese, who had fought the Chinese, the Japanese and the French over the centuries, were not intimidated. By March 1972, only 95,000 American soldiers remained in Vietnam, and only 6,000 of them were engaged in combat. Communist General Vo Nguyen Giap had been promising for months "a great victory over the Americans and their Saigon puppets." He launched the Easter Offensive on Good Friday, March 30, 1972. After a heavy artillery barrage, more than 30,000 North Vietnamese troops, supported by 200 Soviet tanks, crossed the demilitarized zone. On May 1, they took Quang Tri City, about thirty kilometers inside South Vietnam. More Communist forces massed inside Cambodia and still others attacked in the Central Highlands.[11]

Nixon used vigorous air support to prevent the collapse of Thieu's regime. He told General John W. Vogt, Commander of the Seventh Air Force, "to get down there and use whatever air power you need to turn this thing around.... Stop this offensive." Thus, Operation Linebacker unleashed Air Force, Marine and Navy bombers against North Vietnam, with B-52s attacking within a few miles of Hanoi and Haiphong. When Le Duc Tho refused to change his bargaining position, Nixon told Kissinger, "The bastards have never been bombed like they're going to be bombed this time."[12]

The "madman" suspended the Paris Peace Talks on May 4, 1972. He announced that Operation Linebacker would continue indefinitely and that the U.S. Navy would mine and blockade the North Vietnamese coast. Waves of B-52s struck every forty-five minutes around the clock for weeks. On June 18, the North Vietnamese began to withdraw from the captured areas, having been repulsed by South Vietnamese forces supported by massive U.S. firepower. The invaders had not captured a single provinceial-capital, and failed to decisively defeat any major South Vietnamese unit.[13]

The Soviets and Chinese had offered only cautious support for their fellow Communists. Nixon had driven a wedge between the Communist nations and, in late June, he traveled to Moscow to sign the long-awaited Strategic Arms Limitation Treaty. Within just six months, Nixon had walked along China's Great Wall during his February 21, 1972, journey for peace, toasted Mao, issued a communiqué of Sino-American friendship, unleashed a furious air and naval campaign against North Vietnam, withdrawn most U.S. ground troops from Southeast Asia, preserved President Thieu's government, persuaded the Soviet Union's Leonid Brezhnev to sign an arms limitation treaty, and stood on the edge of what he knew would be a landmark re-election. The "madman" had outwitted his foes, or so it seemed.

Chapter 8

Last Chance

"This is your last chance to use military force effectively to win this war."
Richard Nixon, 1972.

Throughout his long life, Richard Nixon proved repeatedly that he could never be counted out. Above all else, he was a survivor. His humble childhood (his father, he said, was "a little man") turned him into a tough combatant. His Quaker mother's pacifism failed to influence him. Fighting was a central part of Nixon's life; he was a fierce competitor, unafraid to march into the arena. His law school years at Duke University prove this point. He earned the nickname "ironbutt" because he sat for hours in his small, unheated garage apartment, poring over his law books. He would not settle for second in his class. Interestingly, he once slid across a faculty office transom in order to scan the instructor's grade book. He was always determined to be in conscious control of his own destiny.[1]

In politics, also, he was alert and ferocious. He demolished Representative Jerry Voorhis in 1946, trumpeting his own World War II naval service while criticizing Voorhis' lack of a military record. Nixon's battle for the U.S. Senate in 1950 was brutal. Helen Gahagan Douglas and her left-leaning Hollywood friends did not deserve to represent California. Nixon, the slayer of Alger Hiss, could be counted on to keep a watchful eye on Communist agents in our midst. He was a vigilant patriot, warning against traitors who had "Ph.D.s from Dean Acheson's Cowardly College of Communist Containment."[2] "Coward" would never appear on his résumé.

Nixon became Dwight Eisenhower's running mate in 1952 so that the general could avoid the hand-to-hand combat of the political trenches. When foes whispered about his alleged slush fund, Nixon went on national television to defend himself and his family. The Checkers Speech transformed the use of that medium for political warfare. When Eisenhower refused to speak up for Nixon's integrity, the Californian liked to claim that he told the general that it was "time to shit or get off the pot." Nixon would stay on the ticket in 1952 and resisted Eisenhower's efforts four years later to ease him from the vice presidency into a cabinet office.[3]

Repeatedly, Nixon outwitted and outfought enemies. When he suffered defeat in 1960 at the hands of JFK and two years later in the California gubernatorial race, he planned a comeback — despite bitterly telling reporters in 1962, "This is my last news conference. You won't have Nixon to kick around anymore." He never really left the stage, endorsing the doomed Barry Goldwater in 1964 and campaigning for Republican candidates in 1966.[4]

The "new Nixon" of 1968 was not terribly different from the "old Nixon." He was not that complex a man — driven, perhaps, but not complex. He sold his "secret plan" for ending the Vietnam War to a war-weary electorate. Voters were certainly in the market for such a product. His Vietnamization policy was a gradual exodus from Southeast Asia. In the process, he would hold the Communists back, pressure North Vietnam, try to graft popular support to Thieu's government, unleash American air power, and keep moving toward the exits. If this plan took until 1972, an election year, so be it. What Nixon failed to comprehend was that the war, which had dragged on much too long for many Americans, had unleashed a poison in our body politic. This poison, mixed with Nixon's hubris, would create what White House Counsel John Dean told Nixon in a fateful June 1972 taped conversation was a "cancer on the presidency."[5]

Of course, in the summer of 1972, the tragic end of Nixon's presidency was nowhere in sight. He stood at the apex of his career. All who had discounted his tenacity had been proven wrong. He had forged a new relationship with Mao's China and Brezhnev's Soviet Union. He had shielded Thieu and brought the North Vietnamese back to the bargaining table for what he was convinced would be an honorable peace settlement — after his re-election.

There was little doubt that Nixon would win in 1972. The Democratic Party had beaten itself to a bloody pulp in the streets of Chicago four years earlier. Robert Kennedy was dead and Edward Kennedy had sunk his presidential ambitions in the waters of Chappaquiddick Island. The Democrats had only "second-stringers" like Senator Edmund Muskie. But Muskie, in March 1972, cried in the snows of New Hampshire, angry about dirty campaign tricks played on his wife. Muskie was not very presidential when contrasted with the architect of a new world order. Richard Nixon would never weep, but he might just allow a dirty trick or two to be played on his behalf in order to insure his victory at the polls.[6]

The seeds of Watergate had been germinating in the soil for years. Those seeds had been fertilized by the war, springing forth as grotesque fruit. Other chief executives had abused their power. Lincoln had arrested critics, shut down newspapers in 1861, and suspended habeas corpus. Franklin Roosevelt had used the Internal Revenue Service to harass Louisiana's Huey Long. Presidents from Herbert Hoover to Lyndon Johnson had manipulated facts, eavesdropped on foes, and protected their policies from scrutiny.[7]

The Vietnam War was born from such abuse. John Kennedy's fingerprints were all over the November 1963 assassinations of President Ngo Dinh Diem and his brother. He did not pull the trigger, but he knew the weapons were aimed at the man Dwight Eisenhower had applauded as the "Vietnamese George Washington" because of his ardent nationalism. Ironically, as Diem tried to evade his pursuers that November, he telephoned American ambassador Henry Cabot Lodge to find out if he knew anything about a plot against him. When the ambassador dodged the question, the uneasy president added, "You have my telephone number." Lodge, like JFK, knew about the conspiracy against our erstwhile ally.[8] Yes, we surely did have the doomed Diem brothers' number.

Lyndon Johnson's Tonkin Gulf Resolution in August 1964 was a document conceived in duplicity. Congress was misled into passing a resolution that "approves and supports the determination of the President, as Commander-in-Chief, to take all necessary measures to repel any attack against the forces of the United States and to prevent further aggression." As Johnson quipped later, the resolution was "like grandma's nightshirt — it covered everything." What the president had failed to do was reveal that the reported second attack on the USS *Maddox* and USS *Turner Joy* in the darkness of the Gulf of Tonkin, his justification for the resolution, had probably never occurred. The vessels were attacked by porpoises, Johnson laughed to close confidants. Nonetheless in waded the U.S. Marines in 1965,[9] and down the slippery slope America tumbled.

Johnson had used dirty tricks domestically. His victory in the 1948 Texas senate race earned him the nickname "Landslide Lyndon" as dead and ineligible voters cast their ballots for him, helping him eke out a seventy-two-vote victory. After Martin Luther King broke his silence about Vietnam, Johnson increased his surveillance of the civil rights leader. However, this domestic spying on King stretched back to Kennedy's administration. Civil liberties were frequently abridged in the tumultuous climate of the 1960s and 1970s as government agencies snooped on students and minorities.[10] Speaking out in criticism could lead to harassment ranging from a tax audit to a wiretap to the sifting through of a citizen's garbage. Richard Nixon felt comfortable in this environment because, as Daniel Ellsberg proved, America was at war on several fronts and traitors must be exposed.

While he was traveling on his "journey for peace," Nixon left his re-election campaign in the hands of John Mitchell, his former law partner and ex–attorney General. Mitchell, however, was distracted by his wife's bizarre behavior. He allowed underlings to plunge into illegal activities. These aids took the burglary of Daniel Ellsberg's psychiatrist's office and the earlier Huston Plan as authorization to do whatever necessary to silence the President's critics and re-elect Nixon.[11]

The Committee to Re-elect the President (CREEP), chaired by Mitchell, operated as a clearinghouse for misinformation and questionable political contributions. Businesses were squeezed until they spewed forth cash for the Nixon campaign. Dirty tricks were practiced. Forged documents and press releases were produced to weaken Muskie and other Democrats. There were no limits to how low the committee would stoop to guarantee Nixon's victory. Discussion was given to hiring prostitutes to entrap Democrats at their 1972 Miami convention. That measure would not be needed, however, because the party was suffering the aftereffects of its Chicago convention of four years earlier.[12]

Nixon's re-election operatives were not willing to glide to an easy victory. In the early morning of June 17, 1972, four men with links to the CREEP were arrested inside the Democratic Party headquarters, located in the Watergate complex. Nixon's press secretary, Ron Ziegler, termed the break-in "a third rate burglary" but the press, especially the *Washington Post*, would not leave the story alone.[13]

The summer of 1972 featured images other than the photographs of burglars. The year's Pulitzer Prize–winning photograph was of a nine-year-old girl, her clothes and her body shredded by napalm. Phan Thi Phuc, running down Route 1, personified the human toll of the war. She had been engulfed in the conflict, scarred by her own government's weapons. That photograph, and the one from the 1968 Tet Offensive in which Saigon Police Chief Nguyen Ngoc Loan summarily executed a suspected Viet Cong on the streets of the capital, recorded for the world the horrors of war.[14]

In Hanoi that August, movie actress Jane Fonda posed with North Vietnamese officials and American prisoners of war who were paraded out for propaganda purposes. Fonda naively spoke of "blushing military girls" who, when American aircraft approached the capital, "became such good fighters." Fonda urged President Nixon "to read Vietnamese history, particularly their poetry, and particularly the poetry of Ho Chi Minh."[15] Nixon rejected such advice; he had never valued Hollywood's opinion.

The President, overwhelmingly re-elected that November over the hapless South Dakota Senator George McGovern, focused on a final display of military power to conclude the war. Linebacker II was the response to Le Duc Tho's suspension of negotiations in Paris in mid December 1972. Kissinger had told the President that he essentially had two options: intensified bombing or waiting until the next year to resume negotiations. Basking in the warmth of his electoral triumph, Nixon chose the first option.[16]

Linebacker II was eleven days of constant bombing of North Vietnamese targets. 3,000 sorties were flown and 40,000 tons of weaponry rained down upon the Communists in what came to be called the Christmas Bombing. The New York Times labeled the offensive "stone age barbarism" as hundreds, if not thousands, of civilians died alongside soldiers. Nixon told the chairman of the Joint Chiefs of Staff, Admiral Thomas Moorer, "I don't want any more of this crap about the fact that we couldn't hit this target or that one. This is your chance to use military power effectively to win the war." On December 26, the North Vietnamese sent word that they were ready to resume discussions with Kissinger in Paris.[17] Finally, the elusive and long-anticipated "end of the tunnel" was coming into view.

Chapter 9
Gravest Consequences

"You have my assurance of continued assistance in the post-settlement period and that we will respond with full force should the settlement be violated by North Vietnam."
Richard Nixon to Nguyen Van Thieu, 1973.

The Christmas 1972 bombing campaign appeared to have accomplished its goal. Le Duc Tho sent the American negotiators the word that he was ready to return to the bargaining table. The history of the negotiations is a tortured one. Desperate to salvage his presidency in 1968, Lyndon Johnson had repeatedly tried to negotiate with the Communists. In the final year of this tenure in office, he shouted, "If I could just get Ho Chi Minh over here." His personal skills at diplomacy — or intimidation — skills were never to be used. His bombing halt on the eve of the 1968 presidential election failed to lead to peace. The Communists settled in Paris, waiting on American opinion to swell against the war, watching Thieu's support erode, and arguing with the Americans about the peace conference table's size and seating arrangements. Finally, it appeared, after five years in Paris, the parties were heading toward a negotiated peace.[1]

From Nixon's first months in office, the Communists tested his support for Saigon. On April 30, 1969, the Provisional Revolutionary Front argued that an end to hostilities could come only if Nixon abandoned the "disguised colonial regime" in South Vietnam. The Communists saw Thieu as a puppet of the United States, lacking popular support, propped up by American "imperialists."[2]

As we have seen, the war raged on, but Nixon implemented his Vietnamization policy. Always a student of history, Nixon realized that there were limits, in terms of materiel and lives, which governed his conduct of the war. In 1877, for example, time had similarly run out on the Reconstruction Era, a twelve-year attempt, begun by Abraham Lincoln, to rebuild America and assist the former slaves. Finally, after more than a decade, President Rutherfurd B. Hayes reached a grand compromise that brought the curtain down on Reconstruction. Unfortunately, the freed slaves were largely abandoned by this arrangement. Howard University philosophy professor Alain Locke called it "the nadir of the Negro."[3]

Unlike his predecessor of a century earlier, Nixon was negotiating from a position of strength. In 1876, Hayes had won a questionable election over Samuel J. Tilden. There was nothing questionable about Nixon's 1972 landslide. In addition, there was no mistaking the effects on North Vietnam of the Christmas bombing. However, the normally politically shrewd Nixon misread Le Duc Tho's motivation. The Communists returned to Paris because they considered the timing to be to their advantage. They had fought and talked for years. Now, in early 1973, they wished to see the last 24,000 American troops leave Vietnam. Then, they could better prepare for the final offensive against Thieu's government.[4]

Like the freedmen of Reconstruction, Thieu was suspicious of those in Washington who now wished to turn their attention elsewhere.[5] Did they really have his country's best interests at heart? He had resisted the conference seating arrangements that were seen as legitimizing the Viet Cong. Additionally, he thought the withdrawal of American forces had been too rapid, destabilizing his military. Would the Americans, if need be, re-enter the war with their B-52s? If worse came to worst, would Nixon re-deploy troops to Southeast Asia?

As we know, Nixon inherited the war. By his inauguration in 1969, the conflict was splitting our nation. Vietnamization had been his strategy. For nearly four years, he had withdrawn American military personnel, but over 25,000 soldiers had lost their lives during his presidency. "Lyndon's War" was now "Nixon's war." The conflict was a liability, an "irritant," which stood in the way of his mission to work on a grand scale with the Soviet Union and China to create an era of cooperation instead of Cold War confrontation. As Nixon had observed in 1972, "The real problem is that the enemy is willing to sacrifice in order to win, while the South Vietnamese simply aren't willing to pay that much of a price in order to avoid losing."[6]

President Thieu would be required to make a sacrifice. He would be assured, in a January 5, 1973, secret cable, that the United States would supply him with adequate materiel to fight the Communists. The implication was that there could be no doubt that, if needed, America would use "full force" to protect Saigon. There also could be no doubt that the peace agreement must have Thieu's assent. For him to raise questions, Nixon informed Thieu, would result in the "gravest consequences" for the South Vietnamese. Only after threats to cut off all aid to South Vietnam and repeated pressuring by General Alexander Haig, Henry Kissinger, and in the end Richard Nixon himself, did Thieu agree to sign the dastardly document. He really had no other choice.[7]

On January 27, the United States, South Vietnam, North Vietnam, and the Provisional Revolutionary Government signed the treaty in Paris. Kissinger and Le Duc Tho would win that year's Nobel Peace Prize for their efforts to forge an agreement. (The North Vietnamese negotiator would refuse to accept the award, however.) The treaty's terms called for the withdrawal of all United States combat military personnel and the release of American prisoners of war within sixty days. A four nation International Commission of Control and Supervision would monitor the cease-fire. No more military action was to be allowed in Cambodia or Laos. The United States could provide military and economic aid to Thieu's

(From l. to r.) Defense Attaché General John Murray, CIA Station Chief Thomas Polgar, General Ralph Magliore and Ambassador Ellsworth Bunker at Tan Son Nhut in early April 1973, shortly after the signing of the Paris Peace Accords. *Courtesy of General John Murray.*

government, but military materiel was to be provided only on a one-for-one "replacement" basis. An organization under the control of the American Defense Attaché would be established to oversee the delivery of military equipment, but its American staff would be limited to fifty uniformed personnel and 800 to 1,000 civilians. A Council for National Reconciliation and Concord would lay the groundwork for elections and the resolution of political questions in South Vietnam.[8]

Nixon's second term began with peace in Vietnam. The U.S. Congress had been on the verge of imposing peace by withholding funds for the war, but Nixon had solved the issues in his own way. The Christmas bombing had been a necessary use of force because, he believed, it frightened the North Vietnamese. In addition, the treaty gave Thieu a chance to work out a favorable agreement with the Communists in the south. Nixon told the American people, "South Vietnam has gained the right to determine its own future.... Let us be proud that America did not settle for a peace that would have betrayed our ally." Former South Vietnamese President Nguyen Cao Ky saw it differently: "I give them a couple of years before they invade the south." In a couple of years, that would occur.[9]

For a few months, the treaty held. On February 12, 1973 nearly 600 American prisoners of war returned to the United States. Nixon would honor them at a White House banquet where they praised their commander in chief. In Laos, the warring parties signed a cease-fire. The four-party international commission, composed of Canada, Indonesia, Hungary, and Poland, began to watch the interaction between Hanoi and Saigon. Kissinger remarked that now we "could heal America."[10] What no one grasped was that political wounds were already festering and they would be fatal for Richard Nixon.

Chapter 10

Under Siege

*"The American people need to know that their president is not a crook.
Well, I am not a crook."*
                                                        Richard Nixon, 1973.

The clashes that occurred in the late 1960s and early 1970s were not restricted to Asian battlefields. In 1962, Helen Gurley Brown published *Sex and the Single Girl*, a book with frank advice about everything from automobile care to having affairs with married men. The next year, Betty Friedan's book *The Feminine Mystique* took aim at "the problem with no name," the male-dominated culture in which women were considered to be mere extensions of their more talented husbands. Thus, modern feminism had been born, nurtured by publications like *Ms.* Magazine, groups such as the National Organization of Women, and court cases like *Roe v. Wade*.[1]

Richard Nixon, like many men of his generation, was awkward in his ability to accept women as equal partners in business, politics, and society. *The Roe v. Wade* ruling, coming in January 1973 with a 7–2 Supreme Court decision, created new options for women to control their bodies. A "right to privacy" existed for women in the first trimester of their pregnancy, the court ruled. After consultation with her physician, a woman could choose to terminate her pregnancy. Nixon was on the losing side of this issue, favoring "the sanctity of life — including the life of the yet unborn."[2]

The *Roe* mandate, coming as it did in January 1973, was a forewarning of the issues that would continue to divide our society. The Paris Peace Accords had been signed but there were other wars to fight. Throughout the decade, Americans would argue about the Equal Rights Amendment. Was it necessary? Would it result in unisex bathrooms? Could it destroy the family unit? What exactly was "the problem with no name" and could it be solved with the amendment's ratification?

For much of his presidency, Richard Nixon had wrestled with similarly perplexing economic questions. By the summer of 1971, the American dollar was under attack by foreigners who wanted guarantees that, if need be, they would be able to convert their dollars into gold. What should be done to protect the interests of the United States? One of Nixon's advisors recalled, "It was absolutely necessary to close the gold window. The old exchange rate policy was basically bankrupt." Nixon's New Economic Policy, unveiled on August 15, 1971, gave the answer. The dollar was no longer to be convertible into gold at a fixed price, and wage and price controls were imposed on the nation. For a while unemployment and inflation were checked, but, by 1973, when the controls were lifted, the economic demons returned with a vengeance. For example, the massive grain deal that Nixon had negotiated with the Soviets the previous year in Moscow resulted in higher food prices here at home. As Kissinger lamented, "They beat us at our own game."[3]

The chill of January 1973 was augmented by the return of the Watergate saga. Since the arrest of the burglars in June 1972, the *Washington Post's* two talented investigative reporters, Bob Woodward and Carl Bernstein, had been writing accounts of high-level complicity in the break-in at the Democratic headquarters. The journalists were aided by a shadowy source, "Deep Throat," who urged them to dig deeper.[4]

By March 1973, cracks were appearing in the ranks of the burglars and their White House supervisors. Judge John Sirica had kept the burglars in prison without bond since their arrest. James McCord, one of the accused, agreed to cooperate with Judge Sirica's court. Another defendant, White House operative Howard Hunt, was demanding hush money to keep quiet and accept his sentence of thirty-five years in prison. Hunt would receive these payments to remain silent.[5]

Leaders of the U.S. Senate authorized a special committee to investigate not just the break-in, but also a wide range of illegal campaign activities during the previous year's presidential election. All of the political ugliness of the era was about to be exposed that spring in the bright lights of televised hearings chaired by North Carolina senator Sam Ervin. While referring to himself as "just a country lawyer," the Harvard-educated Ervin often read from the U.S. Constitution about the powers of the branches of government and lectured Nixon Administration officials about abuse of such agencies as the FBI and the IRS. One columnist observed that the wide range of dirty tricks could become "a political bomb that could blow the Nixon Administration apart."[6]

The upper levels of the White House remained quiet until Ervin began to subpoena them. Tales of illegal activities including fundraising and domestic spying unfolded on nationwide television. Committee member Senator Howard Baker of Tennessee would ask repeatedly, "What did the President know and when did he know it?" Had Nixon authorized the Watergate break-in? Had he allowed CREEP to use any means necessary to secure his re-election? Were there links between the Ellsberg matter, antiwar protests, domestic spying, the pursuit of perceived "enemies," and the use of the executive branch to abridge the civil liberties of citizens?[7]

By April 1973, a key figure emerged. White House Counsel John Dean, who in late June 1972 had warned Nixon about a "cancer on the presidency," began cooperating with Ervin and the grand jury used by Sirica. Dean had sat in meetings with Nixon during which the use of hush money for the burglars was discussed. He knew about Nixon's orders to "screw our enemies." He realized that the dirty tricks went much further than the events at the Watergate office building and included perjury and obstruction of justice.[8]

With Ervin preparing to take aim at the President, Nixon decided to offer three scapegoats to his foes. The weak John Dean would be fired, and Chief of Staff Bob Haldeman and Domestic Advisor John Ehrlichman would be forced to resign. Nixon remembered an April 28 telephone conversation in which Ehrlichman had told him "all the illegal acts ultimately derived from me [Nixon], whether directly or indirectly." Announcing the departure of Ehrlichman and Haldeman two days later, the President called the allies "two of the finest public servants it had been my privilege to know." By this point, Dean was actively cooperating with Sirica and the Ervin Committee.[9]

Dean's photographic memory was striking. Before Ervin, he displayed an impressive recall of dates, places, discussions, and participants at meetings. While Haldeman and Ehrlichman could appear combative and arrogant, Dean seemed contrite and helpful. Ervin asked other witnesses for their recollections. Could a fired employee be believed when the President repeatedly asserted "I am not a crook?" Finally, White House staffer Alexander Butterfield revealed in mid July that an elaborate taping system recorded presidential conversations. Butterfield, an assistant to Haldeman, was one of only a handful of people who knew about the tapes. Ervin would demand the recordings while Nixon claimed on July 23, 1973, that "executive privilege" shielded the tapes from review by the congressional panel.[10]

While this Constitutional crisis boiled, Nixon sought safety in foreign policy. The Soviet Union's Leonid Brezhnev came to the United States for a summit meeting with Nixon. The two leaders discussed China, Jewish emigration from the Soviet Union, weaponry and troop strength, and the Middle East. Brezhnev sympathized with Nixon's "domestic difficulties."[11] Nixon brooded; why could not the Ervin Committee, Special Prosecutor Archibald Cox (appointed by the attorney general), and Judge Sirica be sympathetic? The President was under siege in a hostile world with enemies all around him. South Vietnam, which was under siege of a different kind, was rarely on the President's mind. His survival, not Thieu's, was of paramount importance. Other crises were about to erupt.

Chapter 11

Crises

"Your Commander-in-Chief has given you an order."
Chief of Staff Alexander Haig to
Justice Department official William Ruckelshaus, 1973.

Throughout the Cold War, hot conflicts occurred. The Korean War of 1950–1953 is an example of the superpowers using surrogates to test each other. In Korea, the United States and its United Nation allies fought to prevent a Communist takeover of the Korean peninsula. In Berlin, in 1948, the Communists and anti–communists stalked one another, looking for any sign of weakness or lack of resolve. Vigilance, the United States concluded, must be a weapon in the fight against the enemy. A lack of vigilance would allow the Communists to dominate Asia, Europe, Africa, or Latin America. Thus, Vietnam was part of the Cold War, a struggle between America and the Soviet Union. By 1973, Nixon had brought the troops home from Vietnam, but the Cold War was far from over. Communist states were not far from our borders.

When Marxist Salvador Allende was elected president of Chile in 1970, the CIA had tried unsuccessfully to prevent his coming to power. Allende nationalized American economic interests in Chile. For three years, the United States worked to isolate Chile, withholding funds from the International Monetary Fund and the World Bank, and stirring up political opposition to Allende. By the summer of 1973, Chile's economy was in a shambles and the middle class, with CIA assistance, revolted. On September 11, Salvador Allende was overthrown in a bloody coup, killed, and replaced by a military junta led by General Augusto Pinochet who moved swiftly to align himself with the West. He returned the properties that

Allende had nationalized and arrested leftists.[1] Vigilance had scored another Cold War victory.

In the Middle East, the United States was the chief sponsor of the nation of Israel. A special relationship had been in place since President Harry Truman recognized the homeland for Jews in 1949. When Palestinians protested the creation of a Jewish state from their territory, the United States stood ready to defend Israel. There had been war in the Middle East in 1956 and, in 1967, the Six-Day War was a tremendous Israeli victory over its Muslim neighbors. The Sinai had been seized from Egypt, the west bank of the Jordan River from Jordan, and the strategic Golan Heights from Syria. Egypt and its Arab neighbors were client states of the Soviet Union. They were pieces on the Cold War chessboard, moving about, threatening Israel, and falling back when the United States came to the assistance of the Jews.

On October 6, 1973, the Arabs struck in what came to be called the Yom Kippur War. Better prepared than before, the Muslims made significant progress on the battlefield. Nixon faced a dilemma. He had wished to cultivate better relations with the Arab world and he resented Israeli lobbying efforts in Congress and through the media, but he also accepted America's historic ties to Israel. He urged the Soviets to rein the Arabs in. When these efforts proved fruitless, Nixon authorized an American airlift to Israel. On October 24, he issued a nuclear threat to the Soviets and their Arab clients. Soviet interference "would produce incalculable consequences." While tensions lessened within a few days and a tenuous peace returned to the Middle East, the Organization of Petroleum Exporting Countries (OPEC) punished the United States with an oil embargo. Oil prices zoomed to $11.65 a barrel ($44.92 in year 2000 dollars), nearly four times the price before the Yom Kippur War. Even Saudi Arabia and Iran, usual Western allies, participated in the anti–American boycott. The embargo would remain in effect against the United States until March 1974, radically affecting everything from highway speed limits (lowered to 55 miles per hour) to the cost of electricity to energy policy, all of which further strained an already fragile economy.[2]

Even while Egypt and Israel headed toward conflict in the Sinai, a political drama was unfolding in Washington. Nixon argued with Special Prosecutor Cox and Senator Ervin about access to the Oval Office tape recordings. On August 7, 1973, Cox argued in Sirica's court that the tapes were evidence to be presented to the Congress and to the court. Cox asserted, "there is no exception for the President from the guiding principle that the public, in pursuit of justice, has a right to every man's evidence. Even the highest executive officials are subject to the rule of law...."

Nixon's attorney, law professor Charles Allen Wright, countered that separation of powers protected the chief executive from scrutiny by Ervin and the judiciary. Wright contended that the proceedings were "a serious threat to the nature of the presidency as it was created by the Constitution." Cox replied, "Not even a President can be allowed to select some accounts of a conversation for public disclosure and then to frustrate further grand jury inquiries." Sirica agreed with the special prosecutor and, on August 29, 1973, ordered Nixon to produce the tapes "for my private inspection." Nixon appealed the order in September as did Cox who wanted the tapes placed in his possession. The United States Court of Appeals for the District of Columbia urged the President and the prosecutor to compromise. Nixon remained steadfast, however, and the appeals court issued a formal opinion on October 12 upholding Sirica's ruling.[3]

By October 12 another scandal was grabbing headlines. Vice President Spiro Agnew had vigorously defended Nixon's conduct of the war. As vice presidents often do, Agnew had been on the front lines since 1969 raising questions about the loyalty of antiwar activists like Jane Fonda and former Attorney General Ramsey Clark. He had ridiculed the "nattering nabobs of negativism" in the media and accused the press of bias against the administration.

By late August 1973, rumors had circulated that Agnew was being investigated by a grand jury for illegal acts allegedly committed when he was Baltimore County executive and Maryland's Governor. The allegations centered on kickbacks that Agnew had received from contractors who wanted to receive favorable treatment in Maryland. On September 30, Agnew had responded, "I'm a big trophy. I will not resign ... I intend to stay and fight." Despite his vow to resist, Agnew did resign. On October 10, while the Middle East was at war, the vice president pled nolo contendere to tax evasion; he resigned his office and payed a fine of $10,000. Two days later, under the provisions of the Twenty-Fifth Amendment, Nixon appointed House Minority Leader Gerald Ford to be Agnew's successor. Ford, a popular member of Congress, easily received Senate approval.[4]

Nixon had had enough of Cox's insistence that the tape recordings should be handed over to the special prosecutor. On October 19, Nixon said that the entire Watergate matter had produced "a strain ... on the American people." He agreed to give summaries of the tapes to Senator Ervin, but Cox should "make no further attempts by judicial process to obtain tapes...." Cox responded the next day saying he was "not out to get the President of the United States." The prosecutor then added that he would continue his efforts to review the tapes and other executive branch documents. Enraged, Nixon ordered Attorney General Elliot Richardson to fire Cox. Richardson refused and resigned himself. Then, in the Saturday Night Massacre, as it became known, Richardson's deputy, William Ruckelshaus, also refused to fire Cox — which led to him being fired. Finally, Solicitor General Robert Bork terminated Cox. Newspapers and members of Congress called on Nixon to resign, or face impeachment, or appoint a successor to Cox.

Nixon, under fire from all sides, agreed to comply with Sirica's subpoena "in all respects." Attorney Charles Wright observed, "The president does not defy the law, and ... he will comply in full." Shortly, Sirica learned that some of the requested tapes could not be located and one of the key recordings had an eighteen-minute gap on it. Sensing that he may be signing his own death warrant but aware of the widespread criticism of his actions, Nixon appointed Leon Jaworski, a protégé of Lyndon Johnson, to be a new special prosecutor.[5]

Chapter 12

Expletive Deleted

"If détente unravels in America, the hawks will take over."
Richard Nixon to Leonid Brezhnev, 1974.

Richard Nixon believed that Article II of the U.S. Constitution gave the president tremendous latitude regarding the use of the military. One of the roles of the President was that of "Commander in Chief" of the armed forces. Congress had the authority, under Article I, to declare war, but that branch of government had done so on only five occasions: the War of 1812, the Mexican War, the Spanish-American War, and the world wars of the Twentieth Century. No congressional approval, in a constitutional sense, had been sought by Lincoln in 1861, or by Truman in 1950, or by Johnson in 1964. Troops had fought, but they had fought under the orders of the commander in chief.

Vietnam changed the relationship between Congress and the president. As we have seen, the Gulf of Tonkin Resolution was a fraudulent quasi declaration of war by which the sly Lyndon Johnson manipulated the Congress into giving him permission to defend American military personnel. Throughout the next nine years, Congress re-evaluated its complicity in the nightmare of Vietnam. By late 1973, the Democrat-controlled Congress, seeing a politically wounded Republican president, acted to curtail Nixon's ability to command American troops in the future.

The resulting War Powers Resolution of the Congress must be viewed in the wider context of the era. By 1973, the Paris Peace Accords had been cobbled together; American troops and prisoners of war had returned home. Nixon, however, had endured four years of assault from politicians, the media, Hollywood critics, and students who contended that "peace

69

with honor" could have been achieved much earlier, saving many lives. The tales of domestic spying, harassment of dissidents, and active cover-up of questionable activities had seriously eroded Nixon's domestic support. His efforts to reach out to China and the Soviet Union failed to strengthen his position in the United States. The rise in grain prices in the United States, as the result of grain deals with Brezhnev, demonstrated the two-edged sword of detente with the Communists. The Yom Kippur War and our support of Israel triggered the devastating rise in the price of oil; the American public had to adjust to gas shortages and a fifty-five miles per hour speed limit. Nixon's congressional allies were put on the defensive by all of these developments. Some Republicans—for example, Massachusetts Senator Edward Brooke and Oregon Senator Mark Hatfield — were openly critical of Nixon's conduct.

Thus, the War Powers Act, passed over the commander in chief's veto, had significant support inside and outside of Congress. The resolution limited a president's ability to command troops abroad. Under the law, the president was required to notify Congress within forty-eight hours after dispatching troops where "imminent involvement in hostilities is clearly indicated." Within ninety days, maximum, these troops were to be withdrawn unless Congress authorized the operation. Some Nixon advisors discussed urging the president to resign.[1] As we have seen, he was no quitter and he therefore prepared to direct his attention to the war that was being fueled by the Watergate scandal.

In February 1974, the U.S. House of Representatives began movement toward an impeachment inquiry. That house of Congress, like the Senate, was under Democratic control. Special elections held that month had given the Democrats two more House seats. The House's Judiciary Committee requested access to all the tapes that had been gathered by Judge Sirica — and demanded forty-two more tapes. Special Prosecutor Leon Jaworski, appointed in the aftermath of Cox's firing, subpoenaed sixty-four more recordings. Additionally, Nixon was slapped with a fine of $400,000 for unpaid taxes.[2]

With the courts and the Congress closing in on him, Nixon devised a plan to silence his critics. It backfired. On April 29, 1974, the President published more than 1,300 pages of transcripts of the subpoenaed tapes. The televised scene from the Oval Office was surreal. Nixon seated before rows and rows of notebooks, bearing the presidential seal, telling the public, "The President has nothing to hide." Nixon hoped that the flood of documents would satisfy his enemies. Instead, some of the transcripts had been carefully edited and they contained unflattering profanity, called in the text "expletive deleted," that reflected poorly on the chief executive.

One transcript, to Judge Sirica's dismay, omitted a March 23, 1973, conversation in which Nixon told his top aides, "I don't give a shit what happens. I want you all to stonewall it, let them plead the Fifth Amendment, cover up, or anything else." A majority of Americans, according to a Harris poll, now favored Nixon's removal from office.[3]

Vietnam was far from Richard Nixon's mind. That war was over, "peace with honor" achieved. He focused on foreign affairs, trying to ignore the House Judiciary Committee's findings that the conduct of the President had been despicable. "Obstruction of justice" and "abuse of power" became phrases that joined "expletive deleted" in the vernacular. Nixon escaped to the Middle East, where he received a "tumultuous welcome" in Cairo. Kissinger, who had by now replaced William Rogers as Secretary of State, was making progress in lessening tensions between Egypt and Israel. Nixon rebuked Israel: "Continuous war in this area is not a solution for Israel's survival." With the Saudis, he discussed the oil prices that had caused twenty percent inflation in the United States. He met with Syrian President Hafez el-Assad, resuming diplomatic relations with that nation. Jordan's King Hussein praised Nixon's "journey for peace."[4]

On to Moscow, where the besieged President met with Brezhnev in late June and early July 1974. It seemed to Nixon that some of his aides were trying to sabotage detente, something unthinkable just a few months earlier. He was reluctant to discipline the hard-liners in his administration because he needed their congressional patrons for his own political survival. Nixon confided to his Soviet hosts, "If detente unravels in America, the hawks will take over."[5]

Coming back to Washington on July 3, 1974, Nixon watched as the United States Supreme Court prepared to consider the validity of the President's claim of executive privilege. Four justices, including Chief Justice Warren Burger, were Nixon appointees to the Court. Prosecutor Jaworski had withstood Nixon's claim that he was merely an employee of the executive branch. Before the court, Jaworski dismantled executive privilege, asserting that it could not be used "to shield alleged criminality." Nixon's attorney James St. Clair replied that the President was the nation's chief law enforcement officer and could supply information to the prosecution as he — and he alone — deemed appropriate. St. Clair added, "The framers of the Constitution had in mind a strong Presidency."[6]

St. Clair was correct about the Founding Fathers of 1787. In Philadelphia that summer they had addressed the weakness inherent in the Articles of Confederation. The central government was impotent, weakened by its lack of a chief executive and a federal court system. New York's Alexander Hamilton spoke of the critical need for "energy in the executive."

Hamilton, however, could never have envisioned the turmoil of the 1960s and 1970s. His times had been threatened by the spectacle of Shays' Rebellion, with its tax protesters. The protesters of the 1960s and 1970s had used the media to expose an ugly, divisive war. "Energetic executives" had stumbled into undeclared war, ensnarling us in faraway conflicts that had drained the nation of its "energy." Thus, Nixon fell victim, not just to his own hubris and his crimes, but also to public and congressional outrage with strong presidents.

Congress moved methodically towards impeachment. The Judiciary Committee's chief counsel, John Doar, described the White House's "Byzantine Empire" in which shadowy figures plotted schemes aimed at their foes. He said that the climate of illegality was Nixon's fault. He had failed to "take care that the laws be faithfully executed." Doar proposed several articles of impeachment aimed directly at the chief executive who, Doar suggested, had engaged in a "pattern of massive and persistent abuse of power for political purposes involving unlawful and un–Constitutional invasions of rights and privacy of individual citizens."[7]

On July 24, the Supreme Court ruled 8–0 that Nixon must provide the special prosecutor with complete tape recordings. The Court accepted the doctrine of "executive privilege" but emphasized the "legitimate needs of the judicial process." The President was not "above the law." Stung bye the unanimity of the decision, Nixon announced that evening that he would surrender the material to Judge Sirica.[8]

Within five days, the President's allies on the Judiciary Committee found themselves in the minority. Three articles of impeachment were approved, accusing Nixon of obstruction of justice, abuse of power, and failing to produce evidence in a timely manner.[9] His "Byzantine Empire" had collapsed. Illegal wiretaps, domestic break-ins such as the one authorized against Daniel Ellsberg's psychiatrist, harassment of enemies by the FBI, IRS, and CIA were all crimes that warranted the President's impeachment, the committee declared. They met the threshold of "high crimes and misdemeanors."

Nixon fought on for a while. He refused to resign. He isolated himself from his staff. There were fears that an unstable commander in chief might launch a nuclear Armageddon. Working with Republicans in Congress, Chief of Staff Haig tried to fashion a resignation arrangement, but, until August 7, Nixon refused to accept defeat. On that day, three senior Republicans visited Nixon at the White House. One of them, Senator Barry Goldwater, had commented a few days earlier that he was "mad as hell" at Nixon's conduct in office.[10]

Nixon's August 8 speech to the American people showed little remorse. He would leave office the following day because "I no longer have a strong enough political base in the Congress...." The next morning, in his remarks to his staff, he admitted, "Sure we have done some things wrong...." He was abandoning the presidency, however, because he had lost his effectiveness. A hostile Congress would not enact his policies. He could no longer lead. He was realistic about his loss of authority, he said. As he spoke of his mother, "a saint," and his father, "a little man," he made no mention of South Vietnam or his wife Pat Nixon.[11] Our Southeast Asian ally had been abandoned much earlier, well before Nixon boarded his presidential helicopter that summer day and flew into lonely exile.

Chapter 13

Caretaker

"Are you ready, Mr. Vice-President, to assume the presidency in a short period of time?"

Alexander Haig to Gerald Ford, 1974.

It seemed that everyone in Washington liked Gerald "Jerry" Ford. Lyndon Johnson had said as much — even though the former president joked that the ex-football star "had played football too often without his helmet." To dismiss Ford as a likeable dunce, however, is to fail to grasp exactly why he found himself in the summer of 1974 waving goodbye to Richard Nixon as the disgraced President boarded a helicopter, destined for political obscurity. Ford was a well-educated (University of Michigan and Yale University Law School degrees) Washington insider. He had served, as had Nixon, in the U.S. Navy during the Second World War. After returning to the States, he, again like Nixon, had launched a Republican career. But Ford, by the time Nixon chose him to succeed Agnew as vice president in 1973, had avoided accumulating enemies. With the exception of his quixotic crusade to impeach former Chief Justice Earl Warren, the congressman had built for himself a reputation for decency and fair play. There were no hints of "dirty tricks" on Gerald Ford's résumé. As House Minority Leader, Ford had advocated his party's proposals, but since the GOP did not control Congress, he was rarely in the spotlight. He had loyally supported President Johnson's conduct of the war in Vietnam and had endorsed Nixon's Vietnamization program.[1]

The nation seemed to breathe a sigh of relief on August 9. The Nixon years had been traumatic for the United States. Incursions and presidential paranoia had created cynicism among the public. While America's

74

troops and prisoners of war had finally come home in January 1973, the war had left domestic scars. The anemic economy, political scandals, and gridlock called for a respected leader like Gerald Ford. He would, it was hoped, restore stability and honesty to the Oval Office.

In his first news conference, Ford calmly proclaimed that "America's long national nightmare" was over. When questioned about Richard Nixon's future, Ford replied unequivocally that he would never pardon the former President—"the American people would never stand for that." Within a month, Ford had issued a "full pardon" to Nixon, destroying his own credibility. Thus, Ford became tainted by Nixon; Watergate dirtied his previously clean hands. His September 1974 decision to pardon Nixon was, he thought, an act of "closure," but in reality it reopened the wounds that Nixon had inflicted on himself and the country. Ford, a caretaker, an unelected President, would never recover from his action. Almost apologetically he joked, "I'm a Ford, not a Lincoln."[2] No one would ever confuse the two.

Beginning in 1973, Congress asserted its authority in foreign affairs. On the eve of the Paris Peace Accords, debate in Washington was ongoing concerning Nixon's use of troops in the previous year's military activities in Southeast Asia. As previously recounted, Congress curtailed the president's ability to use American armed forces with the November 1973 War Powers Act. In addition, and as always, Congress reigned supreme in the allocation of funds, which had been sharply reduced with regard to appropriations for the Thieu government since the budget for fiscal year 1973. Aid to South Vietnam that year had been $3.2 billion. It was reduced to $1.1 billion in mid 1974 and the funding for fiscal year 1975 was cut to only $700 million. South Vietnam was suffocating, gasping for the oxygen provided by the American dollars that had sustained it for more than a decade.[3]

During a September 12, 1974, meeting with congressional leaders in the White House, Ford observed, "We must assure that what we are trying to do in Vietnam is not destroyed through lack of funding and that our hands are not tied in using these funds." Secretary Kissinger reviewed the tensions in the Middle East and Cyprus where "passions run high" between Greeks and Turks. Kissinger added that arms talks with the Soviets "are facing the best prospect we have had for some time." But in Vietnam, he warned, the Communists were poised "on the brink of deciding whether or not to go the military route." In conclusion, however, Kissinger admitted, "We realize the funds are agreed."[4]

South Vietnam had been abandoned long before Nixon fell victim to Watergate and Ford begged Congress for aid. With promises that, if need be, the United States would come to the rescue with American firepower,

Defense Attaché John Murray (left) and Ambassador Graham Martin at the Republic of Vietnam Armed Forces display. *Courtesy of General John Murray.*

Nixon had pressured Thieu into de facto recognition of the Communist Provisional Revolutionary Government and had permitted the North Vietnamese to leave 160,000 of their troops inside South Vietnam. Nixon did not anticipate either his own problems or the effects that the oil embargo would have on the American and South Vietnamese economies. The North

Vietnamese were, of course, watching the events of late 1973 and 1974. They correctly sensed weakness and, by the time of Ford's pardon of Nixon, realized that Thieu lacked a strong ally in Washington.[5]

Ford kept Henry Kissinger at the State Department. While he felt some obligation to Thieu, by late 1974 Kissinger was focused on superpower diplomacy with the Soviet Union and China. They were key players in America's future. He was also attempting to create goodwill in the Middle East. Kissinger, who practiced realpolitik, was realistic about the South Vietnamese. With a staggering economy and an assertive U.S. Congress, there was little chance that more funds would be forthcoming for Thieu. They would have to stand up for themselves—without the aid which had been promised Thieu the previous year. Compounding the challenges facing Thieu was a domestic inflation rate of sixty-five percent and a crippling forty percent unemployment. When the Americans exited in 1973, the underpinnings had been knocked from the South Vietnamese economy.[6] How could Thieu maintain a 1.1 million-man army without American financial aid?

The Communists were, as we know, patient and cautious. They had fought enemies for decades. In late 1974, they decided to test Thieu and the United States in Phuoc Long Province, bordering on Cambodia and only thirty miles from Saigon. Twenty-two fully equipped infantry divisions were already in South Vietnam. Repeatedly, the Communists had ignored the provisions of the Paris Peace Accords that mandated good-faith negotiations with Thieu. Instead, they had continued to send troops and supplies down the Ho Chi Minh Trail. Thieu became, in turn, more authoritarian and more corrupt. Dissent was dealt with harshly, and the Communists reasoned that the time was right to launch an attack. Such an act of aggression in Phuoc Long would test the strength of Thieu and the resolve of the caretaker American president. If the Americans vigorously responded to such an attack, the Communists could withdraw and wait a while longer. If the South Vietnamese and their erstwhile ally stumbled, though, the final assault on the south could commence.[7]

Some American civilian workers had been shouting about the weakness of South Vietnam. While the Paris Peace Accords limited the U.S. uniformed presence in South Vietnam to fifty men within the Defense Attaché Office, there were over a thousand American civilians, civil service and contract employees, sprinkled throughout the country. One of them, communications technician John Guffey, sent report after report to his supervisors in 1974 that documented the corruption and ineffectiveness of the South Vietnamese military. Guffey told of tons of military equipment that the South Vietnamese either could not use or would prefer to pilfer. He wrote, "Serious problems in terms of maintenance, training, discipline, quality of leadership and mobility cause the ARVN to get less 'bang for the buck' than most other armies of the world." He warned, "There seems to be a mental paralysis in lower level commands when decisions need to be made, as everyone waits for the Corps Commander's decision" Concerning unused technical equipment, Guffey added, "The average Vietnamese soldier (who had little formal schooling and had been drafted from the countryside) is not a technician and all things mechanical are generally alien to him."[8]

Not all of these problems were entirely the fault of the South Vietnamese. Large quantities of military equipment and supplies had been rushed to Vietnam just prior to the signing of the agreement in Paris. The crash program, called Enhance Plus, was an attempt to "beat the clock" and provide our ally with as much materiel as possible before the "one-for-one" replacement rule came into effect. As often happens in such efforts, large quantities of the equipment provided were out of date. This prompted one of the Hungarian Air Force colonels assigned to Hungary's embassy to say to the American CIA station chief, that while he had asked for the assignment so he could have a chance "to see the latest in American equipment," what he had found instead was "an air museum."[9]

While Guffey did not directly accuse the South Vietnamese of stealing material, he painted a sad portrait of soldiers who faced the dilemma of fighting the enemy while trying to provide for their families on already low incomes that had been greatly eroded by inflation. Morale was "deteriorating" because, "The soldier has come to expect little from his commanders in the way of concern for his health and welfare. He is faced with the problem of dividing his time between military duties and activities which permit him to survive."[10]

Other American civilian personnel told of supplies arriving in Saigon only to be taken away to be sold on the black market. Air Force secretary Rosalie Redmond recalls that this pilfering even applied to small materials such as typewriters and toilet paper.[11] Americans became accustomed to buying these items, stamped with United States markings, from black-market profiteers. As the offensive in Phuoc Long began, the military preparedness of Thieu's forces was in question — as was his government's ability to wisely use the scarce supplies intended to fight the enemy.

Chapter 14
The Razor's Edge

"Peace with honor was and is a fantasy in Vietnam; can we not face the glaring fact of our failure in Southeast Asia?"
An open letter from John Guffey to Gerald Ford, 1975.

It was not as if Washington did not have advance warning of the deteriorating situation in South Vietnam. Policymakers were just not being attentive. Throughout 1974, the acrimony produced by Watergate overflowed into Vietnam. The nation's attention was focused on the sputtering economy, with spiraling inflation and rising unemployment, and the death throes of the Nixon Administration. Public support for, and interest in, the Thieu regime had largely evaporated. To many, if not most, Americans, the signing of the Paris Peace Accords had concluded the war. Congress was in step with this mood; the legislative branch had spent most of 1974 asserting its prerogatives. Vietnam was a painful experience that had cost too many lives and too much money.

Civilian communications expert John Guffey had repeatedly warned his superiors that the South Vietnamese were becoming weaker. In January 1974, Guffey noted that the military suffered from a "shortage of junior officers and high personnel turnover." They also "had significant deficiencies in intelligence gathering." Troops suffered from the high rate of inflation. Their response to economic pressures was "to moonlight to make ends meet and engage in corrupt practices for the same reason." But Guffey added, "At the same time, the ARVN soldier shows considerable staying power once engaged." (It needs to be pointed out, however, that there were some senior officers in the South Vietnamese government and armed forces who engaged in corrupt practices simply to enrich themselves and their families. This was just one more example of the debilitating effect of the politicization of the RVNAF hierarchy.)

Guffey was pessimistic about improvements in morale and effectiveness. Just because South Vietnam had a million-man military, it did not mean that Thieu's armed forces could repulse the Communists. Guffey closed his gloomy assessment by using the analogy of the Polish Army in 1939. With the second-largest army in Europe, the Poles "conducted a static defense on its borders with no other plan than to dig in and hold on, and was crushed in little more than three weeks by an army that was numerically inferior in every respect."

Guffey sensed that South Vietnam was doomed. He repeatedly called attention to the systemic deficiencies in Thieu's government and military, he knew about them. North Vietnam knew about them, also; so did many in Washington. The Congress' reducing funding for South Vietnam, instead of forcing Thieu to lessen his authoritarian hold on the country, caused him to desperately tighten his control of the populace and increase the harassment of his domestic opponents. In addition, as dollars became scarce in 1974, and as inflation accelerated, so did the corruption in South Vietnamese society.[1]

Guffey was far from alone in warning about the critical situation escalating in Southeast Asia. In Saigon, Deputy Chief of Mission Wolfgang Lehman sent his superiors at the State Department a cable in August 1974. Nixon had just left office; Ford was cautiously picking up the pieces left behind by the Watergate scandal. Lehman said that he and Defense Attaché General John Murray had reviewed the most recent funding reductions. Congress' action, Lehman was convinced, meant that the $700 million "would at best leave $475 to $500 million to the RVNAF in actual assets...." In his corresponding message to the Pentagon, Murray started his analysis with what had been the bare bones budget of $1.126 billion and then he decreased it in "hundred million dollar, country killing, increments." He ended his blunt cable this way: "$600 million level — write off [the Republic of Vietnam] as a bad investment and a broken promise."

Lehman reported that the Communists were spending their time rebuilding the infrastructure of North Vietnam that had been decimated by American bombing missions. No one should mistake Hanoi's intentions, however, Lehman said. He made absolutely clear to the State Department that "Should the North Vietnamese conclude that the U.S. is disengaging politically and economically from the South, they would suspend serious economic planning and hold their resources in reserve to use militarily against South Vietnam at some opportune moment." Some intelligence reports suggested that the Communists would launch a military attack "as early as the spring of 1975 when the Vietnamese government's equipment and material shortages could be more severe if there is no additional U.S. assistance." Reflecting later on the events of late 1974 and early 1975, Lehman recalls, "We had to walk on the razor's edge."[2]

The "decisive" assault that Lehman predicted would come sooner rather than later. Observing Thieu's domestic problems and America's distraction, the North Vietnamese made their decision in September 1974 to test Thieu and the new American President. Additionally, a large North Vietnamese delegation traveled to Moscow that November to inform the Soviets of their plans to attack South Vietnam in the strategic province of Phuoc Long.[3]

From December 18, 1974, to January 8, 1975, the Political Bureau of the Government of North Vietnam held an extremely important meeting in Hanoi. In addition to the members of the Bureau, participants included "leading party members and commanders from all battlefields, members of the Central Military Committee, and the vice chiefs of staff in charge of combat operations." A backdrop to this gathering of the North Vietnamese leadership was the critical battle for the southern province of Phuoc Long, the capital city of which was about 120 kilometers north of Saigon. In addition, there was heavy fighting going on in Bin Tuy, Long Khan, and Tay Ninh provinces on the eastern and western flanks of the South Vietnamese seat of government. However, it was the outcome of the battle for Phuoc Long's capital city, Phuoc Binh, which had the most influence upon the attitude of the North Vietnamese leadership. This battlefield victory, which was completed on January 6, 1975, led these leaders to conclude that the Armed Forces of South Vietnam no longer had the strength to mount large-scale, encircling operations to recapture regions. It was also a clear indicator that the United States would not come to the support of its ally in the south. This did indeed turn out to be the case, in spite of the fact that at the time of the 1973 Paris peace agreement Nixon had promised to intercede in the event of an overt attack in the south by the forces of North Vietnam.[4] Nixon was out of office and Gerald Ford was crippled by the pardon of the ex–president and the anemic American economy.

On January 9, 1975, General Van Tien Dung was appointed representative of the North Vietnamese Central Command to supervise the Tay Nguyen (South Vietnamese Central Highlands) campaign. General Dung had been a member of the Communist Party of Vietnam since 1937. From then on he had been an aggressive fighter for the causes of his party, even to the extent of having been condemned to death by the French after being captured for the second time in 1944. In both instances, he demonstrated his resourcefulness by escaping and rejoining the fight against his country's occupiers.[5]

General Dung's mission for 1975 had been outlined by the party's First Secretary Le Duan at the conclusion of the Political Bureau's meeting: "The situation has become quite clear. We are resolved to complete our two-year plan [to conquer South Vietnam] ... [T]he Americans have withdrawn, we have our troops in the South, and the spirit of the masses is rising. This is what marks the opportune moment. We must seize it firmly and step up the struggle on all three fronts: military, political, and diplomatic.

"In the South we have new strength: we have the initiative on the field of battle, and have linked our positions together from Tri Thien [in the north] all the way to the Mekong Delta [south of Saigon].... We must strike the strategic blow in 1975. [While we must bring pressure to bear on Saigon and other major cities in the South,] we agree that the year will open with attacks on the [Central Highlands]." In particular, these attacks were to begin at the strategic city of Ban Me Thout, a crossroads that had been critical to control of the region over the entire Indochina War.

The Communists' two-year strategic plan for 1975–1976 called for widespread attacks in 1975 designed to create conditions favorable "to carry out a general offensive and uprising to liberate the South completely" in 1976. The plan also provided for taking advantage of any unforeseen opportunities to "immediately liberate the South in 1975."[6]

At exactly 10:30 A.M. on February 5, 1975, the airplane carrying General Dung to the front lines took off from Hanoi. Upon his arrival in South Vietnam's northernmost province, Quang Tri, the gruff, square-faced fifty-eight-year-old Army chief of staff and his fellow generals immediately began making their plans for the coming battle for the strategic highlands.

In the years following the 1973 agreement in Paris between Henry Kissinger and Le Duc Tho, the North Vietnamese had prepared themselves for their intended conduct of "revolutionary warfare [to] destroy the enemy and liberate the South." This was a huge effort involving more than 30,000 troops and members of the Vanguard Youth. It resulted in more than 20,000 kilometers of eight-meter-wide paved roads capable of supporting trucks, tanks, and other weapons of war. The logistical complex also included 5,000 kilometers of oil pipeline, major storage facilities, and extensive telecommunication lines. In addition, over 80,000 troops had been moved south of the demilitarized zone giving the North Vietnamese Army a total force of some 200,000 soldiers in combat units supported by another 100,000 men in administrative and logistical outfits. The number of armored vehicles available to these forces exceeded 700. This gave the Communists as many tanks as were available to the South Vietnamese defenders. In addition, the number of artillery pieces in the hands of the invaders had quadrupled to 400. Clearly, the "peace" of 1973 was what John Guffey labeled it in his open letter to President Ford, "a fantasy."[7]

It was during the Political Bureau's meeting that the tactical decision was made to begin Campaign 275 with a massive attack in the Central Highlands. On January 8, 1975, just two days after the fall of Phuoc Long province, party First Secretary Le Duan declared "We must strike the strategic blow in 1975. We must open with attacks on Ban Me Thuot and Tuy Hoa. We must liberate [the area] from Binh Dinh [on the coast east of Ban Me Thuot] on up. In [the northeast] we must gain control from Hue to Da Nang. Such great victories will greatly change the balance of forces. We must sustain the fighting until the rainy season starts [in the late spring] and pile up repeated victories. If we strike powerfully, the enemy will face the danger of disintegration sooner. To fight around the cities we must smash the enemy's main force troops. When we enter the cities we must crush the enemy's nerve centers. The North must guarantee adequate material and technical support to the infantry. These are the basic principles of victory." No international body stepped forward to force the Communists to honor the Paris Peace Accords. And the United States was not about to unleash its B-52 bombers.[8]

If one were to draw lines on a map from the coastal city of Qui Nhon west to Kontum City in the highlands, down through Pleiku Province to Ban Me Thuot, and then back to Nha Trang on the coast, he would be roughly following first Route 19 west, then Route 14 south, and Route 21 back east. These highways were the principal lines of communications supporting the South Vietnamese Armed Forces defending the Central Highlands. The Communists' strategy was apparently like that of Union General Ulysses S. Grant at Vicksburg in 1863: they would split South Vietnam into two pieces and then surround Saigon from all directions.

In early January, the South Vietnamese captured a member of the North Vietnamese Third Army Division in the vicinity of the An Khe Pass, a potential choke point on Route 19 some 70 kilometers west of Highway 1 on the coast. Reconnaissance on the part of the South Vietnamese in late February and early March confirmed the existence and extensive nature of the network of roads built by the northerners for the purpose of bringing massive forces into the area. They also took note of the heavy truck traffic that was making use of these highways. Concerned that his forces in the highlands might have their lines of communications to the coast cut, the Commander of Region II, South Vietnamese General Pham Van Phu, began repositioning his forces.[9]

General Phu had established his reputation as a division commander, but he had never been in a position with as much responsibility as he held

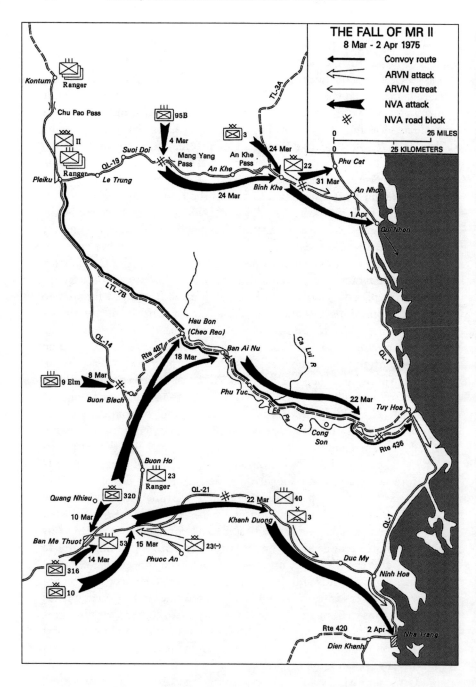

Military Region II.

in these early months of 1975. According to General Homer Smith, who had relieved General Murray as defense attaché in September 1974, Phu's lack of experience in commanding such large forces meant that he "apparently had little concept of the logistics of large troop movements, particularly under conditions which would introduce large masses of civilians into the problem."[10] As will be seen, this ignorance was a contributing factor to a debacle of major proportions.

The battle for the Central Highlands began in earnest early on the morning of March 4, 1975, at the Mang Yang Pass on highway 19 about 35 kilometers east of Pleiku City, the military headquarters for the region. Attacks along the southern connector between the coast and Ban Me Thuot, Route 21, were carried out simultaneously. As a result, by March 6, the Communist forces had successfully isolated the Central Highlands.[11] As we know, it was not that these attacks were a total surprise. For some time both American and South Vietnamese intelligence had monitored not only the construction of the vast logistical network described above, but also the movements of troops and supplies across that network. Lehman had sent a message to Washington expressing the view that the drastic reduction in military assistance being provided to South Vietnam combined with the resignation of Richard Nixon would likely lead Hanoi to make an all-out effort to conquer the south sometime in early 1975.[12]

The main question that faced General Phu at this point was not so much whether or not he would have to defend against a major, full-force, attack by the Communists, but where the attack would come. General Phu's intelligence officer, Colonel Trinh Tieu, insisted that the enemy's principal objective would be Ban Me Thuot, with intermediate and supporting objectives at Buon Ho to the north of Ban Me Thuot on Route 14 and Duc Lap to the south. Based upon sporadic attacks in the Kontum and Pleiku areas immediately following those along Highways 19 and 21, the general became convinced that his intelligence officer was wrong and that Pleiku was the enemy's main objective. Since he had only two regiments protecting the western approaches to his headquarters, he decided not to weaken this front in order to reinforce Ban Me Thuot where nothing of significance had yet taken place.[13]

Upon his arrival in the Central Highlands, General Dung and his deputy, General Le Ngoc Hien, spent their first night in the region pondering their next course of action. General Dung raised the questions, "How could we carry out the Political Bureau's resolution on liberating the South? How could we win in the [Central Highlands]? Especially, how should we attack Ban Me Thuot so the enemy would collapse quickly?" While Dung was thoroughly familiar with the north's conventional approach to fighting, he had, over the years, developed his own style; attack the enemy "like a bolt of lightning straight at their command center and smash it first."[14]

General Dung conducted a study of the deployment of South Vietnamese forces. He made note of the fact that General Phu had concentrated the bulk of his assets in the northern portion of the highlands around his headquarters at Pleiku. The North Vietnamese commander decided that, rather than confront his enemy across the entire region, he would concentrate his armies in the area around Ban Me Thuot. The result was that even though there was rough military parity in the region, at the point of the planned major attack, the North Vietnamese outnumbered their adversary by 5.5 to 1 in soldiers, 1.2 to 1 in tanks and armored cars, and 2.1 to 1 in large artillery. The South Vietnamese were spread too thinly.[15]

As formal plans for the attack on Ban Me Thuot were being prepared, Dung was visited by "some people in the revolutionary structure in [the] town." These party members had come to report "about the local political situation and the local political movements, and the status of our network within the town." Additional information relating to the deployment of the defending units was obtained from a captured South Vietnamese spy. This knowledge was all integrated into the planning process.

General Dung outlined his plans for the capture of Ban Me Thuot in his book *Our Great Spring Victory*:

1. The attack on Ban Me Thuot must be made using concentrated forces so as to "wipe out the enemy there."

2. All units must be closely coordinated, especially the mechanized units that are to strike deep inside the town.

3. The fact that Ban Me Thuot is a political and economic center for the region must be recognized. The fact that its residents are members of a diverse collection of ethnic groups that include members of various religions, citizens of foreign countries, and members of the bourgeoisie who have become accustomed to life under neocolonialism must be considered. This means that when our soldiers enter the town they must have "the correct attitude and behavior ... in order to win the hearts of the people and quickly stabilize people's lives after liberation."

4. Upon the liberation of the city, a military administrative structure must be quickly put in place. Colonel Ly Bloc, a man from one of the local ethnic groups who "has the confidence of the people and is loved and respected by everyone in the area," will be made chairman of the Ban Me Thuot military committee.

5. Since the city has a large system of military storage areas as well as a considerable industrial base belonging to the bourgeoisie, it will be necessary to protect these assets and put them back into operation. While South Vietnamese government property will be confiscated, the property of the people must not be touched.

6. Based upon the experience of the fight for Phuoc Long, it will be possible to put prisoners of war to work in such capacities as drivers of cars, tanks, armored cars, and road repair vehicles. In sum, "utmost attention [must be paid] to using war booty and prisoners of war immediately for the battle."[16]

It should be noted that while these plans contain instructions to treat South Vietnamese civilians and prisoners in a constructive way, the fact is that, in their implementation, many who were suspected of being "collaborators" with the Americans or the Thieu government were summarily executed once in custody.[17]

During the period of March 5 through March 9 the North Vietnamese forces implemented the plan to strike several outlying ARVN posts. Dung also ordered additional shelling of the Cu Hanh airfield at Pleiku. In a final directive to his commander in charge of these operations, he said that the commander should "strike once and shout ten times."

These attacks served two purposes. One was to confuse the ARVN and lead it to believe that Pleiku or Kontum in the northern part of the region or both were to be the principal point of attack. The other was to further cut off and isolate Ban Me Thuot. Dung observed that "by March 9 we had completely set our forces in their strategic and campaign positions, had cut [the highlands] off from the lowlands, had cut the northern and southern [sections of the highlands] apart, and completely surrounded and isolated Ban Me Thuot. The first stage in our test of wits with the enemy was over and the victory was ours."

Jay Scarborough, an American civilian on a leave of absence from Cornell Law School, was in Vietnam under a Ford Foundation grant to photograph thousands of pages of old Cham manuscripts. The Chams were an ancient ethnic group that had been nearly extinguished by the Vietnamese as they has driven south out of China centuries earlier. On Sunday, March 9, he decided to fly to Ban Me Thuot to visit some students that he had taught for four years at a local high school. Scarborough had been in country between the time he had completed his undergraduate work at Cornell in 1967 and when he entered law school in 1973. Over these years he had served with a U.S. Government-funded private organization called the International Voluntary Services. This was a Peace

Corps–like entity used to place young Americans who were willing to contribute their time and energy to help people in areas where the dangers of conflict precluded the insertion of Peace Corps personnel. During this period he had become fluent in Vietnamese and made many friends. It was with one of these friends that he stayed that night. At three o'clock on the morning of the 10th, Scarborough was awakened by his host with the shouted words, "Incoming! Incoming!"[18]

It had been exactly 2:00 A.M. that morning when the North Vietnamese sapper troops opened the battle for Ban Me Thuot with an attack on its airfield. Simultaneously, artillery and rockets were fired at the ARVN 23rd Division headquarters in the city itself in a barrage that lasted until 6:30 A.M. Under cover of this heavy fire, tanks, armored cars, troop transports, trucks pulling artillery, and antiaircraft guns raced toward the heart of the town in accordance with Dung's "blossoming lotus" tactic of "smashing [the enemy's command center] right at first."[19]

When the shells first landed, John Miller, his wife, Carolyn, and his five-year-old daughter, LuAnne, were shaken awake by the noise and shock of the explosions. The Millers were in Vietnam as missionaries for the Wycliffe Bible Translators and had been in the country for fifteen and fourteen years respectively. LuAnne had two older brothers and a sister who were attending school at Nha Trang on the coast. Also living in Ban Me Thout were other missionaries, a Canadian couple, and three other Americans. Shortly after dawn on the 10th of March, these westerners converged on the USAID compound where Paul Struharik, the local U.S. consulate representative, took them in. By then there were twenty people in the compound, the others being a mix of local USAID employees, a visiting Australian Broadcasting Corporation official, and a Philippine agriculture expert

Struharik herded his charges into a 12 by 20 bunker that had once been used by the CIA and he radioed the consulate in Nha Trang, advising them of their precarious situation. While a helicopter was immediately dispatched on a rescue mission, Communist ground fire repeatedly drove the aircraft off. In the end, all were taken prisoner by the invaders.

Struharik was suspected of being a CIA officer and was therefore isolated from the others in solitary confinement, and all were held as prisoners of war for the next eight months. In the meantime, the Wycliffe Bible Translator's staff had seen that the three older Miller children were taken to the Philippines. The family was ultimately reunited and the Millers continued their mission as Bible translators.[20]

By nightfall on March 10, the North Vietnamese had completed their conquest of Ban Me Thuot itself, but at the Phung Duc airfield about eight kilometers east of the city, a fierce battle continued. In addition, a South Vietnamese Ranger group that had been moved by General Phu to the town of Buon Ho, about forty kilometers northeast of Ban Me Thuot on Route 14, began a counterattack against the still not heavily occupied city.[21]

It has been said throughout time, and in every part of the world, that soldiers do not fight so much for their country, as they do for their buddies. It has therefore been the challenge to military leadership across the ages to direct this fighting spirit in such a way as to best serve the country's interests in time of war. However, in South Vietnamese society, as in many others, the loyalty to family supersedes virtually all others. It is this loyalty that led to what General Homer Smith has referred to as the "family syndrome," (i.e., the willingness of ARVN soldiers to leave their posts in order to protect their wives, children, and other relatives from danger.) In the battle for Ban Me Thuot, one of the earliest and most destructive of these derelictions of military duty took place. As the Ranger group was fighting its way toward the city, the commander of the 23rd Division diverted it to a training center just outside town to prepare a defended helicopter landing zone. The ARVN II Corps chief of staff later described what happened:

"...General Tuong, the 23rd Division Commander, worried a lot about his family. His wife and children were still in Ban Me Thuot city. So he had them go to the training center southeast of Ban Me Thuot. He had them gather there in an open place. He then directed the Ranger group to go back to the training center in order to protect the landing zone for his helicopter to pick the family up. The Ranger group was advancing; they were fighting with the enemy. The enemy was not strong inside the city. Most communist main forces were outside the city possibly afraid to concentrate within Ban Me Thuot for fear of air attacks. Tuong directed the Rangers from the air to go back to the training center. The commander must obey the order of his general, his division commander. They went back to protect the landing zone, and he picked up his family and when the soldiers tried to go back to Ban Me Thuot city, the enemy had sealed it off."[22] While this particular action had only a marginal effect upon the ultimate fate of Ban Me Thuot, it illustrates a problem that faced the South Vietnamese armed forces as the Communist army advanced from one battlefield success to another.

In the meantime, the ARVN defenders of the Ban Me Thuot airfield continued to vigorously resist repeated Communist assaults. As the Communist encirclement tightened around the division command post, air strikes were requested in a desperate attempt to relieve the North Vietnamese Army pressure. However, one bomb struck the defenders' tactical operations center cutting communications with II Corps headquarters. In the end, Ban Me Thuot fell into enemy hands by 11:30 A.M. on March 11.[23] The Ford Administration failed to respond.

Beginning on March 12, Phu attempted to position a counterattack force in the village of Phuoc An about 45 kilometers east of Ban Me Thuot. It has been alleged by a number of the South Vietnamese military that one of the consequences of having had the Americans be the de facto leaders in the war for so long was that many South Vietnamese officers had become "conditioned" to an American way of fighting (i.e., accustomed to vast amounts of logistical and air support). Whether for this reason or some other, Phu greatly underestimated his ability to move the troops and materials necessary to carry out this effort. As a consequence of this, and because of the tactical skill of the North Vietnamese commander and the fact that the ARVN soldiers brought into Phuoc An were not prepared for combat, the counterattack was totally ineffective.

Adding to his shameful behavior at the Ban Me Thuot training center, General Tuong "was slightly wounded as his helicopter received fire and had himself evacuated to a hospital," turning command of the 23rd Division over to a colonel.[24]

On March 11 there had been a meeting in Saigon between President Thieu, Joint General Staff (JGS) Chairman General Cao Van Vien, Lieutenant General Dang Van Quang, and Prime Minister Tran Thien Khiem. The President is reported to have declared that he believed Ban Me Thuot to be more important to the defense of South Vietnam than either Pleiku or Kontum, and that it had to be retaken "at all cost." He then went on to describe his strategic concept of "light at the top, heavy at the bottom." This plan consisted of conceding to the enemy much of the territory to the north of Saigon, and it was based upon Thieu's concern that without the American aid that had been promised to him by President Nixon, the balance of forces was now "severely tipped in favor of North Vietnam." Moreover, there was a disastrous morale crisis prevailing in South Vietnam at that time as a result of the aid reductions. In a postwar interview, the ex–Speaker of the South Vietnamese House of Representatives is quoted as saying that Thieu's change in strategy "cannot be regarded as an inspiration of the moment, nor as a move by an exhausted man stunned by the loss of Ban Me Thuot," but rather as being motivated by "highly important political necessities." Speaker Can went on to say, "At the time, Thieu was in a very bad posture." The growing domestic opposition was about to urge him to resign. Word of a coup spread around Saigon, and additional U.S. aid seemed to be uncertain despite efforts by President Ford to convince Congress that more aid was vitally needed. Besides satisfying the purely military needs, Thieu's decision to abandon the highlands would also create a state of emergency in the country that would consequently muzzle the mounting opposition. Moreover, Thieu would naively expect that because of worldwide repercussions resulting from the catastrophic retreat, the U.S. would appropriate the requested military aid in order to avoid being accused of betraying an ally and thus losing all confidence abroad. Since Phuoc Long had fallen into enemy hands, President Thieu repeatedly blamed his reverses on Washington's failure to keep its promises, and once exploded; "If they [the U.S.] grant full aid we will hold the whole country, but if they only give half of it, we will only hold half of the country." Can was surprised by such reasoning which sounded like President Thieu was defending the U.S. and was fighting for the Americans themselves." Half a country could quickly become "a quarter of a country," or less. Neither the U.S. embassy nor the Defense Attaché's Office (DAO) was notified of President Thieu's decision to withdraw from Pleiku and Kontum.[25]

President Thieu wished to discuss the new strategy, and the force movements impelled by it, face to face with General Phu. However, the hazardous situation in the highlands decreed that any such meeting be held outside that area. It was therefore scheduled for Cam Ranh Bay on the coast for March 14, at which time the President outlined his new strategy to his Region II commander. In view of the fact that the only two major highways from the highlands to the coast (Routes 19 and 21) were blocked by Communist forces, the decision was made to use Route 7B, described as "an old logger's road" that was "overgrown with brush, with fords in disrepair, and an important bridge out.

The meeting that Friday was attended by only five men: President Thieu, General Phu, the Presidential Security Advisor, Lieutenant General Dang Van Quang, Prime Minister Khiem, and Joint General Staff (JGS) Chairman, General Vien. After only an hour and a half, four basic decisions were reached: (1) the regular ARVN forces in Pleiku and Kontum were to be pulled out of the highlands; (2) the Regional and Popular Forces, consisting "overwhelmingly" of Montagnards, along with dependents, civilians, and government administrators of Pleiku and Kontum were not to be told of the retreat and therefore not to be withdrawn; (3) the redeployment was to be executed within a few days and in secrecy; and (4) the route for the evacuation was to be the long unused Route 7B. There seems to be some question as to whether or not this movement of troops was intended to be preparatory to a campaign to recapture Ban Me Thuot, but in the end this question was made moot by the actions of General Dung and his superior forces. President Thieu's recounting of this point came in his

April 21 farewell address, "After Ban Me Thuot fell we wondered where we could get the troops to recapture it. We came to a political decision not to insure the life or death of Kontum and Pleiku.... We decided to re-deploy our forces from Kontum and Pleiku to recapture Ban Me Thuot." In any case, upon his return to his headquarters Phu made his decision to pull out all at once. General Homer Smith has expressed the view that if Lieutenant General Dong Van Khuyen, chief of staff of the JGS and senior logistician in the South Vietnamese armed forces, had not been in Japan where his father was being treated for cancer, the withdrawal may have been executed quite differently. Smith is convinced that General Khuyen would have directed Phu to develop a detailed plan for any such large-scale movement before putting it into effect.[27]

When General Phu announced the decision to his staff, "all of those assembled were surprised." Colonel Le Khac Ly, who as chief of staff for the II Corps had the responsibility for planning, recounted these exchanges at the meeting: " Nobody believed him. All of us asked him again, we are to abandon Kontum and Pleiku? Yes, this decision has already been made. We have no discussion on this. I asked him how? He said some by air, some by road. I asked him what road? He said Route 7B, through Phu Bon. That has already been decided. No discussion again. It was the President's decision."

Colonel Ly then said to Phu, "Please give me a week or three days at least for me to present you with a plan." Phu responded, "No. You have no time. Everything starts tomorrow." Ly later recounted, "I opened my eyes widely, my mouth, and everyone looked at him except [newly promoted Brigadier General] Tat." Phu then said, "Tomorrow I will fly to Nha Trang and Cam and Ly will stay here. Tat will be overall commander. That is the plan."

In giving his orders for the conduct of evacuation, General Phu con-fused the chain of command for the withdrawal by giving Brigadier General Cam, his assistant for operations, "verbal orders to the effect that he was to 'supervise' the retreat." According to Ly, this "created more prob-lems between Tat and Cam, more disagreements." Phu then directed his staff to "go ahead and prepare tonight and start moving tomorrow." The movement orders were to be issued to the units just one hour in advance of the execution of the operation. He also then revealed that only the reg-ular units were to be withdrawn.

Colonel Ly remembered this part of the conversation vividly: "I asked him another question, how about the province and district personnel, the Regional and Provincial Forces (the RF/PF), the troop's dependents and the people? He said, [and] I will never forget, 'Forget about them. You have no responsibility to take care of them! ... If you tell them about it, you cannot control it and you cannot get down to Tuy Hoa [on the coast] because there would be panic.'"

The discussion then turned to the decision to use Route 7B. Ly argued that Route 19 was a better road whereas Route 7B "required a lot of engineer effort to open the road, because [of] mines, enemy mines, friendly mines, and Special Forces mines. The bridges were also down and the route had not been used for a long time. So we had to rebuild it. And it would take time and equipment to rebuild. Engineering equipment. Do we have enough, can we move it? If the American troops were here, they could use flying cranes for the movement of engineering equipment in the area. It would be easy. But now, we Vietnamese are alone, do we have enough assets to move heavy equipment to the place where it is needed? That's a problem. It's good for surprise, I agree with you. Yes, surprise. For the enemy to move into this area to attack us would take time. But we have to build roads, to build bridges, and it's easy for them to harass us. The enemy will have enough time to overcome the surprise. But he didn't buy my opinions. He said the President had already decided."

Later, when Colonel Ly was asked whether or not the II Corps had sufficient engineering assets to repair Route 7B he responded: "We did not have enough. We had just a fair amount of equipment and engineers. It requires a lot of time; it's a tough job. To move equipment it takes time. It's heavy equipment and can't move fast. He [Phu] said the President discussed that, knew that. The President and Vien knew that, they all knew about the difficulties and they decided to take this road, a big surprise to the enemy. We would be down to Tuy Hoa by the time the enemy came and we would have no problem at all. We would use air support."

The next morning, March 15, General Phu and a number of key staff officers took off for Nha Trang, ostensibly to supervise the overall operation from there. However, those left behind were left with feelings of betrayal and anger. General Cam, the putative "supervisor" of the difficult operation, immediately left for Tuy Hoa leaving Colonel Ly to cope with the withdrawal on his own. The II Corps chief of staff described his situation as follows: "I was the only man to assume the responsibility for everything [other than General Tat's Rangers]. Cam [went] to Tuy Hoa, Phu to Nha Trang, and Tat stayed at the old American 4th Division headquarters in Pleiku [at Ham Rong Mountain] to take care of his Rangers. I stayed of course in corps headquarters. Every report from all units came to me and they reported, 'Enemy attack, enemy attack—surrounded.' I could communicate with General Phu on the 'hotline' phone only. And Saigon said they could not get information from Phu in Nha Trang. I forgot to tell you one more thing. Phu took all the key staff members. The Chiefs of G3, G2, G1, all his key staff went with him. He left only the deputies of each staff agency with me. The total troops we had in II Corps at that time were about 165,000 including lowland troops. And you withdraw a corps like that with no planning! With no planning at all he withdrew the troops. I had to do my best. I called the unit commanders; I had to let them know the situation. I personally informed the Americans there, the CIA, the consulate, the DAO, and told them that they must go right now. At first they couldn't believe me. But I said, 'Go, don't ask.' They called Saigon and checked with headquarters, and they didn't know.... Later on, of course, they knew and they were asking me questions, 'Where is Phu?' and I said, 'Phu is not here, Phu is in Nha Trang.' And Phu couldn't provide enough information for the JGS. So the JGS contacted me directly in Pleiku."

Once the ARVN regular units began their preparations for leaving Pleiku, the Montagnard and PF/RF realized that they were being abandoned and panic broke out. In Colonel Ly's words, "The people, the troops, the dependents became undisciplined. Troops were raping, burning things, and committing robbery. The troops became undisciplined when they heard the order. I can't blame them. There was no plan to take care of the troops' dependents. The airfield at Pleiku was in a state of panic. Sometimes the planes could land, but they couldn't do the job. I had to go there and use my pistol to restore order. Of course, I didn't shoot anybody, just shot in the air. And when the people saw me, there was order. But soon I had to go back to headquarters. And the enemy kept shelling the headquarters at Pleiku. We left all of the old airplanes in Pleiku, helicopters and fixed wing, and heavy equipment, and the important equipment like the sensors left by the Special Forces. All types of equipment like that. We moved only about seventy percent of what we had. What we left behind we destroyed by air later. "However, Colonel Uoc reported later that not all 'operational planes' were destroyed at Pleiku and that over 100,000 tons of ammunition were left behind. The final report of the DAO, dated June 18, 1975, stated that "[l]ittle, if any, materiel was destroyed, although the Vietnamese Air Force did bomb the ammunition storage areas at Ban Me Thuot and Pleiku."[28]

In the meantime, the ARVN engineering units were dispatched down Route 7B at the column's head with the mission of clearing the path for the rest of the corps. By noon on March 16, a mass of humanity — troops, dependents, civilians, and deserters — was clogging the old road. Some 400,000 civilians, 60,000 regular forces, and 7,000 Rangers began the attempted escape to the sea.[29]

On the same day that General Phu and his staff left Pleiku for Nha

Trang on the coast, North Vietnamese General Dung received cables from Le Duc Tho and Vo Nguyen Giap confirming plans to accelerate the timetable for the conquest of South Vietnam. In addition, Western news reports heard on the radio described a crush of departures for Saigon from the Pleiku airport. Intercepted messages on March 16 from South Vietnam Air Force (SVAF) planes indicated a mass exodus of the SVAF to Nha Trang, in spite of the fact that the airfield had not yet been heavily shelled. At 4:00 P.M., reports were received of long convoys of vehicles headed south from Pleiku. At 9:00 P.M. that day, the convoy was reported to be headed down Route 7B.

As General Dung described it, "Our headquarters came alive. A map of [the highland] road network was spread out on the table, with flashlights and magnifying glasses spread out along Routes 19, 14, and 7B to find points we could 'cork up,' encircling routes, and attack routes, and measuring the distance between the nearest unit and Route 7B to calculate the time for each action. I picked up the telephone and talked directly with Kim Tuan, who was then Commander of the 320th Division. Before we attacked Ban Me Thuot I had asked many times about Route 7B, and it was reported that Route 7B had long been abandoned, bridges were out, there were no ferries, and the enemy could not use it. Two days before, I had again asked Kim Tuan about this road, and he, too, had given the same answer. Now having heard that the enemy were retreating along Route 7B, but that his unit still had no concrete hold on that road and was not yet urgently pursuing the enemy, I spoke very severely to the unit's highest responsible person. I emphasized twice to Kim Tuan, 'That is a shortcoming, negligence that deserves a reprimand. At this time if you waver just a bit, are just a bit negligent, hesitate just a bit, you have botched the job. If the enemy escapes it will be a big crime, and you will have to bear the responsibility for it.'"[30]

Meanwhile, the convoy became stalled near Cheo Reo, the provincial capital of Phu Bon Province located about halfway down Route 7B. Again, according to Colonel Ly, the repair work on the bridges took much longer than had been anticipated. "General Phu's estimate was that in about two days the roads would be open. He was completely wrong. Just one bridge took about three or four days." There was little interference with the column by the North Vietnamese along the road to Cheo Reo until March 18, but late that day the 320th Division began executing General Dung's orders to prevent an escape by the fleeing South Vietnamese.[31]

The withdrawal from Pleiku was now turning into a major disaster. Colonel Ly described the situation as Kim Tuan's forces began their intense attacks on March 18. "The road from Pleiku was terrible. I saw many old people and babies fall down on the road and tanks and trucks would go over them. Accidents all the time but everything would keep moving.... Nobody could control anything. No order. The troops were mixed with the dependents and civilians and were trying to take care of all the children and wives. You can't imagine it. It was terrible. No control. And the enemy squeezed them. Refugees were strung out all the way from Cheo Reo back to the point where Route 7B and Route 14 fork [a distance of about 40 kilometers]. I walked under fire."[32]

Even before the mass of refugees was halfway toward their goal of reaching the coast, any semblance of discipline among the soldiers had disappeared. Food supplies ran out and the men began to pillage the villages along Route 7B. There were many incidences of murder and rape. By March 18, some 200,000 desperate people were trapped in the vicinity of Cheo Reo. And the Communists continued to fire at them with small arms and artillery from the hills on both sides of the road. General Smith has called it a "turkey shoot."

The former commander of the ARVN Artillery Command, General Thin, described the retreat as follows: "We must salute the battalion commanders and lower officers for having marched with their units but they were no longer able to control their famished and tired men. The soldiers kept shouting insults at President Thieu for this impossible and terrible retreat. Some reached the limit of their despair and killed their officers. An artillery battalion commander who was marching in the retreating column was shot to death by some Rangers who wanted his beautiful wristwatch. The despair was so great that at one point two or three guerrillas arriving at the scene could make prisoners of a hundred Rangers. Wives and children of retreating soldiers died of hunger and sickness along the road. It was a true hell."[33]

The journalist Nguyen Tu, who was in Cheo Reo on March 18, wrote: "On the heels of the refugees evacuating Pleiku and Kontum, the people of Cheo Reo were also leaving their city. Refugees evacuating Pleiku and Kontum who reached Cheo Reo in small groups made the long journey in two days. The majority [were] still far behind, dragging their feet on the dirty road under a scorching sun by day and chilled by night in the forests. It was not possible to say how many children fell during the walk, how many helpless old people were standing alongside the road unable to move, how many others were suffering from thirst and hunger during the walk to freedom and democracy. A Ranger officer told me, 'This time, I can never look straight ... [at] my people again.' A private said, 'Damn it, we got away without any fighting. I prefer to fight and run away if we lose. I will accept that.' An Air Force captain said, 'It is sad, very sad, especially when we look back at Pleiku, a deserted city now. We can see only fires and fires. I am very sad.' Another soldier added, 'I am stunned.... Look at these people, the young ones. Isn't this miserable?'"

He continued, "Women, children, youngsters, and the elderly — all in small groups with their belongings either on their backs or in their hands — rushing out of their houses as they saw the convoy approaching. The same scenes of plundering and ransacking of homes by unidentified people reappeared.... Many sections of town were set on fire.... Cheo Reo has capitulated not to the enemy but [to] its own.... After Kontum and Pleiku on Sunday, Cheo Reo became a lost town on Tuesday."[34]

The next day Tu's dispatch read, "the leading part of our convoy got through the ambush point under a screen of supporting fire. But the tail end had to leave the road and pass through the jungle. I was in the tail end. Rebel mountain tribesmen armed with our [American] weapons and Communist B-41 rockets and AK-47 rifles shot into the convoy, while Communist artillery struck from all directions. Many trucks were hit by shells and burst into flames and exploded. The trucks were crammed with soldiers, children, and old people. They fell everywhere. Those who walked fell to machine gun bullets. Their blood flowed in tiny streams. The roaring artillery, crackling small arms, screams of the dying and crying of the children combined into a single voice from hell.

"The Rangers resisted all night, permitting the tail end of the convoy to flee into the jungle.

"At last, 200 of us succeeded in climbing up Chu Del hill, about six miles from Cheo Reo, 210 miles north of Saigon. Helicopters contacted us and moved in for rescue. The operation was difficult, because Chu Del is a narrow and steep hill. Finally, in an operation that evening and the next morning, 200 people were lifted out and rescued."[35]

The following Sunday, March 23, a photographer for United Press International named Lim Thanh Van was able to get a ride on a helicopter piloted by Captain Huynh My Phuong. The pilot's mission was supposed to be "to destroy Communists." However, Captain Phuong spotted a group of refugees huddled on top of the same hill from which Nguyen Tu had been rescued earlier. Captain Phuong dropped down to pick up as many of them as he could. As he pulled up, an old woman and an old man holding a child lost the grip that they had managed to get on the skids and fell to the ground. The pilot was quickly notified of the fact that the child's mother had made it on board in the mad scramble, and he started to turn back. Lim Than Van later wrote, "Phuong, tears in his eyes, tried to swing his helicopter around and pick up the abandoned child. He could not, because he already had so many aboard. We dropped his load of refugees

at the province capital of Tuy Hoa and flew back, Phuong urging his helicopter on in an attempt to pick up the ones left behind. When we got
there, they were gone....

"Communist artillery, attacks by mountain tribesmen and dissident
troops, the heat, the sheer struggle, the hardships have killed — who knows
how many died?

"Vehicles lie along Highway 7B, route of retreat from the Central
Highlands provinces of Pleiku, Kontum, and Phu Bon. So do the dead
children, women and old men. For miles and miles, people look up to us,
falling on their knees, begging for rescue. Phuong saw a communist mortar team firing at one group of persons in the convoy. He and his following gunships furiously attacked. The mortars stopped."

Journalist Lim recorded, "It is against Phuong's orders to stop and
pick up people, but he said he must. The door gunners ran out to pick up
children, old people. Others, including government Rangers, ran for the
helicopters. I fell down and had ten persons on my back. I didn't even feel
any pain, worrying only that the children wouldn't get on the chopper. In the
helicopter, I was pinned down by people. I couldn't even click my camera.

"No one knows how many people have died in this most incredible
convoy down Highway 7B. No one likely ever will. Babies are born on the
route. More die. The sheer incomprehensible terror is not only on Highway 7B.

"At Pleiku last Sunday, the last planes took off before the town was
abandoned to the communists. Old Mrs. Khien told me the huge crowd
trying to get on the last three C-130 transports looked like a huge dragon
dance, pushing, shoving, up and down, back and forth. People grabbed for
the tail, falling off as the plane taxied. Just as the last one took off, a small
baby fell out of the aircraft, killed instantly as it hit the tarmac, she said.

"And at Tuy Hoa [on the coast] sits major Ly Van Phuc, generally recognized as the best field information officer in the South Vietnamese Army.
Phuc was away at training school when Pleiku was evacuated. His wife and
eight children were somewhere between Pleiku and Tuy Hoa on the convoy of death."

Richard Blystone, then working for the Associated Press, reported
from Tuy Hoa. "The helicopters spill out weeping women and children
limping on bare feet and soldiers in blood-caked camouflage fatigues.
Some carry satchels and straw baskets; some have nothing but their lives.
An Army major, hoping his family has made the 150-mile march from
Pleiku, watches each incoming helicopter intently. An old woman drops
down on the grass near the helicopter pad. 'Now I know I am alive,' she
says. She has been on the road a week.

"'It was such misery I cannot describe it,' says a mother after frantically searching for her ten children and finding that they are all there.

"Two children arrive alone. Their father put them aboard a helicopter thinking that their pregnant mother was on board. But she was not.

"A school teacher says that his family walked through the jungle to avoid North Vietnamese shellfire and thought their luck had changed when they were able to climb aboard a truck. But later they realized that their five-year-old child was missing in the scramble.

"The refugees are flown to this coastal province headquarters about 240 miles northeast of Saigon from a stalled refugee column that ends 15 miles to the southwest. Outgoing choppers carry ammunition, rice and bread — some of which the helicopter pilots pay for out of their own pockets. Flying from Tuy Hoa toward the column, the reasons why the refugees cannot move soon become evident. Six miles from the city, a blackened armored truck sits in the road beside a flattened burned out hamlet. This is as far as relatives of the refugees hoping to meet their loved ones dare to go....

"The retreating soldiers at the head of the column have set up several camps beside the road. Farther on, cars, trucks and busses are clustered in a bizarre traffic jam in the middle of nowhere. Other vehicles are backed up at a half-completed bridge across a river. Viet Cong shells have been hitting near the river crossing, killing and wounding many persons, the refugees say.

"Earlier in the week, they say, more than 100 persons, mostly civilians, were killed by shellfire near Cong Son, ten miles back.

"The column trails out of sight into the foothills where a cloud of gray smoke rises; officers say that there are about 35,000 refugees near [that fire] and anther 30,000 stretching back to Cong Son, where a Ranger group harassed by communist fire brings up the rear. How many hundreds are left behind along the rest of the more than 150 miles to the abandoned Central Highlands capitals of Pleiku and Kontum no one knows."[36]

By the time that the last straggling men, women, and children had reached Tuy Hoa on the coast 300,000 civilians, 40,000 ARVN, and 6,300 Rangers were missing, never to be accounted for. While General Phu had said that the withdrawal could be completed in three days, some of those who had left Pleiku on or about the 16th of March were still staggering down Route 7B when the North Vietnamese captured Tuy Hoa on April 1.[37]

General Cao Van Vien, the last chairman of the South Vietnamese Joint General Staff, summarized the situation this way: "Psychologically and politically, the self-inflicted defeat of II Corps in the Highlands amounted to a horrible nightmare for the people and armed forces of

South Vietnam. Confusion, worries, accusations, guilt, and a general feeling of distress began to weigh on everybody's mind. Rumors spread rapidly that territorial concessions were in the making. The immediate impact of the rumors was to unleash an uncontrollable surge of refugees seeking by all means and at all costs to leave whatever provinces remained of Military Region II. To the north, Military Region I also felt the repercussions. Its population soon joined the refugees and battered troops streaming south along the coast. First, they rushed into Phan Rang and Phan Thiet (on the coast south of Nha Trang), and then moved on toward Saigon. In the national capital itself, the opposition increased its activities and irreparably widened the government's credibility gap. Confidence in the armed forces also swung down to its lowest ebb. Demonstrators angrily demanded the replacement of President Thieu; they also vigorously voiced anti–American sentiment. A pervasive hope still lingered, however, for some miraculous thing to happen that could save Vietnam."[38]

The debacle on Route 7B is only part of the story of the North Vietnamese success in defeating the ARVN forces in Military Region II. Prior to achieving his overwhelming success in the defeat of General Pham Van Phu's forces at Ban Me Thuot and their subsequent rout down the infamous logging road 7B, General Van Tien Dung had isolated his main target from the other ARVN forces in the Central Highlands. Dung described his strategy thus: "For our attack in the [Central Highlands] campaign, we would have to use relatively large forces, of regimental and divisional size, to cut Routes 19, 14, and 21, thereby establishing positions dividing the enemy's forces: strategically, this would cut off the [Central Highlands] from the coastal plains, and tactically, it would isolate Ban Me Thuot from Pleiku and Kontum. At the same time, we needed diversionary maneuvers to tie the enemy's feet and draw their attention and their forces towards the northern [part of the Central Highlands], enabling us to maintain secrecy and surprise in the south until we began the attack to take Ban Me Thuot."[39]

The first of these tactical maneuvers occurred on March 1 about 25 kilometers west of Pleiku on Route 19 where two small ARVN outposts were wiped out. General Phu reacted by shifting one regiment of troops to that area on March 3 to reinforce his defenses of Pleiku. It was at this point that General Dung directed that the airfield there be shelled while the division commander "shouted ten times." While Phu was reacting to the action to the west of his headquarters, North Vietnamese Army attacks were carried out on 4 March at key choke points on Route 19 to the east. This closed that highway to reinforcements that might try to come from the coastal areas. On March 5, Communist forces overwhelmed an ARVN outpost west of Khan Duong on Route 21, the southern connector between the highlands and the coast. There they established a roadblock that was about 65 kilometers east of Ban Me Thuot. This completed the isolation of Phu's armies from the South Vietnamese units based on the plains below without revealing Dung's immediate objective.

Dung explained his decision to hold back from completely isolating Ban Me Thuot at the outset as follows: "We didn't cut Route 14 (between Pleiku and Ban Me Thuot) at the same time we cut Routes 19 and 21 although our plan included, besides strategic roadblocks, the campaign blockade of Route 14 in order to cut Ban Me Thuot off from Pleiku. The problem was when we should put it into effect. If we cut Route 14 too soon, our intention to attack Ban Me Thuot might be discovered." He went on to explain that his intention was to cut Route 14 when he began the attack on Ban Me Thuot.[40]

Since Route 21 had been defended by relatively light forces, the establishment of a roadblock there was accomplished by Dung's forces with relative ease. That was not the case along Route 19. The eastern portion of this vital connector from the seacoast to the highlands was defended by the 22nd ARVN Division, commanded by General Phan Dinh Niem, and by South Vietnamese Air Force units located at the Phu Cat Air Base on Route 1 in the north of Military Region II.

The coordinated attacks by Dung's troops on March 4 were at several points along Route 19. These included the Mang Yang Pass about 45 kilometers east of Pleiku, the airfield at An Khe about 25 kilometers further toward the coast, the An Khe Pass, the intersection of Route 3A and Route 19 just west of the city of Binh Khe, and the air base at Phu Cat. While the 22nd Division was attempting to maintain some semblance of control in Binh Dinh Province to the east, the South Vietnamese forces near Pleiku were under heavy rocket, mortar, and recoilless rifle fire. These were the attacks that reinforced General Phu's belief that it was his headquarters that was the principal target of the invading North Vietnamese army.

In the first couple of days of the battle along Route 19 between Pleiku and the coast, the Communists achieved some success. However, General Niem began re-deploying several of his units on the 8th and 9th of March in an effort to stop the advance of General Dung's armies and to protect Phu Cat Air Base.

On March 10, the day General Dung's lotus bloomed in Ban Me Thuot, troops of the 22nd Division fought off repeated attempts by the North Vietnamese Army to clear a path east of the An Khe Pass. By the 11th, the attacking army had been badly hurt by South Vietnamese artillery and air strikes. In fact, two companies had been virtually annihilated.

However, truckloads of replacements and ammunition continued to reinforce the Communist forces, demonstrating once again the value of the huge complex of highways and depots constructed by North Vietnam between the signing of the Paris Peace Accords in January 1973 and the aggressions initiated in 1975.

On March 13, a representative of the Defense Attaché Office visited the battlefield along Route 19. While his report of the situation faced by the South Vietnamese forces described General Niem's general confidence and optimism, the situation was, in fact, shaky. On the 12th, the command post of a company of Regional Forces had been overrun, and heavy attacks by North Vietnamese units had killed four successive commanders of one regular ARVN battalion and had left it at half strength. As it turned out, the superior numbers and resources of the North Vietnamese units slowly overwhelmed General Niem's forces attempting to open the An Khe Pass. For example, despite killing nearly 500 of the enemy in two days, the 42nd Regiment was unable to make any real progress in dislodging the three North Vietnamese Army battalions holding the high ground at each end of the pass. On March 17, the division commander concluded that they could not succeed in breaking the North Vietnamese resistance so he ordered his troops to hold in place. This left several hundred territorial soldiers cut off in the city of An Khe. By March 19, some 500 people were struggling to escape from this besieged city to the coast over rural roads and trails. On March 24, the massed forces of the North Vietnamese 3rd Division began their assault of the city of Binh Khe. In other words, General Niem's 22nd Division had been pushed back to within less than 50 kilometers of the coast by this date.[41]

As the 41st and 42nd Regiments of the 22nd Division dug in for the defense of the port of Qui Nhon on March 27, orders came to evacuate what remained of General Niem's troops. On the 31st, the Communists attacked Phu Cat Air Base and the Vietnamese Air Force flew out 32 aircraft, leaving about 58, mostly disabled or destroyed, on the ground. General Thinh, commanding general of the Artillery Command of the Joint General Staff, described the final act of this drama as follows: " Finally isolated, at the end of [its] supplies, and deprived of the necessary area support, the 22ed ARVN Division was forced to lead a heroic delaying action toward the ocean, abandoning the province of Binh Dinh to the enemy." Only a fifth of the division's complement, some 2,000 officers and men, remained to be evacuated by sea on April 1. "The rest having been dispersed or killed, wounded, or made prisoner.... The general commanding the 22ed Division, in his command post on [the] boat, fainted several times at the news of [the] severe losses of his unit.[42]

While the South Vietnamese forces were attempting to stop the Communist advances on Route 19, a similar effort was under way on Route 21, the connector between Ban Me Thuot and the cities of Ninh Hoa and Nha Trang on the coast. Even though General Dung's forces had been able to quickly overcome the defenders of Ban Me Thuot, a number of the surviving ARVN troops had been able to regroup at the city's airfield about ten kilometers outside of town. There they fought valiantly before superior forces finally overwhelmed them.[43]

First Lieutenant Nguyen Troung Toai described this part of the battle as follows: "At Phung Duc air base, where our Corps Headquarters 53 and 44 were stationed, we fought with them for almost ten days, and the number of casualties on their side was greater than on our side. The ratio was seven deaths on their side to two on our side. We fought until our ammunition ran out. We had helicopters supplying us with ammunition. But under the intense fire our pilots became afraid and they flew too high and didn't aim right. They dropped boxes of ammunition closer to the communist side than our side and we were not able to retrieve the ammunition. So we fought to the last bullet, and all of us were nearly wiped out."[44]

In contrast, however, the attempt by the ARVN to retake Ban Me Thuot from Phuoc An city about 40 kilometers to the east, which was briefly mentioned earlier, was another disaster. In response to President Thieu's order to reoccupy Ban Me Thuot right away, General Phu apparently planned to airlift the entire 44th Regiment of the 23rd Division from Pleiku to Phuoc An. In the event, there were insufficient helicopter assets to move more than two battalions, and those could not be provided with artillery or tank support. General Thinh described what happened: "Ban Me Thuot was the rear base of the 23rd Division, with many barracks of married men from all units. For this reason, it was hoped that the men would push quickly toward the city in order to liberate their families in the city. Unfortunately, the opposite took place. As soon as they landed with their copters, ... most of the soldiers, seeing by chance their families who had left the city several days earlier, threw their uniforms and weapons away and disguised themselves as civilians in order to lead their wives and children to Nha Trang, which city was still under friendly control."

The chief of staff of II Corps confirmed this account in these words: "...the defensive troops worried too much about their families in Ban Me Thuot city. So when they got out of the helicopters they would run to find their wives and children rather than fighting the enemy. When they departed from Pleiku the spirit of fighting was very high, the morale was very high. And Tuong and Phu felt very good about it. But actually, when they got on the ground at Ban Me Thuot, they ran away to take care of their families. Nobody could control them."[45]

Once the Rangers at Phung Duc airfield were eliminated and the soldiers of the 23rd Division dispersed at Phuoc An, the path down Route 21 was wide open to the North Vietnamese armies. In an effort to block their anticipated drive to the sea, the Joint General Staff decided on March 17 to provide reinforcements to those still defending Military Region II. An Airborne brigade that had been withdrawn from Military Region I to provide additional strength to the defenses of Saigon was diverted to Nha Trang. This force of about 2,000 men moved quickly to the Deo Cao Pass about 50 kilometers west of coastal highway Route 1 and the city of Khan Duong. There they joined two battalions of the 40th Infantry that had come down earlier from Binh Dinh Province some 200 kilometers to the north. These two battalions had taken up positions just west of Khan Duong city while the Airborne units dug in on the high ground in the pass behind the infantrymen.

After defeating the failed ARVN counterattack at Phuoc An, General Dung's forces moved rapidly down Route 21 toward the defenders of Khan Duong and the Deo Cao Pass. On March 22, the North Vietnamese Army 10th Division, with supporting tanks, overwhelmed the two infantry divisions on the western approaches to the city, forcing them to withdraw from their positions.

Since the possibility existed that the Communists could avoid the Airborne-protected Deo Cao Pass by using a network of logging roads and local Route 420 to get to Nha Trang, the 40th Infantry was directed to take up new defensive positions in that area. However, the North Vietnamese Army did not deviate from the most direct route to the most important city and it moved quickly to engage the outnumbered Airborne units directly. General Thinh described the battle: "Quite a number of [North Vietnamese] T-54 tanks were hit and burned, artillery duels terminated in silence by North Vietnamese artillery but also by the loss of South Vietnamese artillery. The paratroopers were the only hope for the port of Nha Trang, but they were only a light brigade, whereas the enemy facing them consisted of at least a division, supported by many heavy tanks, long-rang cannon and intense antiaircraft. On our side there remained no tanks and only a few 105's and 155's."[46]

After a week of heavy fighting, the Airborne soldiers were forced back down Route 21 and then Route 1 toward Nha Trang. As the fighters moved toward the coast, students and staff of the three ARVN training centers located in the area joined them in retreat. Colonel Loi of the Joint General Staff described the consequences of the evacuation of these cites.

"Along the road from Ban Me Thuot to Nha Trang we had two or three training centers, so when the Airborne withdrew along the road, all these training centers just disbanded and ran with the Airborne. When the Airborne and these troops ran out of the camp, and Nha Trang knew about this, then Nha Trang ran too. If we had had responsible people to hold Nha Trang and to organize a defense of Nha Trang, I think that we could hold it for a while."[47]

First Lieutenant Loi, one of the few survivors of the battle for the airfield at Ban Me Thuot, managed to hide from the Communists, but he was still trapped inside the city. He finally decided to make a break for it and he described his experience this way in the oral history *Tears Before the Rain.*

"In early April, I was able to escape from Ban Me Thuot and I fled to Nha Trang. By that time Nha Trang had already fallen to the Communists. It was the home of my maternal relatives but by the time that I got there my sister and her husband had already fled to Saigon.

"Let me tell you about the trek from Ban Me Thuot to Nha Trang. It was unbelievable. On the route the many busses that carried people, like big American Greyhound busses but not as nice, got shot at by the Communists on the way. They didn't care that they were shooting at civilians. To have survived that trip required a tremendous amount of luck.

"My bus was stopped by the local guerrillas, and they said, 'There must be military men on this bus, and if you don't get off, we will shoot everybody on the bus.' The term that they used for us was 'Nguy Quam.' They threatened to shoot everybody on the bus and so others and I got off the bus. And, lucky for us, at the moment we got off the bus, there were two A-37 bombers that came by and dropped bombs in the area. The local guerrillas ran away and the bus drove away. But, bless his heart, the bus driver was so kind that he stopped a short distance away and picked us up again.

"One of the most unforgettable scenes we witnessed was something that really hurt us in our guts. There were two companies of South Vietnamese Airborne men who got captured by the Communists and were ordered to march without any shoes or uniforms, and they looked so pathetic. Those of us on the bus looked out at this scene and we just wanted to cry because it hurt us so much, and we were so angry. Another thing that really hurt us was to see so many corpses of the Airborne troops along the road. Too many corpses. There were many corpses of the Communists, too, but they were removed, so what were left were just the bodies of the Airborne men, especially in the area of Phung Hoang. The Phung Hoang route leads from Ban Me Thuot to Nha Trang."[48]

Thus, the Communists' two-year plan to "liberate" South Vietnam had been replaced by an accelerated assault, assisted by Thieu's errors and American inaction. Members of the U.S. Congress were not about to send more money to Thieu. In the final two months of the war, visiting Congressmen arrived in South Vietnam — not to voice outrage at Communist violations of the 1973 peace agreement, but to criticize Thieu's treatment of dissenters. The former staff director of the House Foreign Affairs Committee Jack Brady remembers New York representative Bella Abzug's insistence on meeting every imprisoned foe of Thieu's government. California's Paul McClosky spent his time on the February 1975 visit posing for photographers, "flashing his pearlies," as James Piner, General Homer Smith's executive officer, put it. While South Vietnam collapsed, Congress refused to provide more money for its defense. By March 1975, South Vietnam had become, as Defense Department consultant Richard Armitage explains, "a pregnant lady" — abandoned by her lover to face her fate.[49]

Chapter 15

Nothing Happened

*"Our whole army had been given singular, unprecedented strength because
the strategically decisive battle bore his name: Ho Chi Minh, for every one
of our cadres and fighters, was faith, strength, and life."*
North Vietnamese General Van Tien Dung, 1977.

It was almost as if the ghost of Ho Chi Minh haunted President Thieu.
The tenacious Ho, who had fought colonialism since the 1930s, had died
during Nixon's first year in office, but his body, preserved in a Hanoi mau-
soleum, served as a shrine for the Communists. His death in 1969 had no
discernible effect on the North Vietnamese. As we have observed, they
fought on, shouting Ho's name, as their military sliced South Vietnam
into pieces.

On the other hand, Thieu became increasingly unpopular in the
period after the peace agreements were signed. A Roman Catholic in a
Buddhist nation, Thieu relied on people like himself for advice. In a bit-
ing characterization, John Guffey called them "French lackeys," the left-
overs of the French colonial system. Without a large American presence
in South Vietnam, Thieu survived on a dwindling pool of sycophantic
advisers.[1] Even these counselors had objected to Thieu's decision to abandon the Central Highlands. The retreat had cost the lives of more that
100,000 civilians and 15,000 soldiers trapped in the maelstrom. That had
not been the only tragedy to befall the defenders of South Vietnam in the
fateful month of March 1975. While General Dung was wreaking havoc in
Military Region II, the North Vietnamese General Command directed
Brigadier General Le Tu Dong to attack in Military Region I (MR I) just
south of the DMZ.

As of March 1, the North Vietnamese Army had had the equivalent of seven divisions positioned strategically throughout Military Region I. In addition, there were several divisions held in reserve just across the demilitarized zone that formed the de facto border between the two Vietnams. The defending forces consisted of five divisions, which included both ARVN and Marine units, plus some 220 Regional Force companies. However, the defenders were faced with the problem of protecting not just such major population centers as Hue, Da Nang, and Chu Lai, but also the logistical lifeline that connected them (i.e., Route 1).

Just as the Communists had developed an extensive network of highways and supply depots in the highlands, so had they done in MR I. Therefore, the northerners were in a position to pick and choose points of attack much in the way that they had been able to do in MR II.[2]

Coordinating their efforts in the northern provinces with those in the highlands, the Communists initiated attacks throughout MR I on March 8. While the military defenders of the region were resisting these aggressions, much of the population of Quang Tri Province immediately south of the DMZ left their homes and headed for hoped-for safety in Hue. Over the next several days, the fighting continued with some successes reported on both sides. General Dung describes those of the Communists thus: "Our armed forces circled enemy bases over a broad area, wiped out and forced evacuation of a number of outposts, and at the same time stepped up damaging attacks on the enemy's rear bases and storage areas, and cut communications routes." But the southerners responded with a vigorous defense by Marines, 1st Division, and local units that were able to beat back these attacks, which reportedly cost the VC and NVA over 1,000 killed. The DAO intelligence officer, Colonel William LeGro, noted that "by 8 March, NVA and local VC were in control of seven hamlets [in the northernmost area of fighting]," but that an ARVN task force had "succeeded in driving the enemy from nearly all populated areas by afternoon on 9 March."[3] In other words, at the outset, neither army could be said to have defeated the other. However, the existence of 100,000 refugees leaving their homes and heading for safety in Hue was a precursor to the events yet to come.

As the North Vietnamese army was striking straight into the heart of Ban Me Thuot on March 10, the 1st ARVN Division under the command of Brigadier Nguyen Van Diem was initiating counterattacks in the coastal lowlands about 20 kilometers south of Hue and just west of Dam Cau Hai Bay. These efforts were designed to negate the successes of the NVA in that area over the previous two days.

One battalion of Communist soldiers had been able to seize 12 fishing boats and ferry itself across Dam Cam Hai Bay. This unit was then able to push north up the barrier island on the other side of the bay in an attempt to reach Hue from the east. However, they were met by a reinforced Airborne battalion and dispersed. In the end, all but 38 of the invaders were either killed or remained unaccounted for when the remnants of the NVA battalion were captured. It is noteworthy that prisoners said that they had received no support from the local population.[4]

While the defenders of Military Region I were struggling to hold their own, the Joint General Staff, on March 10, ordered the commander of these forces to return the Airborne Division under his control to Saigon. This decision seems to have been made without considering the consequences on the overall defense of the South; rather, it appears to have been made on the perceived specific need to strengthen the defenses of the capital city, Saigon. Buu Vien, close advisor to Prime Minister Tran Thien Khiem, described the circumstances leading to this decision. "Along with the attack of Phuoc Long, fighting became more and more intense around Tay Ninh province [northwest of Saigon]. Unlike Phuoc Long, Tay Ninh was considered as a strategically important province that had to be defended at all costs. Its loss would directly threaten the security of the Capital Military District.

"Even though the enemy had already succeeded in occupying several key positions around the provincial capital of Tay Ninh City, especially the Black Virgin Mountain which overlooked the city and where ARVN had its radar installation, he still wasn't able to get through to the city, thanks to the valiant resistance of the defending units, particularly those of the 25th ARVN Division under the command of General Ly Tong Ba. Ba was one of the most able ARVN generals. It was he who had successfully defended Kontum with the 23rd ARVN Division under his command, and had driven off the communists from the city in the 1972 communist offensive.

"But the pressure exerted by the enemy with heavy artillery shelling into the city created a population exodus to Binh Duong [province] and Saigon and shook the morale of the Cao Dai [religious sect] dignitaries who were quick to declare the Cao Dai Temple neutral to military activities.

"As enemy pressure persisted, President Thieu deemed it necessary to strengthen the defense of the capital area and decided to pull the Airborne back to Saigon."[5]

Whatever the motivation, or justification, for ordering the withdrawal of the airborne from MR I, the effect was to greatly reduce the chances of defending the region with the South Vietnamese armed forces that remained.

Besides being the occasion for President Thieu's announcement that he intended to implement his "light at the top, heavy at the bottom" strategy, the meeting of the country's leadership that was held in Saigon on March 11, resulted in decisions critical to the defense of MR I. According to General Cao Van Thien, the last chairman of the Joint General Staff, President Thieu described his views of the situation with an "impassioned monologue on geopolitics."

"In the Central Highlands, he said, indicating the area [on a map] by a sweeping motion of his hand, the Ban Me Thuot area was more important than Kontum and Pleiku taken together, because of its economic and demographic preponderance. So were the coastal provinces of MR II because they bordered on the potentially [oil] rich continental shelf. As to MR I, it was largely a matter of 'hold what you can.' Here he sketched his idea by drawing a series of phase lines cutting across MR I at different locations of the coastline from the north downward. If we were strong enough, he said, we would hold the territory up to Hue or Da Nang. If not, then we could deploy farther south to Chu Lai [in the southern end of MR I] or even Tuy Hoa [halfway down MR II]. This way, he emphasized, we could redeploy our own capabilities, hold a more important part of our national territory with a better chance of surviving and prospering as a nation."

General Cao Van Thien went on to say, "And so, with a few peremptory statements, a momentous decision had been made. Its full implication was still not clear, but it certainly carried wide-ranging problems, militarily speaking. As the senior military advisor, I felt obliged to voice my opinion. I said something to the effect that this redeployment was indeed necessary, and I had embraced such an idea for a long time. But so far I had kept it to myself considering it an improper proposal. First of all, it conflicted with prevailing national policy, and, second, if I had made such a suggestion, it could well have been interpreted as an indication of defeatism. What I refrained from adding though was that I believed it was too late for any successful redeployment of that magnitude. Besides, it looked to me like a decision that precluded any unfavorable comment. After all, as commander-in-chief, it was the president's prerogative and responsibility to dictate the conduct of the war. He must have known exactly what he was doing."[6] This is just one of several instances where the leadership of South Vietnam seems to have made decisions that might be called suboptimal; that is, they were based upon short-term considerations without regard to their overall effect upon the long-term defense of the country. In this particular case, although various strategies that included a truncation of South Vietnamese territory had been advocated in the past, President Thieu had always rejected them.

As President Thieu discussed his new strategy for defending his country, the fighting throughout Military Region I continued with mixed results. On the one hand, in Quang Tin Province, some 65 kilometers south of Da Nang, North Vietnamese Army forces overran the defenders of the districts of Tien Phuoc and Han Duc. As a result, large numbers of refugees left their homes and headed for the coastal city of Tam Key. That same day, March 11, a rocket attack was launched against Da Nang Air Base, and artillery-supported infantry attacks were made from Dai Loc to Que Son about 45 kilometers south of Da Nang. Here, however, nearly all NVA assaults were repelled with heavy losses. On the 12th of March, the commander of the ARVN forces located in Tam Key established a defensive perimeter designed to hold off his attackers, but by this time, the enemy had been able to move within artillery range of the city.

In the meantime, General Ngo Quang Truong, commander of MR I, was faced with having to adjust to the loss of the Airborne Division. He had protested the order to send these excellent troops down for the defense of Saigon, but his protest had been denied and he was told to begin their transfer on March 17. The general therefore began the task of redeploying his assets so as to compensate for this significant force reduction. His first step was to relieve the Marine Division in the northernmost portion of MR I with a Ranger group so that the Marines could participate in the defense of Da Nang. One brigade of Marines was to be positioned just south of the Hai Van Pass about halfway between Hue and Da Nang and the rest were to reinforce Da Nang itself.

On March 13, General Truong was called to Saigon for a meeting with President Thieu, Prime Minister Khiem, General Vien, Lieutenant General Dang Van Quang, presidential assistant for security affairs, and Lieutenant General Nguyen Van Toan, commander of Military Region III.

The meeting began with a briefing by General Truong on the military situation in MR I. This was followed by a relatively optimistic review by General Toan of the situation in his area of responsibility. It was then President Thieu's turn to speak. This is how General Vien described his remarks: "First he made an analysis of the general situation and pointed out the difficulties we were facing in military aid. He admitted that he did not entertain any hope of intervention by the U.S. Air Force in case South Vietnam was subjected to an all-out offensive by North Vietnam. He sympathized with the difficulties and handicaps of the corps commanders. Up to now, he admitted, he had given many instructions that he knew could not possibly be carried out.

"The president said there was little he could do under the circumstance except to change strategy, to re-deploy our forces to hold those vital areas where our national resources were concentrated. Even if we were to lose the jungle and mountainous areas to hold the remaining resource-rich areas [to include the continental shelf], such losses would be definitely much better than a coalition government with the communists. The resource-rich areas defined in the president's new strategic plan included the Da Nang region of MR I. As part of the redeployment plan, conceived in private by the commander-in-chief himself, the Airborne Division was slated to leave MR I. Although this strategy was not mentioned at this meeting, the Airborne Division was to be followed by the Marine Division, if possible, without endangering the I Corps defense posture. These moves would allow the reconstitution of a general reserve that was vital to the success of the president's plan. President Thieu also instructed General Toan to temporarily withdraw his forces from An Loc to employ them wherever they were more needed in MR III."[7]

In addition to learning of the President's new ideas concerning a response to the North Vietnamese Army invasion in MR I, General Truong was advised of the decision to evacuate the highlands. He was also granted a short reprieve of the redeployment of the Airborne Division. The first brigade was now scheduled to leave on March 18 with the rest delayed until March 31.[8]

While the generals were discussing strategy in Saigon, the North Vietnamese Army was making advances throughout Military Region I. Two South Vietnamese Regional Force positions were overrun in the northern portion of MR I; the Marines found themselves under heavy pressure west of Da Nang, and enemy tanks were bearing down on Tam Key further south.

The movement of the Marines away from their positions just south of the DMZ toward Da Nang had a significant impact upon the subsequent events in the region. According to the I Corps chief of staff, Colonel Dang, the withdrawal of the Marines "had three bad effects. It reduced [the defender's] fighting strength; it reduced the morale of [the] troops; and it hurt the morale of the population. It upset the balance of forces." Once the word of the redeployment of the Airborne and Marine divisions became common knowledge, the civilian populations lost confidence in the ability of the South Vietnamese Armed Forces to protect them. Buu Vien, an advisor to the Prime Minister, explained this reaction this way: "In the minds of the people of Quang Tri and Hue the presence of these two divisions was so essential to the security of the area that the news of the withdrawal of the Airborne Division completely confounded them." Colonel Dang, I Corps chief of staff, explained further: "When we took the Marines out of Quang Tri, it upset the population there so when we withdrew the

Marines to replace the Airborne, we had the same effect in Quang Tri as we had had withdrawing the Airborne from Quang Nam. The people and the soldiers got upset. As soon as we started to withdraw the Marines from Quang Tri the collapse started already. They went down by truck over Highway 1."[10] A debacle not unlike the one that occurred on Route 7B was born.

After returning to his headquarters, General Truong met on March 14 with General Thi, I Corps troop commander, and General Lam, the Marine Division commander. He explained to them the new strategy for defending only portions of MR I and directed them to begin redeploying their forces accordingly. It should be recalled that it was on this same day that President Thieu was directing General Phu to withdraw his forces from Pleiku and Kontum. In other words, the south was now poised to concede large areas of its territory to General Dung's invaders in an effort to preserve the most important regions of the country from total defeat. The problem with this approach was that it was not simply a question of ceding real estate. This action precipitated the flight of hundreds of thousands of frightened civilians at the same time that the military was trying to establish new lines of defense without benefit of a coordinated plan for these re-deployments.

Over the next three days, the 15th, the 16th, and the 17th of March 1975, the South Vietnamese forces in MR I were pulling back from their forward positions toward the coastal cities of Hue, Da Nang, and Chu Lai. They were not permitted to go in peace as the Communist army continued its offensive. At each sign of retreat by the South Vietnamese military, the civilians in the areas being left unprotected gathered what they could of their possessions and headed for what they hoped would be a safe haven on the coast.

On March 18, the day that General Dung's 320th Division caught up with the mass of humanity attempting to escape down Route 7B, Prime Minister Khiem flew to Da Nang. His mission was to assess the impact of the North Vietnamese successes to date in MR I and advise the President on what part of the region could be held, given the defenders' current force levels. The Prime Minister also used the occasion to "make it clear to General Truong that no additional troops would be sent to his corps; that [a previously] promised new Marine brigade would remain in defense of Saigon."

While in Da Nang, the Prime Minister was also briefed by five province chiefs and the mayor of Da Nang. They did not mince words. Colonel William LeGro, of the DAO, Saigon, described the report this way: "The mayor told him that civilian morale was very low, that many families had already gone to Saigon, and that the lack of support by the United States at this critical time was deeply felt by the people. The Quang Nam Province chief, Colonel Pham Van Chung, told him that morale among his troops was still good, but the people were very worried about the departure of the Airborne Division. The reports from Quang Ngai and Quang Tin, by Colonels Dao Mong Xuan and Le Van Ngoc, were grim; the territorials had all but given up, and were deserting in large numbers. Units were below half strength. The Quang Tri province chief, Colonel Do Ky, gave a similar report; almost all civilians had left the province, morale was low and the territorials could not be expected to offer serious resistance to an attack now that the stiffening presence of the Marines had been removed. Colonel Nguyen Huu Due of Thua Thien, unduly optimistic, said that although people were beginning to leave Hue in large numbers his territorials were in good spirits and would fight."[11]

The North Vietnamese Political Bureau and Central Military Committee reacted to the successes of their forces in the Highlands by directing their armies in the northern portion of Military Region I "to recognize their opportunity clearly and change the thrust of their attacks." While the Prime Minister was being briefed in Da Nang on March 18, the NVA 2nd Army Corps sent its "forces in a daring thrust past the outer defense lines to cut off Route 1 [south of Hue] and close in on [the Imperial City]."[12]

The day after General Truong hosted the Prime Minister in Da Nang, the commander of I Corps was called to a meeting in Saigon. This is how General Vien described the meeting at the Presidential Palace: "The session began at 1100 with Vice President Tran Van Huong also present. As expected, General Truong briefed the President on his MR 1 withdrawal plan. This was well worked out, presenting a choice between two alternate courses.

"Course 1 assumed the use of National Route 1. It prescribed two opposite but simultaneous withdrawals via National Route 1 from Hue to Da Nang and from Chu Lai to Da Nang.

"Course 2 assumed enemy interdiction of National Route 1 and hence the necessity of withdrawing all troops into three enclaves: Hue, Da Nang and Chu Lai. However, Hue and Chu Lai were only to serve as layover stations for troops who would be sealifted to Da Nang during the final stage. So Da Nang, the major enclave to be held as part of the redeployment plan, would become a stronghold defended by four divisions and four Ranger groups.

"Less than a week separated the two meetings at the palace. By the time of the second meeting, it was obvious that only the second course stood any chance of success. Any phased withdrawal along National Route 1 had become almost impossible. The pressure that the enemy had exerted on it had increased tremendously between Hue and Da Nang and Chu Lai. Two Ranger groups, the last units held in reserve by I Corps, had been thrown in to relieve the pressure, so far to no avail. The balance had been irretrievably lost. Besides, even without enemy pressure, I Corps could hardly conduct any major troop movement on an artery jammed beyond control during the last days by refugees moving toward Danang.

"This was in summary what General Truong told the President. 'We have only one choice,' he said, 'we had better act before it is too late.' The only choice was to withdraw our troops toward Hue and Chu Lai as well as Da Nang and take advantage of existing fortifications in these cities, in particular, those scattered in the hilly terrain around Hue, in order to destroy enemy troops to the maximum of our ability. General Truong had also heard unconfirmed reports that the Marine Division was to be re-deployed to MR III. If this should occur, it would affect General Truong's plan, and he accordingly asked for President Thieu's decision.

"President Thieu's position was excruciating. It was he who had conceived and ordered the whole thing and already the re-deployment from the Central Highlands had given signs of turning sour. Worst of all was the psychological impact on the civilian population that now threatened to throw his plan into utter disarray.

"Understandably enough, when it came to giving specific instructions to his field commander, President Thieu sidestepped the withdrawal plan altogether. Instead, he told General Truong to make an effort to hold onto whatever territory he could with whatever forces he now had, including the Marine Division. Then turning aside and away from the problem, he asked General Quang to prepare a speech. He was going to address the people on TV, he said, to try to calm their emotions and let them know that the government was going to defend Hue at all costs. He also seemed to ignore the refugee problem; neither he nor Prime Minister Khiem said anything about General Truong's headache. But in contrast with the previous meeting, there was a feeling of encouragement this time, if only because the momentous withdrawal decision had been set aside for the time being."[13] But now, in late March 1975, the ghost of Ho Chi Minh marched toward the South Vietnamese coast.

In his own way, Thieu had attempted to persuade Washington to help him. He had sent emissaries time and time again to plead his case. He recalls, "every week of every month I sent delegates to Washington — military men, political men, Vietnamese Senators — to explain. I wrote to the American President and I explained the dangers to the ambassador in Saigon — and nothing happened." U.S. Army colonel William LeGro, the

Chief of the Intelligence Branch of the Defense Attaché Office, had escorted two of these delegates on a tour of the Pentagon, State Department, and the Central Intelligence Agency. The Deputy Director of the CIA, Vernon Walters, met with the representatives. Walters spoke French fluently with them and lectured the supplicants about the danger posed by the Soviet Union.[14] By March 1975, the United States was engaged in "other wars"— the one in Southeast Asia seemed forgotten.

One of Thieu's few American allies was Ambassador Graham Martin, called by congressional staffer Jack Brady, the "general." Martin's diplomatic credentials were impressive. He had served as a colonel in World War II. His diplomatic postings had included ambassadorships in Thailand and Italy. At the end of his service in Rome, Secretary of State Kissinger had persuaded Martin to delay his planned retirement to a villa in northern Italy and accept the Saigon assignment. Martin had been scarred by the war; his adopted son had been killed in Vietnam in 1965. Thus, Martin was determined in early 1975 to do everything that he could to save South Vietnam from a Communist dictatorship. In his efforts to do so, he wrapped his arms protectively around the Thieu regime. He routinely lobbied congressmen — both back in the United States and during in-county visits— for more resources with which to fight the fight for the country's survival. On the February tour of the area by Representatives Abzug, McClosky, and other skeptical members of Congress, the ambassador accompanied the delegation on their flight back to Washington. Still, Martin could not obtain more aid. The commitments made to Thieu were ancient history as far as those on Capitol Hill were concerned. Brady gives us a glimpse of a frustrated ambassador: "Martin didn't suffer fools gladly. And he thought that there were a lot of fools in Congress. I liked him."[15]

On March 20, 1975, Colonel Edwin F. Pelosky, chief of the Army Division of the Defense Attaché Office and the DAO's principal logistician, flew to Danang on a twofold mission: first, to find out why the radio relay station at Tam My, a port just to the east of Hue, had been evacuated by the contractor that had been hired to run it; and, second, to evaluate the logistical situation in the northern portion of MR I. The next morning he took off in a South Vietnamese helicopter to survey the area from the air. This is how he described what he saw: "No sooner had we started to climb toward the Hai Van Pass than I noticed that one-third of the way down the slope of the pass, vehicles were blocked bumper to bumper. We made several passes over the area and saw that a culvert had been blown and that repairs were being made. A half-mile away, a firefight was in progress and we assumed that it was ARVN fighting with sappers or North Vietnamese elements trying to cut the pass. Since the top of Hay Van Pass was fogged in, we dropped down and followed the coastline north. The further we went, the lower we flew, until we were fifty feet over the water. Then, to my amazement, I noticed a large number of small watercraft in the water. It reminded me, as we progressed up the coast, of the motion picture *Dunkirk* where every available watercraft was used to evacuate the beachhead. At first, the small boats were in small groups and many were being pulled — even rafts! Also, on the beaches, we could see where the people had camped overnight. Further north, there were more boats, and they were all flying the South Vietnamese flag.

"One observation that boggles my mind yet to this day is what some believe to be the most important possessions to take with them when they are abandoning their homes. I saw ducks, dogs, pigs, bed frames, old clocks, along with the normal pots and pans and bundles of firewood."

Pelosky's helicopter then landed at the basic training camp at Phu Bai just south of Hue. From there the small party went by jeep to a supply base about two miles to the south and astride Route 1. Pelosky's story picks up there: "At the Direct Support Group, I met the commander and his staff and he briefed me on how he saw the situation, which, I admit, left a lot to be desired.

"Several rounds [of artillery fire] hit in the depot complex, and a number of soldiers and dependents were wounded. The soldiers and officers were completely demoralized and fear was written all over their faces. All the dependents that I talked to said that if they could get to Danang, all would be saved. I hated to disillusion them, but it was obvious that Danang could not hold out under a prolonged attack. We finally received word that the 325th North Vietnamese Army Division had cut Route 1 in the vicinity of Phu Loc [about halfway between Hue and Danang] and everything had stopped in the middle of the road. It appeared that the only thing that could move was helicopters. Since I had known the Direct Support Group Commander and his staff for four years, all of my suggestions were taken as orders and immediately carried out. [In the end, however], the commander and his staff were all killed on the 25th of April."[16]

The refugees fleeing the Communists descended upon Danang from all sides. The population in the city became swollen to as many as two million desperate souls, twice the normal size. On March 28, NVA artillery shells began to fall on the overcrowded city. On the 29th, General Truong gave the order to evacuate the city by sea. Unable to beach because of a low tide, the South Vietnamese Navy ships sent to evacuate the soldiers in Danang anchored offshore. General Truong and his men had to wade and swim to reach them. Many were drowned or killed by Communist artillery fire. However, 6,000 Marines and 4,000 ARVN soldiers were saved and moved south to assist in the defense of Saigon.[17]

Over the weekend of March 29 and March 30, a tugboat that belonged to the Alaska Barge and Transport Company and under contract to the Military Sealift Command Office in Saigon, pulled a string of barges through the harbor acting as a pick-up point for people who had headed out toward the sea on anything that could float. In the end, 15,000 thirsty, hungry Vietnamese soldiers and civilians were taken aboard the barges. On Monday the 31st, the American cargo ship SS *Pioneer Contender*, also on charter to the Military Sealift Command, began taking these refugees on board. After several hours of tedious loading, the last of the struggling crowd was trying to climb the gangplank to the relative safety of the big ship. All of a sudden, a woman pushed her way down the ladder against the tide. When she reached the barge, she found what she was looking for. There were the bodies of three infants at the foot of the gangplank ... trampled to death. The woman reached down and picked up one of the dead babies. Her wailing filled the night air.[18]

While thousands were trying to escape the doomed city by sea, a huge mob of people had gathered at the Danang airport in hopes of boarding a flight to Saigon. Chaos reigned. Soldiers fought with civilians in their effort to board any aircraft that was trying to take off. These scenes of panic were broadcast by television worldwide. One of Ed Daley's World Airways Airlines Boeing 727 aircraft was the last flight to take off. When the loading ramp had been lowered for boarding, it was immediately swamped. Daley was at the stairway trying to pull women and children up, but soldiers from the Hac Bao— Black Panther — unit of the 1st ARVN Division literally shot their way onto the airplane. In the end it was loaded with 285 passengers— mostly armed soldiers. One photograph that was widely published showed Ed Daley physically forcing members of the mob off of the ramp. Even as the aircraft taxied away to start its take-off roll, desperate men were trying to hang on to the undercarriage. When the plane finally landed at Tan Son Nhut, bodies had to be pulled from the wheel wells where they had been crushed when the pilot tried to retract the landing gear.

Danang had been the site, a decade earlier, where American Marine units had landed and were welcomed by schoolgirls bearing flowers. On March 30, 1975, the city, with its strategic port, fell to the Communists. The South Vietnamese ambassador to Washington poetically observed, "On us the night is descending beyond which there is no dawn."[19]

Thieu had prayed that American troops would wade ashore at Danang as they had ten years earlier. Secretary of Defense James Schlesinger briefed President Ford on the deteriorating situation. The secretary gave Ford one option to prevent the fall of Danang: the use of tactical nuclear weapons. Ford rejected that option. Schlesinger remembered receiving word of the seizure of Danang: "I don't blame the Vietnamese for holding out little shreds of hope. I sympathized with them. I grieved for them."

The Speaker of the South Vietnamese House of Representatives and the President of the nation's Senate had written Ford a few days earlier. They eloquently stated the nature of the relationship that had existed between the United States and the Republic of South Vietnam: "Together the U.S. and South Vietnam signed the Agreement in Ending the War and Restoring Peace in Vietnam; together we gave our word and guarantee that we would respect it and fulfill our commitments as they are defined by the Paris Agreement." But the Communists, since 1973, had violated the treaty, according to the two South Vietnamese legislators, 80,000 times. They asked Ford for emergency aid "to deter North Vietnam once and for all from carrying out its ambition." Ford responded by sending Army chief of staff General Frederick Weyand to South Vietnam to survey the situation. Thieu and his legislative friends would probably say, "Nothing happened."

Weyand was in country from March 28 to April 4, 1975. Thus, he arrived after the collapse of the Central Highlands and the fall of Hue and Chu Lai on March 25. He was in South Vietnam as Danang surrendered on March 30 and the enemy seized Nha Trang and Cam Ranh on April 3. Weyand painted a pessimistic picture of a country "on the brink of a total military defeat." Weyand, who had preceded General Murray as America's chief military presence in South Vietnam, reminded Ford, "We reached out our hand to the South Vietnamese people, and they took it." Weyand estimated that 20,000,000 of these people were in imminent peril. The $700 million provided by Congress "guarantees GVN defeat." The Thieu government planned to fight on, but they needed immediate help. He added that plans should be under way to evacuate "U.S. citizens and tens of thousands of South Vietnamese and Third Country Nationals to whom we have incurred an obligation and owe protection." As he saw it, it was a question of honor and a question of credibility. Weyand concluded, "The United States credibility as an ally is at stake in Vietnam. To sustain that credibility, we must make a maximum effort to support the Vietnamese now."[20]

A month earlier, General Alexander Haig had argued the same position with Ford. Haig had helped ease the transition from Nixon to Ford in August 1974. As Nixon's Chief of Staff, he had laid the groundwork for the disgraced President's resignation. By 1975, Haig was serving in Brussels as NATO commander. Seeing the slow strangulation of our ally, Haig had flown back to Washington to meet with Ford. He urged the commander in chief to aggressively back Thieu and lash out at congressional critics who wished to abandon South Vietnam. He met with Ford for over an hour, making the same argument verbally that Weyand made in writing. Ford replied, "I just don't think that the American people have the stomach for a resumption of this." Haig rose to his feet and replied, "I think that you'll be a one term president."[21]

By early April 1975, Ford and Congress could not be bullied or persuaded to provide more assistance for Thieu. Secretary of State Kissinger tried one last time to seek an emergency allocation, but he was rebuffed.[22] Neither money nor B-52s would be forthcoming. All that remained was for the final evacuation of Americans and South Vietnamese allies from the dying country. Operation Frequent Wind would become the final chapter in the story of America's longest war.

Chapter 16
Will ARVN Fight?

"I don't care how many divisions the other side sends against me. I will knock them down."
        18th ARVN Division Commander, General Le Minh Dao, 1975.

Le Duan, Ho Chi Minh's successor as Secretary General of the Lao Dong (Worker's Party), had spent more than two decades directing Viet Cong forces in the South. His instructions to the guerrillas were simple: "When the enemy masses, we disperse. When the enemy passes, we harass. When the enemy disperses, we mass." He had applied this maxim thousands of times. By March 1975, he had seen this strategy take root in Cambodia, where the Khmer Rouge were on the outskirts of the capital city of Phnom Penh; and in Laos where Communist Pathet Lao guerrillas had launched an offensive against the capital Vientiane. Years of dispersing and regrouping were about to yield fruit for Communists throughout Southeast Asia. Thus, on March 31, Le Duan, who had been imprisoned by the French and fought the Americans since the 1954 Geneva Accords, smelled victory—a "once in a thousand years opportunity to liberate Saigon before the rainy season."[1]

Many Americans employed in South Vietnam's defense had sensed that it would come to this. Army captain Stuart Herrington, an intelligence officer who routinely traveled to Hanoi as part of the delegation seeking resolution of missing-in-action issues, had shipped most of his belongings back to the United States in December 1974. General Haig believes that the eventual collapse of Saigon was realized at the time of the Paris Peace Accords. Civilians serving throughout the country also accepted the need to be ready at a moment's notice to evacuate South Vietnam. Rosalie Redmond,

121

an Air Force secretary, kept her bags packed for months, as did other support personnel. They were told to be prepared "just in case." The U.S. Congress allocated $300 million in early April for humanitarian aid and for the evacuation of Americans and vulnerable South Vietnamese.[2]

Ambassador Graham Martin had resisted ordering a large-scale evacuation. However, Air Force general Richard Baughn began a small-scale evacuation of South Vietnamese personnel on his own without notifying the ambassador. When Martin found out about it in mid April, he stopped it and had Baughn relieved of his duties and sent home. Another unauthorized evacuation effort was an "underground railroad" established by several officers within the Defense Attaché Office. This was a network of safe houses and caravans of official vehicles used to move South Vietnamese intelligence and other sensitive personnel, along with their families, to Tan Son Nhut Airbase for evacuation on special mission flights code-named "Black Flights." These were secretly authorized by the State Department on April 17, 1975. With a few exceptions, they left from the CIA-managed Air America terminal under semicovert and covert conditions. About 1,000 very sensitive evacuees were spirited out of the country on these aircraft. The DAO personnel who organized and managed the "railroad" risked their careers to do so, just as General Baughn had risked his. The DAO personnel who ran the "underground railroad" are persuaded that few, if any, of these South Vietnamese allies could have made it to freedom by other means.[3]

Military Sealift Command employees slipped Vietnamese friends out of harms' way. Contract workers loaded Vietnamese on trucks, hidden among boxes, and smuggled them out on cargo planes returning to the Philippines after delivering supplies to Saigon. Marriages of convenience became common and long-lost dependents surfaced. State Department counselors also identified people who should be targeted for rescue. General Smith was able to persuade the ambassador to allow him to begin sending some of his staff to safety by explaining to Martin that the money budgeted for the salaries of those who left could be transferred to the accounts that were used for logistic support of the RVNAF. This authorization had the effect of creating a loophole through which the DAO was able to move large numbers of refugees out of Vietnam without violating the letter of Ambassador Martin's law.[4]

The ambassador would not — could not — bring himself to the realization that South Vietnam would soon fall. CIA station chief Thomas Polgar had assured Martin that the Communists would surely accept a coalition government in Saigon. Thus, there would be no need to evacuate all Americans at that point. Richard Armitage, who had been sent to

Vietnam along with Eric Von Marbod on April 24, 1975, to attempt to save as many Defense Department assets as possible, believes that Polgar was unduly influence by the Polish-Hungarian members of the International Commission of Control and Supervision when they hinted at this possibility. Martin was also influenced by a message from Soviet Union leader Leonid Brezhnev that had been forwarded to him by Kissinger. CIA analyst Frank Snepp described it as "a masterpiece of ambiguity." Polgar and Martin optimistically interpreted it to mean that the hints coming from the ICCS were more than just hints but truths. There would be no last-minute cease-fire; there would be no coalition government — despite what Polgar's Hungarian sources told him or what the real meaning of Brezhnev's message was.[5]

In spite of the loophole that had been opened for him by Martin, Smith walked a thin line. The ambassador had made it very clear: no evacuation could take place that would create panic in Saigon. Thieu already felt abandoned by the United States. Wholesale departures under American auspices could easily create a panic similar to the one that had occurred in Danang. Americans might be held hostage by the Thieu regime. But in spite of all this Rosemary Taylor, a representative of Friends for All Children, one of the largest organizations trying to bring Vietnamese orphans to the U.S. for adoption, was able to obtain permission from both the Vietnamese government and the American embassy to use the American military transports that were delivering materiel to the RVNAF to take these children out of the country rather than simply return home empty. General Smith and his DAO staff became the conduits for connecting the orphanages to the Air Force cargo aircraft departing from Tan Son Nhut Airbase. The effort was labeled Operation Babylift. Since these orphans, many the offspring of American fathers and Vietnamese mothers, were either very young or infants, they would have to have escorts to accompany then on the flight. This gave Smith another vehicle for reducing, in an orderly fashion, the number of Americans still in Vietnam. So Operation Babylift now served a twofold function: to save orphaned children, and lower the number of Defense Attaché Office employees remaining in country. The escorts, of course, would not be returning to Saigon.

The tragedy that befell Operation Babylift on April 4, 1975, is symbolic of the war in its entirety: noble intentions, aided by supposedly infallible American technology, gone terribly awry. That day a giant C-5A transport aircraft loaded with weapons for the RVNAF was reported to be inbound to Tan Son Nhut. In a flurry of activity, 243 children were quickly loaded into busses and taken to the airfield. Thirty-seven secretaries and analysts, mostly female, from the DAO were identified to serve as escorts.

After the cargo of seventeen 105 mm howitzers was unloaded, the children and their escorts were taken on board and made as comfortable as possible, some in the troop compartment on the flight deck and the rest down on the cargo deck.

The aircraft then took off without incident. While still climbing at an altitude of 23,000 feet and ten miles off the coast over the South China Sea, the C-5A suffered a massive structural failure in the rear cargo door area. There was an explosive decompression that blew out a huge section of the cargo ramp and door and severed all control cables to the rudder and elevator. The pilot, Captain Dennis Traynor, using only ailerons and engine power for pitch control, was able to turn back for an attempt at a landing at Tan Son Nhut. Traynor was later to say that as he descended toward the runway on his final approach he thought that he had the landing assured. But, suddenly, for unknown reasons, the aircraft pitched down. The pilot was able to nose the C-5A up to an almost level attitude when it touched down in a rice paddy. It then bounced and flew about a half mile across the Saigon River. On the second touchdown, the aircraft disintegrated. Only the tail section, the troop compartment, and the flight deck remained intact. The remainder of the C-5A became a huge fireball. Thirty-six of the thirty-seven DAO employees on board died in the accident. However, the unparalleled feat of airmanship by Captain Traynor that brought the fatally damaged aircraft to the brink of survival, saved the lives of 150 of the orphans and twenty-five of the others on board. Nonetheless, the remaining Defense Attaché office personnel understandably felt that death was all around them. John Guffey remembers being ordered to collect the belongings of three of the American women who died in the crash. Others have more macabre memories of bodies being sprayed with water to see if they were alive. At a memorial service that evening in the DAO theater, the mourners cried and embraced, and they sang "Amazing Grace." A sense of urgency grew among the remaining Americans. They felt that they had to accelerate the evacuation, using the "underground railway" and any other means that could be devised to get Americans, and vulnerable South Vietnamese who had worked for the Americans, as well as their families, out of the dying country. Ultimately, though, twenty-five years after the fall of Saigon, General Smith spoke for most of his colleagues in the DAO when he declared April 4, 1975, to be "the worst day of my life."[6]

On April 9, the tremendous momentum of the invading North Vietnamese armies was brought to a halt at Xuan Loc, the capital of Long Khanh Province, about thirty-six miles east of Saigon. This was the home base of the 18th ARVN Division. Although this outfit was not especially

known for its fighting prowess, under the leadership of Brigadier General
Le Minh Dao, it proved in the end to be the best division in the Republic
of Vietnam Armed Forces. The battle began with the invaders launching
a barrage of 4,000 rounds of artillery accompanied by an infantry and
armor assault on the city's northwest perimeter. After some initial gains,
the attackers were repulsed with heavy losses. Every day the North Vietnamese renewed their attacks, bringing in reinforcements. Nevertheless the
ARVN soldiers fought back heroically, continuing to hold off the enemy.
By the 12th, the NVA losses were estimated to be over 800 killed and 11 T-
54 tanks destroyed while the defenders had suffered only moderate losses.
The next day, General Smith sent a message on the "Battle of Long Khanh"
to the chairman of the Joint Chiefs of Staff, General George S. Brown. It
said, in part, "We have a victory in the making. In the battle of Long Khanh
RVNAF has shown unmistakably its determination, its will and its courage
to fight even though the odds are heavily weighted against them. Although
the battle may have only passed through Phase 1, we can say without question that RVNAF has won round one…. The valor and aggressiveness of
GVN troops, especially the Long Khanh Regional Forces, is certainly indica-
tive that these soldiers, when adequately equipped and properly led, are,
man-for-man, vastly superior to their adversaries. The battle for Xuan Loc
appears to settle for the time being the question 'will ARVN fight?'" Con-
sistently, Smith had asserted that, when guaranteed that their families were
safe, as was the case here when they were virtually all back in Saigon, the
South Vietnamese would fight as courageously as soldiers anywhere.

The battle raged on. The South Vietnamese Air Force, using CH-47
helicopters, brought in ninety-three tons of ammunition on the 12th and
another 100 tons on the 13th. A modified C-130 transport was fitted to
carry 15,000-pound bombs that had recently been brought in to Tan Son
Nut by the U.S. Air Force. These aircraft, flying against heavy antiaircraft
fire, took a heavy toll on the NVA units around Xuan Loc. General Dung
threw more and more reinforcements into the battle until on April 20 the
defenders were finally forced to withdraw from the now demolished city.
By this time, however, the "stubbornness of" the 18th ARVN Division, as
the fighting spirit of the defenders was described by the North Vietnamese
commander, General Dung, had virtually destroyed three NVA divisions.
The "Battle of Long Khanh," though was to be the last major battle of the
Vietnam War.[7]

The opportunity of a thousand years continued to unfold for the
Communists. Phnom Penh was about to be evacuated by the Americans
as the rebels there cut off all land routes to the besieged city. Lon Nol, who
had overthrown Prince Sihanouk at the behest of the U.S. in 1970, had fled

to Indonesia. Secretary Kissinger tried to negotiate the return of Sihanouk, but the communists rejected any coalition government. On April 12, 1975, the execution of Operation Eagle Pull, as the evacuation effort in Phnom Penh was codenamed, commenced with the launching of a dozen U.S. Marine Corps CH-53 helicopters from the deck of the USS *Okinawa* just off the coast. Landing on a soccer field adjacent to the U.S. Embassy, 82 Americans, 159 Cambodians, mostly employees at the embassy, and 35 third-country nationals were quickly taken on board. Ambassador John Gunther Dean, with the American flag neatly folded by his side, was the last American to leave. Within six days, the Khmer Rouge set about terrorizing the civilian population, emptying the city of its people, and marching a million Cambodians into the countryside's killing fields.[8]

In South Vietnam, Ambassador Martin continued to refuse to order an evacuation. Various plans had been developed over the previous two years. They called for those at risk to be taken to predetermined locations from which they would be evacuated out of the country by air and sea. Estimates of the numbers involved ranged up to one million, and even two million people. Not unexpectedly, there was behind-the-scenes resistance in Congress to bringing into the U.S. anything like that many refugees from Southeast Asia. Key elements of these plans included the use of large fixed wing aircraft flying out of Tan Son Nhut and ships sailing from both Saigon and the port of Vung Tau.[9] As the final evacuation actually developed, however, it involved helicopters, remnants of the Vietnamese Navy, ships, tugs, and barges under charter to the Military Sealift Command, small craft sailing down the rivers in the Mekong Delta, and boats and airplanes commandeered by fleeing South Vietnamese military and civilians. The carefully formulated plans would be useless because the order for the evacuation came too late. The Communists would shell the airport in the final days and the ultimate means of escape had to be developed ad hoc. As we shall see, the evacuation was carried out piecemeal. While the ARVN had proven at Xuan Loc that they would indeed fight, their heroism was academic. The decision had been made in Washington that this war was over and it was time for evacuation. All that needed to be done was to convince Graham Martin.

Chapter 17

Final Betrayal

"The Vietnam debate is over. The administration will accept the Con-gress' verdict without recrimination and vindictiveness."
Henry Kissinger, 1975.

In May 1973, only four months after he had posed for a toast with the Communists in celebration of what was supposed to be an agreement to end the killing in Vietnam, Secretary of State Henry Kissinger traveled to Paris to meet with North Vietnamese Foreign Minister Le Duc Tho to dis-cuss Communist violations of the peace accords. He found Le in a combat-ive mood, unwilling to concede that the Communists were violating the agreements. Le countered by accusing the Americans and the South Viet-namese of trampling upon the cease-fire arrangement. Despite scores of examples of Communist aggression, Le dismissed the evidence and said that the Americans were attempting "to deceive public opinion, as you have done with Watergate." The two diplomats issued a weak commu-niqué reaffirming the earlier treaty. Dejected, Kissinger returned to Wash-ington where he told journalists that he was going to move on to other issues "in order to preserve my emotional stability."[1]

As described earlier, the Congress had asserted itself with funding restrictions and the War Powers Act. Nixon found himself distracted, weak-ened by Watergate. Kissinger watched change occurring all around the world: in Chile, in the Middle East, in Portugal, where a coup replaced the long-time dictatorship, and he spent his time on these matters— as well as try-ing to preserve détente with the Soviets and China. Finally, with the August 1974 resignation of Nixon, it became apparent, to President Ford and Henry Kissinger, that the future of South Vietnam was not a priority item.

Ambassador Graham Martin, however, was a true believer. He continued to believe that America had made a commitment to President Thieu in 1973 and that that commitment needed to be honored. That's why he lobbied visiting members of Congress. A question of credibility was at stake. To Ford and Kissinger, the question was political. Congress had reduced funding levels and, given the antiwar sentiment abroad in 1975, was not about to come to Thieu's aid, despite courageous stands at places like Xuan Loc. Seemingly, such heroism mattered little to a caretaker President and a Secretary of State with other matters before him. In April 1975, they were poised to conclude the Vietnam story. As Ford explained to the American Society of Newspaper Editors on April 16, we had "no legal commitment, only a moral commitment" to Thieu.[2] As if a "moral commitment" was no commitment.

Nguyen Tien Hung, a top aid to Thieu, had come to Washington to make a desperate last attempt to regain the attention of the administration. His plan, a Freedom Loan, would be a request for $1 billion a year in funds, borrowed from the United States using collateral guaranteed by Saudi King Khalid, a staunch anti–communist. Hung recalls explaining his effort this way: "In the anti–Vietnam atmosphere we should go to the Americans and tell them that we have not come to beg from them but to borrow." The loan would be directed to a truncated South Vietnam that would include the territory from just north of Saigon through the entire Mekong Delta. In the end, though, the U.S. Senate Foreign Relations Committee had already told Ford and Kissinger to get Americans out of harm's way. New York senator Jacob Javits explained the view of the Senate's leaders: "I will give you large sums for evacuation but not one nickel for military aid." Thus, Hung's Freedom Loan proposal was vetoed even before he had a chance to explain it. The only funds that were allocated were for evacuation purposes. Henry Kissinger announced on April 18, 1975, "The Vietnam debate is over. The administration will accept the Congress' verdict without recrimination and vindictiveness."[3]

Graham Martin refused to accept the Congress' decision. He had sent Kissinger a second cable, which the ambassador typed himself, on April 17. Martin argued, "The ARVN can hold the approaches to Saigon for quite a while...." He asked the administration, in light of Congress' denial of additional funds for 1975, to "calmly announce you are going all out to win the fight for the fiscal year '76 appropriation. As unrealistic as this may seem, it will have a great effect here...." He added, "The one thing that would set off violence would be a sudden order for American evacuation...." The message then focused on President Thieu. Some South Vietnamese generals were rumored to be plotting a coup, so Martin offered to meet with Thieu to urge him to resign so that a settlement could be reached with the Communists. The Ford Administration authorized Martin to proceed with such a conference with Thieu.

The April 20 meeting between Thieu and Martin was brief. They reviewed the critical military situation. Then Martin informed Thieu, "I believe that in a few days your generals will come to tell you to step down." It must have sounded to Thieu like the last conversation Ambassador Henry Cabot Lodge had with President Diem in November 1963, on the eve of the deadly coup that resulted in Diem's assassination. Diem had asked Lodge, "Do you have my number?" In April 1975 Thieu asked Martin, "If I step down, will military aid come?" Martin responded, "I cannot promise you, but there may be a chance." Thieu vowed, "I will do what is best for my country." Thieu met with his advisers, discussed his dwindling options, and sent word to Martin that he would resign the next day. The ambassador sent the news to Kissinger who, interestingly, asked that the announcement be delayed until Kissinger met with the Soviets. Angry, Martin ignored Kissinger's request: "It just went from the incoming basket to the file with absolutely no action at all."[4]

Thieu's public resignation speech blasted the United States. We had deserted him and his people. He had told visiting congressmen "it was a question of complying with the U.S. pledge to assist the Vietnamese people in the struggle to protect their independence and freedom and the ideal of freedom for which the Americans fought together with our people here and for which some 50,000 American citizens were sacrificed." The $300 million in supplemental aid was not a large sum, Thieu observed, but Congress had rejected it while his troops were dying on the battlefield. Therefore, he would resign, turning over power to his aging vice president, Tran Van Huong. On April 25, 1975, Thieu left South Vietnam, headed for Taiwan where he confided to Mrs. Anna Chennault, the Chinese-born widow of General Claire Chennault, commander of the Flying Tigers in World War II, "It is so easy to be an enemy of the United States, but so difficult to be a friend."[5]

On the day of Thieu's resignation, Kissinger met with the House of Representatives' Committee on Appropriations. He reviewed with the members the dire situation in Southeast Asia. When asked what promises had been made to Thieu at the time of the Paris Peace Accords, he commented, "The commitments that were made to South Vietnam are all on the public record." In fact, Nixon, Ford, and Kissinger had promised Thieu that, if necessary, the 7th Air Force, based at Nakhon Phanom, Thailand, would be used to punish Communist aggression. These secret promises would now be ignored.[6]

At Tulane University on April 23, President Ford explained, "America can regain the sense of pride that existed before Vietnam. But it cannot be achieved by re-fighting a war that is finished as far as America is concerned." In South Vietnam, Defense Department aid Eric Von Marbod had just arrived in country with Richard Armitage to retrieve such American assets as F-5E fighter-bombers. Von Marbod said of Ford's statement, "He raised the white bed sheet. I felt overwhelmed and ashamed."[7]

Chapter 18

Exit

"I'll tell you something. I felt like we were vacuuming up the whole country."

Housing Officer Sally Vinyard, 1975.

Despite Graham Martin's reluctance to order the evacuation of South Vietnam, people had been leaving the country since the latter part of March. The means of evacuation could be ingenious. The "underground railroad" used canopy-covered mail trucks, loaded with vulnerable Vietnamese. When planes flew into Tan Son Nhut, supplies were unloaded and a convoy of mail trucks replaced the supplies with human cargo. Operation Babylift, as we know, was another guise for evacuation. The April 4 crash of the C-5A did not halt the use of orphan flights as a way to lower the total of willing American "escorts" remaining in the country. "Black Flights" by the CIA's Air America evacuated special groups of people through its terminal. Still, between April 1 and April 19, only about 5,000 evacuees had left South Vietnam. General Homer Smith had urged American civilians, such as contractor employees and retired military personnel, to leave, but he could not force them to do so.[1]

On April 1, an Evacuation Control Center (ECC) at Tan Son Nhut was opened for business. This unique organization, born of necessity, was established by General Smith to "Coordinate the evacuation related activities of all U.S. mission agencies." Nine officers drawn from all four services initially staffed it. At this point, no one could have predicted that South Vietnam would fall so quickly. The functions and staffing of the ECC would grow as the demand for its services grew.[2]

The first problem assigned to the ECC was to coordinate the movement of refugees from the ports in Military Regions I and II as they tried to escape the advancing North Vietnamese forces. This proved to be a nightmare for both the South Vietnamese government and those Americans trying to help. An average of eight ships under contract to the Military Sealift Command would be operating at any one time. In addition, there were South Korean, Taiwanese, British, and Philippine vessels that participated in the rescue efforts. The South Vietnamese Navy committed every available asset to the backhaul of troops, refugees, and material.[3]

The first movements brought escaping civilians and soldiers from the Danang and Hue areas down to Cam Ranh Bay and Nha Trang in MR II. However, it was not long before these same refugees had to move further south to once again escape the forces of General Dung. In this second lift, many of the RVNAF troops were taken to Vung Tau, a major port on the coast about 45 miles southeast of Saigon. Many others and thousands of civilians were forced to go to Phuoc Quoc Island further to the south and west, almost to Cambodia, where the facilities for taking care of these unfortunates were totally inadequate.[4]

All of the vessels involved in the sealift were extremely overloaded. In the case of the SS *Pioneer Contender*, a mix of 16,000 military and civilian refugees had crowded aboard. Many of the ARVN still had their weapons and they did not hesitate to use them if they suspected an individual of being a Viet Cong. In these cases the suspect would be summarily shot and his body dumped overboard. In an especially gruesome example of this vigilantism, one suspected Communist collaborator was taken down into a refrigerated compartment, and tied to the ringbolts in the deck. His judge and jury then pulled the pin from a hand grenade, stuck the now live grenade under him, and closed the door. As the chief of Saigon's Military Sea Command Office, Donald Burney, put it, "We know about that because there was a hell of a mess to clean up."[5]

Many of the evacuees died from thirst and exposure while at sea. The surging crowds crushed others. In at least one case, the South Vietnamese soldiers mutinied, forcing the ship's master to take them to Vung Tau instead of Phouc Quoc Island. As the movement of refugees continued, Marine Corps security guards and medical personnel were added to the crews of the American contract vessels participating in the evacuations. This move not only provided for control of what would otherwise have been an unruly mob, but provided minimal health services to those most in need: the very young and the very old.[6]

By the end of the first week in April, the frequency of cargo aircraft bringing supplies into Tan Son Nhut Airbase accelerated. They were used to take increasing numbers of people out on the return trips. For example,

Vietnamese refugees crowd the decks of the U.S. Merchant Ship *Pioneer Contender,* April 6, 1975. *Courtesy of U.S. Navy.*

504 people were evacuated on April 7; 585 on April 8; 804 on the 9th; and 841 on the 10th. There was a slowdown for the next ten days when the average number of departures fell to 334. But after the fall of Xuan Loc on the 20th, the average number of people departing by fixed-wing aircraft jumped to over 5,500 per day. The enforcement of required exit documentation became less and less strict as the month went on. With very few exceptions, however, uniformed RVNAF personnel did not leave with their families. In one incident, a group of South Vietnamese Marines approached one of the American officers who manned the ECC and said, "If you will take our families out, we will fight to the end." The American then requested that two C-130s come to pick up these Vietnamese families. When the airplanes arrived, the dependents rushed aboard while the Marines kept everyone else off. The South Vietnamese Marines kept their word.[7]

As thousands of frightened refugees waited their turns to be added to an aircraft's manifest, they were housed and cared for by DAO personnel. Sally Vinyard, the DAO housing officer, describes the activity of the ECC succinctly: "I felt like we were vacuuming up the whole country."[8]

Thieu's resignation speech and Ford's declaration of the end to America's involvement in the war contributed to the eagerness of many to leave

On April 7, 1975, Vietnamese refugees disembark from the U.S. Merchant Ship *Green Port* at Phu Quoc Island, Republic of Vietnam. *Courtesy of U.S. Navy.*

while they still could. Ambassador Martin, now determined to rescue as many South Vietnamese as possible, sent word to Washington that the total number of refugees could reach 1,000,000. Bottlenecks arose unexpectedly. Philippine President Ferdinand Marcos decreed on April 23 that no more than 200 evacuees could be in his country at any one time; there were already 5,800 there. Negotiating with Marcos slowed things down for a brief period.[9]

As the end of the American presence in Vietnam approached, Ambassador Martin and others pressed for a closing of the books in regard to paying off Vietnamese nationals who were either employed by the Americans or held contracts for providing services to the U.S agencies in Vietnam. In addition, the ambassador insisted that these South Vietnamese be paid in U.S. dollars, a violation of the local law. The individual who had to actually make these payments was the DAO disbursing officer, Ann Hazard, a twenty-six year veteran of the U.S. civil service. $11 million in cash had been flown to Saigon for this express purpose. Day by day the pressure on Hazard and her staff grew as those who were due money pressed for payment. More than once, it took the display of an M-16 or a pistol by a guard to keep the frantic crowds under control. By late on April 29, three and a half million of the dollars as well as eighty-five million in Vietnamese currency remained in the disbursing officer's possession. Hazard was instructed to see that this money was destroyed. The plan called for the cash to be placed in a 55-gallon steel drum along with a large quantity of highly flammable thermite and for the whole thing to be lit off as the last members of the DAO left Tan Son Nhut on their way out to the U.S. Navy ships off shore. As it turned out, no one actually saw the barrels of money burn. However, the entire complex, including the 55-gallon drums, was wired for destruction and this effort was a success. Aerial photographs clearly showed the building to have been totally destroyed by the explosive and flammable charges set off as the last Americans boarded their helicopters. Even with that, Ms. Hazard had to endure an official investigation, which, in the end, absolved her completely.[10] The investigation, which included innumerable interviews and paperwork reviews, demonstrated the lack of understanding by the Defense Department bureaucracy of what had actually been happening in Vietnam after the last of the American prisoners of war came home. It was as if they believed that those last days of April 1975 were comparable to springtime on the Tidal Basin. Like so many in the United States, to them the war had been over since early 1973.

The North Vietnamese seemed, on April 27, to hold back their advance on Saigon. President Huong, after being in office for only a couple of days, had turned power over to General Duong Van "Big" Minh. There were rumors that a coalition government might form. Some believed that Kissinger had made some sort of an arrangement through the Soviets to allow the Americans to leave the country unopposed, if the departure was prompt and complete. Tran Trong Khanh, a twenty-five year-old Viet Cong officer who was at Tan Son Nhut in April 1975 said in an interview given in 1996, "In my opinion, there was a kind of 'gentleman's agreement' to allow the evacuation to go forward. We just stopped fighting and shelling a few hours. We didn't shoot much. Then you were gone." Any hopes for a sharing of power with the Communists were dashed just after 6:00 P.M. on April 28 when Tan Son Nhut came under attack by a flight of three A-37 aircraft. Using 250-pound bombs the attack destroyed several aircraft parked on the flight line and badly damaged base operations. The timing of the bombing made it clear that the North Vietnamese could attack any time they chose to do so. Adding insult to injury, the attackers flew captured South Vietnamese Air Force aircraft.[11]

In the very early hours of the 29th, between 3:00 and 3:30 A.M., three U.S. Air Force C-130s arrived from the Philippines loaded with ammunition for the RVNAF. After discharging their cargo at the ordnance storage area, the three aircraft moved toward the passenger loading area. The first C-130 was quickly filled with refugees, but before the second could take anybody on board, a barrage of 122 mm rockets began to fall all across the airfield. The third airplane was hit and destroyed, but the crew somehow escaped serious injury. They quickly jumped in the empty C-130 and the pilot wasted no time in getting it into the air. U.S. Air Force lieutenant colonel Arthur E. Laehr gave this account of the attack: "Intelligence had warned us that we would be hit by rockets and artillery on the 29th. However, we had been issued the same warning for two or there days in a row. I guess the 'cry wolf' story pervaded our thoughts. Rather than sleep in the DAO complex the night of the 28th, I returned to my trailer.

"I should mention that I firmly believe the NVA were ready earlier. I think that they waited until we got our numbers down to the point where we could make the helicopter evacuation work.

"One of the first rockets hit near the DAO killing two U.S. Marines (Corporals Darwin Judge and Charles McMahon). It was a near direct hit. When the first rocket hit it woke me up. Another rocket hit the gymnasium area as I looked out the window of my trailer. A sick feeling ensued as I knew the EPC (Evacuation/Evacuee Processing Center) was located in the area. A third rocket hit in the vicinity of the DAO compound. It impacted within six feet of the generals' quarters 1 and 2 and blew all of the occupants, fourteen personnel, out of bed while collapsing much of one wall. There were no injuries."[12]

At this point, some members of the South Vietnamese Air Force began their own evacuation using C-130s, C-119s, C-7s, and helicopters. A scene similar to the one at the Danang airport occurred as people fought to board the aircraft. One C-130 took off on a parallel runway. Another took off on an old runway and barely cleared the old airfield control tower on climb-out. A C-7 tried to take off on one engine and spun off the runway onto the grass infield and burned. As it began to get light, F-5s and A-37s took off to escape to U-Tapao Airbase in Thailand.[13]

Not all of the South Vietnamese Air Force personnel made a run for it. At least one C-119 gunship was airborne most the night expending flares and ordnance on the advancing enemy. The pilot would land, refuel and rearm, and take off again. At about 7:00 A.M., an SA-7 antiaircraft missile fired by Communist troops close to Tan Son Nhut hit the C-119. The airplane broke up and plummeted to earth in flames. Three parachutes were spotted, but one became entangled in burning debris and it burned.[14]

Lieutenant Colonel John F. Hilgenberg described the scene at the EPC. "The crowd was tense, but controllable. However, when the C-119 went down, you could see a new phase of depression set in. When I realized SA-7s were almost on the perimeter of Tan Son Nhut, I personally felt the fixed wing lift was over and that even helicopter extraction would be hazardous and costly. To reduce some of the anxiety, I directed that all remaining refugees be manifested and formed into planeload groups. It was a token gesture but seemed to reduce the open fear."[15]

In spite of the shelling and the resulting destruction, direction was received from higher authority that the fixed-wing evacuation was to continue if the shelling stopped by dawn. The word was that president Ford had convened an emergency meeting of the National Security Council and that the decision to continue with the fixed-wing evacuation was made at that level. However, after making an on-site evaluation of the airfield's condition, General Smith concluded that it was not safe for use by fixed-wing aircraft. Ambassador Martin was not convinced at first. It was only after he had made a personal inspection of the airfield, and was reassured by CINCPAC that Tan Son Nhut could no longer be used by large cargo aircraft, that Martin would agree that the time had come for helicopters to begin the final phase of the extraction of the remaining Americans and endangered Vietnamese.[16]

Throughout the month of April 1975, the consul general for Military Region IV, Francis Terry McNamara, haggled with the embassy's evacuation coordinator, George "Jake" Jacobson, about how best to get both his American and Vietnamese employees out of the country should the need arise. McNamara was of the opinion that if the end should come quickly, the only way that he could get all of his Vietnamese workers and their families out was by boat down the Bas Sac River. He correctly assumed that the large number of potential evacuees already in Saigon would make it very difficult for his people to leave from there, even if they could be moved the more than 100 miles overland from Can Tho, where the consulate was located, to Saigon. Jacobson believed that they could be moved either by road or air to Tan Son Nhut and that it would be too dangerous to try to escape by river. McNamara also had to deal with a recalcitrant CIA station chief who wanted no part of his boat trip to the South China Sea. The CIA personnel would only consider using their Air America aircraft. In the end, all three escape routes were used. One American member of the consulate staff, Glenn Rounsevell, took fifty of his Vietnamese employees to Saigon where many had family. The CIA staff, with only a couple of exceptions, left Can Tho for the fleet in Air America helicopters, and Terry McNamara went down the river with everyone else in two LCM landing craft that belonged to the Alaska Barge and Transport Company, but were under contract to the Military Sealift Command Office in Saigon.[17]

Rounsevell had been in the field "helping a South Vietnamese major keep a unit alive" when, on April 24, he heard that President Ford had declared the war "finished" in his speech at Tulane University. He described his reaction this way: "I was totally astonished since here I was in the middle of the Delta, yet with no assurance from my government that they would come to get me out. From all that was going on, I knew damned well that the war was not 'finished.'"[18]

When Rounsevell arrived in Saigon on April 28, he made arrangements for himself and those in his care to leave from Tan Son Nhut the next day. Of course, that was the day that all fixed-wing flights were canceled.

Waking to the sound of exploding rockets on the 29th, Rounsevell headed to the American embassy to try to find out what was going on. His fifty charges, in the meantime, were with their families at various places scattered across the huge city.

In an interview in August 1995, Rounsevell described the situation that he faced. "It soon became clear that the embassy and Washington were dead wrong [about a negotiated conclusion to the war]. Instead, the North Vietnamese Army was going for broke. Tan Son Nhut was shut down. The primary means of evacuation was therefore gone.

"So my only hope was that, if I could still somehow make contact with those on my list, I would have to have them come and try for evacuation from the embassy. Since I had been posted to the consulate in Can Tho, neither myself nor my charges were included in the evacuation plans. I had to fend for myself."

Once he got to the embassy, Rounsevell tried to contact his people and tell them to come, with their families, to the American embassy. The phone lines were largely out of commission and all he could do was post himself atop the wall around the embassy compound and hope that those who were looking to him for help in escaping would show up.

Some did, and he would physically pull them up and over the wall. Many, however, did not. He went on to say, "In the end, to my everlasting regret, I only succeeded in getting out seventeen on my list of fifty. What happened to the others— those left behind? I learned that some went to the river and escaped by boat, some later fled to other parts on Vietnam, to Thailand, Malaysia, the Philippines. Others, no doubt, spent years in communist reeducation camps. I can only pray that those who were left will not believe that I willingly deserted them. It haunts me to his day."[19]

Shortly after 12:30 P.M. on April 29, Consul General Terry McNamara called for his little two-ship "navy" to cast off from the pier in Can Tho and he and about 300 nervous souls started down the river. At times they were the targets of small-arms fire coming from the riverbanks, but no one was hit. Part way to the South China Sea, they were stopped by three South Vietnamese Navy gunboats. A Lieutenant Commander Quang was in charge. He told McNamara that he had been ordered to stop the two LCMs and bring them back to Can Tho. McNamara refused, and he suggested to the young officer that he make radio contact with his commanding officer, Commodore Thang. McNamara's hope was that Thang would act on a promise that he had made a week earlier when the consul general had arranged for Thang's wife and children to leave Vietnam from Tan Son Nhut. True to his word, the commodore told his subordinate that he should allow the Americans and their employees to proceed down the river and that the South Vietnamese Navy gunboats should return to Can Tho.

The rest of the trip was not without excitement. At one point they were fired upon by rockets, and they were hit by a sudden storm that reduced visibility to about fifty yards. At last, though, they made it to the open sea where they would be safe from Communist attack.

The question then became, where is the U.S. Navy? McNamara had been told that a ship would be positioned near the mouth of the Bas Sac River and would pick him and the other refugees up there.

As it turned out, the word had not been passed to any U.S. Navy ship. But Lady Luck was smiling on the consul general. The SS *Pioneer Contender* was down in that area standing by in case she was needed to pick up more refugees. Her master, Edward C. Flink, was not particularly happy to have been given this assignment, especially after his ordeal with the ARVN personnel who had come aboard in Danang. As he told James E. Parker, Jr., one of the Can Tho CIA agents who had been transferred to the *Pioneer Contender* after his escape in an Air America helicopter, "I ain't set up for this. I've no food, no sanitation equipment. I'm supposed to carry cargo. That's C-A-R-G-O. I don't want this ship ever again considered a people carrier. I want boxes of things that don't talk some foreign language, carry guns, eat, and shit." The master was an honorable man, however, and he saved the lives of many who were desperate to escape Vietnam before the Communists took the country over. Among those he saved were the escapees from Can Tho who had slipped the grasp of the invading Communists by boat. McNamara's crew had spotted the *Pioneer Contender* lying at anchor not far off the coast shortly after midnight. Within an hour, the two-ship convoy was able to pull alongside the big ship, and Master Flink's crew took aboard its human cargo.[20]

Back in Saigon, once Ambassador Martin realized that Tan Son Nhut could no longer accommodate fixed-wing aircraft, he gave the word that Operation Frequent Wind, the planned massive helicopter evacuation, should commence.[21]

This would be a complex military maneuver that would include four aircraft carriers, two of which were reconfigured for helicopters, the shipping for two amphibious squadrons totaling fifteen vessels, and assorted escort and support ships. Seventy-five U.S. Marine Corps and ten U.S. Air Force helicopters were involved. Three Marine battalion landing teams (BLTs) consisting of almost four thousand Marines and sailors were there, plus two alert battalions on hand at Subic Bay in the Philippines and on the island of Okinawa. From first light on April 29 until 8:30 A.M. on April 30, 682 sorties were flown. The average crew flight time was thirteen hours, and Captain Gerry Berry, the pilot of the aircraft that carried Ambassador Martin from the embassy's roof to the USS *Blue Ridge* in the early hours of the 30th, was the "high time aviator" logging 18.3 hours of flight time during the operation.[22]

Brigadier General Richard E. Carey, commanding general of the 9th Marine Amphibious Brigade, was the man in charge of the helicopter operations and the Marines who would be brought ashore to provide security for the landing zone at the DAO compound on Tan Son Nhut Airbase. After assuring himself that the prelaunch activities in the fleet were running smoothly, General Carey flew in to the DAO compound, landing at 1:50 P.M. on April 29. At 3:06 P.M. the first wave of twelve CH-53 helicopters carrying two companies of the battalion landing team designated to protect the landing zone arrived. As soon as the aircraft had discharged their cargoes of Marines, 679 evacuees were taken aboard for the return flight to the fleet. From then until General Homer Smith boarded the last

U.S. Air Force helicopter launches from the USS *Midway* to begin Operation Frequent Wind, April 29, 1975. *Courtesy of H. C. Haynsworth.*

helicopter to carry evacuees at 9:00 P.M., there was a steady flow of aircraft ferrying refugees out to the ships off shore. At 11:00 P.M., General Carey ordered the complete withdrawal of all brigade elements from the DAO compound. At ten minutes after midnight, the thermite explosives were ignited in selected buildings and vital areas, and the last two CH-53s lifted off two minutes later. As A result of the activation of the thermite, the fires at the DAO compound grew in intensity and were visible for some distance as the helicopters departed the Saigon area. A total of 395 Americans and 4,465 other refugees were evacuated in an orderly procession of U.S. Marine Corps and U.S. Air Force helicopters.

While the operation at Tan Son Nhut had gone smoothly, especially considering the fact that firefights were in progress just beyond the airfield boundaries and that the airfield had been heavily damaged, the extraction of refugees from the embassy compound was anything but smooth.

No sooner had the Marines landed at the DAO compound and the evacuation had begun than word was passed to General Carey that there were 2,000 people at the embassy waiting to be evacuated from there. There had been no plans made to pull large numbers of refugees from the embassy compound. All refugees, except embassy personnel, were supposed to have

U.S. Marine Corps landing team arrives at Tan Son Nhut Air Base on April 29, 1975. *Courtesy of Colonel Edwin Pelosky.*

been rounded up from predetermined pickup points and taken to Tan Son Nhut. But the streets of Saigon became gridlocked and there was nothing to do but improvise. An inhibiting factor faced by the Marine Corps aviators was the fact that the embassy compound could take only two aircraft at any one time, one in the courtyard and one on the roof.[23]

The evacuation from the embassy began at about 5:00 P.M. on April 29. A platoon of General Carey's marines was flown in to augment the embassy guard force already there. U.S. Army captain Stewart Herrington was a member of a joint military team that was working with the North Vietnamese searching for American missing-in-action (MIA) personnel. Fluent in Vietnamese, he was in the embassy courtyard on the 29th assisting in the processing of refugees for boarding the helicopters that would take them to the ships offshore. He scoffs at the reports that appeared in the media that there was a panicked crowd of 10,000 surrounding the embassy.[24]

The number of potential evacuees that was reported to General Carey was 2,000. As some were airlifted out of the compound, others would either be brought in by Air America helicopters or, like Glenn Rounsevell's charges, called in from around the city.[25]

Herrington described the procedure for processing those leaving:

South Vietnamese scale the wall of the U.S. Embassy in Saigon, April 29, 1975. *Courtesy of Colonel Edwin Pelosky.*

"The CIA was going out and picking up people whom they had promised to get out, and they were bringing them to the embassy with the idea that they could be [taken to Tan Son Nhut] in busses ... the bus thing broke down, [and] they kept bringing them here with the idea that we could get them out with heavy lift [helicopters]. People were frightened. You could see these folks praying before their turn on the helicopter comes." After dark "we backed all of the black sedans around us, all pointing in, and ran the engines and turned the headlights on. Then the embassy engineer and I found a carousel projector and we put it on the roof of the firehouse and when the choppers came in we just turned it on. Big white square line.... all night the CH-53s came.... the media reported 10,000 people around that embassy. I am here to tell you that they weren't there. I was there from roughly 9:30 in the morning on the 29th all the way to the end. And there were confrontations at the gate; poignant things, poor people holding up letters.... A couple of hundred people pushing and screaming and shoving and young people climbing up on the walls and being screamed at by the Marines. And another crowd, the secondary crowd, standing along the far side of the street just basically gawking."[26]

One of the problems encumbering the evacuation was that, in the end, it was being run out of the White House. When Henry Kissinger was asked why this was, he replied, "We had it by default. The Pentagon didn't want to touch it. The Pentagon position was, basically, if there was to be an evacuation they wanted to pull the Americans out and leave. Period! The ambassador wanted to take out as many Vietnamese as possible. The president wanted to take out as many Vietnamese as possible, and I wanted to take out as many Vietnamese as possible. If [Secretary of Defense James] Schlesinger was left to do it, Schlesinger ... was going to come in and take out the Americans and go."[27]

In the early hours of April 30, confusion existed in Washington as to the number of refugees left to be taken out. A decision based upon an erroneous count resulted in a premature order to stop all evacuation flights except one last flight that was to take Ambassador Martin out to the fleet. The ambassador didn't want to go. There were still people to save. But President Ford gave him a direct order to leave, so he boarded Captain Berry's helicopter and flew to the *Blue Ridge*.[28]

Once the ambassador was safely on his way, the Marine security force of 120 men was extracted ... except for eleven Marines on the embassy roof who had somehow been overlooked.

It wasn't until about 6:30 A.M. on the 30th that General Carey's people on the *Blue Ridge* discovered the oversight. They immediately sent another helicopter into Saigon to retrieve the eleven Marines.

Sergeant Terry Bennington, one of the eleven, gave this account of what happened next. "We stayed up there [on the roof], and were as quiet as we could be. We watched the firefights going on. We could see the North Vietnamese Army. We could see some of the tanks and everybody forming up. I remember that it was light when they came and got us. I know that it was 0759 on April 30—one minute before the North Vietnamese Army commenced its major assault. We were in the air while they were assaulting."[29]

At the embassy, 420 people had been left behind by mistake. Stuart Herrington had been assuring them in fluent Vietnamese that neither he nor they would be left behind. But before the ambassador left, Herrington and the very few Americans still there were ordered to get into a helicopter and just leave. He described the abandoned group that he had assured would be saved as "a significant number from the South Korean Embassy ... the poor [U.S.] embassy employees ... a German priest ... [and] a hodge-podge of Vietnamese." Among them were a team of Vietnamese fire fighters who delayed their exit to provide protection should an emergency occur.[30]

At the Military Sealift Command office in Saigon, its chief, Donald Berney, and its operations officer, William "Bill" Ryder, were trying to find ways to help their Vietnamese employees and other at-risk people get out of the country. On April 21, Berney was at the United Seamen's Club in the Newport area of Saigon when he ran into the master of the SS *Green Wave*, a ship owned by the Central Gulf Lines, but under contract to the MSC. When Berney asked him if he would be willing to take some refugees with him when he sailed that night, the answer was, "Yes." The ambassador had not yet given approval for the evacuation of Vietnamese, but Berney and the *Green Wave* master went ahead anyway. Then Berney decided that he had to tell somebody in authority what he was doing so he contacted Admiral Hugh Benton, the CINCPAC representative for the evacuation in Saigon. Berney described the admiral's reaction this way: "My impression is that he was very unhappy to hear about this. But he didn't deny it or anything like that. I think that he just didn't want to, officially, know about it." In any case, Benton sent a message to CINC-PAC alerting his bosses to the probable "outflow of South Vietnamese watercraft to off shore U.S. ships in near future." The message also included a "related item: approximately 1,000 refugees aboard SS *Green Wave* on route Subic with Ambassador Martin's approval." So Berney's spontaneous effort to help save Vietnamese lives was given official, if after-the-fact, sanction.

On April 26, Berney was directed to establish a coordinating center on the *Blue Ridge* for the movement of MSC ships while they were in Vietnamese waters. He and Bill Ryder decided to flip a coin to see who would go out to the fleet and who would stay and man the office in Saigon. The coin chose Ryder to stay behind.

Even after the big MSC ships had been ordered out of Saigon, there were still five tugboats and their barges at the Newport piers. The barges had been used to haul ammunition up the Mekong River to Phnom Penh and they all had sandbag walls. Five of the Alaska Barge and Transportation Company employees, who had been given airplane tickets home, voted to stay in Saigon as long as Ryder did. They too wanted to do what they could to save Vietnamese lives.

On the morning of April 29, Bill Ryder was preparing to make his way down the Saigon River on the *Touchi Maru,* one of the tugs that had a barge in tow, when two CIA agents contacted him on the radio. They said that they had twelve busloads of Vietnamese agents with them that they had collected from around the countryside and that they had been unable to get to Tan Son Nhut for evacuation. Ryder told them to meet him at the Saigon piers. When they got there, they and a large number of escaping Vietnamese filled the five barges that were to be towed to open water. There were more people wanting to leave than there was space, so there was a lot of jostling and shoving going on as the crowd tried to board the barges. One of the walls on one barge collapsed under the pressure. An old woman holding a baby was knocked overboard. The two of them sank like rocks. In their rush to escape, no one even looked to see what had happened to them. At one point, Ryder said, "We literally had to threaten to shoot women and children to stop people from getting on the barge after we figured we had all of the people we could actually carry. You know, who the hell am I to play God!"

The acting engineer of the *Touchi Maru* was really an automobile mechanic and he was unfamiliar with the fuel system on the tug. As a result, partway down the river the engine died of fuel starvation. As the engineer searched for the problem, the tugboat and its barge were grounded on the east bank of the river. Somebody on the riverbank started taking potshots at the vessels. Ryder called out to the flagship by radio and asked, "Is there any chance of just getting a couple of aircraft to come in real low ... just to get these guys to put their damned heads down so that they don't get serious and decide that they really do want to blow us out of the water." It wasn't long before Admiral Donald Whitmire, the task force commander, came on the air. He said, "Bill, the State Department says the we cannot intrude on Vietnamese airspace. Now ain't that a shit?" As Ryder commented, "That's the way things were."

In the meantime the auto mechanic had figured out what the problem was and the tugboat was able to get under way again. Once out at sea, the barge passengers and Bill Ryder were taken on board one or the other of the large ships under the control of the MSC. The tugboats were then used to pick up people from the multitude of small craft that the Vietnamese were using to escape, and then take them to the MSC ships for transfer to the refugee centers on the island of Guam.[31]

The Vietnamese Navy fleet commander in the spring of 1975 was Captain Leon Nguyen. He was in Danang when his ships participated in the evacuation of RVNAF troops from MR I. After that region had fallen to the North Vietnamese, Captain Nguyen and his staff held a meeting at his headquarters in Saigon. It was now mid April and the question was how to keep the ship's crews intact and fighting. It was agreed that in order to be able to do that, they "needed to provide some safe haven for their families." Nguyen added, "That was the conclusion of my staff. So we loaded our ships with provisions ... dry fish and rice. I sent men to get as much rice as possible. Then I passed the word out, 'Whoever wants his family with you in a safe place, fill out an application and send it to the commanding officer.' There was lots of response. That was my plan. And that was two weeks before the fall of Saigon.

"I was relieved of my command because this plan was considered by headquarters to be counterproductive. They said that this plan, having the families on board with my men, produced a false sense of alarm among the troops. But the plans were ready. The plans were there.

"When the final days came, we were able to execute my plan without me in command. By that time there were eighty-one ships in the command: landing craft, troop transports, patrol craft, cutters.

"They came to me and said, 'Show us. Forget what headquarters had done to you.' So I took the fleet again and we headed to Subic Bay [in the Philippines].

"I was able to contact the [U.S.] Seventh Fleet and alert them to our whereabouts. We got some fresh water. I have tried to get some figures of how many people left with us. It was 22,000 or 23,000 people."

When the fleet of Vietnamese Navy ships approached Subic Bay, a new problem arose. The President of the Philippines, Ferdinand Marcos, was wary of admitting the fleet into Philippine waters now that the Communists were the government of all Vietnam. Admiral George Steel, commander of the Seventh Fleet, interceded for the Vietnamese sailors and their families. This is his description of the solution to the problem: "As [the South Vietnamese Navy ships] got closer, the problem grew more immediate of what we were going to do with the ships. Or could we get them all in? Marcos didn't want them in with a Vietnamese flag on them. So I proposed that just outside Subic that we reassume them. They were military assistance ships anyhow. We would put an American CO on each one to raise the American flag and take them back into U.S. custody."

Captain Nguyen described the execution of Admiral Steel's solution: "We went straight to Subic Bay and we turned our ships over to the U.S. Navy. We had an emotional ceremony as we lowered our flag. The Seventh Fleet assigned to each one of our ships a junior officer—a figurehead. We raised the American flag on our ships and saved them from the communists."[32]

After the last of the Marines had been lifted from the roof of the American Embassy in the early hours of April 30, 1975, the flood of refugees

South Vietnamese helicopters descending upon the USS *Midway*, April 30, 1975. *Courtesy of H. C. Haynsworth.*

leaving Vietnam continued. Many left by boat, but many also escaped in South Vietnamese Air Force aircraft. The larger planes, like the C-130s, flew to Thailand, but the helicopters could not make it that far and they headed in the direction of the U.S. Navy fleet out in the South China Sea. Some found ships with space to land helicopters, but others just ditched their airplanes in the water alongside navy vessels. On the ships that were able to actually take the helos on board, their landing areas quickly filled up. In these cases the sailors just pushed the empty helicopters over the side and made room for the next one to land. This went on for hours and thousands more lives were saved this way.

The aircraft carrier USS *Midway* alone took on forty-eight helicopters, some of which carried as many as fifty people. Once on board, the ships crew went all out to make their "guests" as comfortable as possible before they were finally transferred to the MSC ships still in company.

On the afternoon of the 30th, a lone Cessna O-1 spotter plane flew over the *Midway*. The ship's flight deck was covered with helicopters, but the pilot of the little plane flew in low over the big ship. On a third try, the pilot was finally able to get a note to land on the flight deck and not blow over the side. The note read, "Can you move these helicopter to the

Vietnamese refugees led to safety upon arrival on the USS *Midway*, April 30, 1975.
Courtesy of H. C. Haynsworth.

other side. I can land on your runway. I can fly 1 hour more. We have enough time to move. Please rescue me. Major Bung Ly wife and 5 children."[33]

The note was rushed to the ship's bridge and delivered to the *Midway*'s skipper, Captain Lawrence C. Chambers. Once he realized that there were seven lives at stake, he quickly ordered the flight deck crew to make room on the angle deck so that Major Ly could try to save his family. Those naval aviators watching the events unfold could only shake their heads. Not only was it highly unlikely that this Air Force aviator had ever tried to land on an aircraft carrier before, but even worse, his Cessna had no tail hook.

Once enough room had been cleared, Bung Ly began his approach. This is how he described what happened next. "When they moved the airplanes, I said, 'Humm, I've never landed on a carrier before.' The family and I were very nervous and everything. So I came down for a first pass. I had to measure how strong the wind was, how the carrier was moving, and how fast. I came in once, and thought I'd do it in the second one. The second time I came in, I just shut off the whole engine. That way I could keep it short and stay there. I believe I was back on about one third of the

deck." The sailors in the flight deck crew rushed over to the plane. They wanted to make sure that it didn't go over the side. Major Ly, his wife, and five small children climbed out of the airplane and were immediately mobbed by the welcoming crewmen.

The entire episode had been shown on the ship's closed-circuit television system. When the O-1 rolled to a stop, the entire ship's company let out a great cheer. It was a wonderful moment.

As Captain Chambers said, "The courage and skill that the major demonstrated in making his first carrier landing a successful one captured the admiration of the *Midway*'s crew and for most of us, was the highlight of the eventful period of Operation Frequent Wind."[34]

Opposite, top: Major Bung Ly and his family land on the USS *Midway* in their O-1 Birddog on April 30, 1975. *Bottom:* Crewmen from the USS *Midway* greet the Bun Ly family after their successful landing on the *Midway*'s flight deck. *Courtesy of H. C. Haynsworth.*

Chapter 19

Who Lost South Vietnam?

"When we abandoned the use of power in Indochina, we also abandoned its people to a grim fate."

Richard Nixon, 1985.

The news media covered the collapse of South Vietnam extensively. Television broadcast scenes of chaos at the embassy walls. Marines clubbed desperate civilians as they attempted to squeeze through the gates. The May 1, 1975, issue of *Stars and Stripes* featured a photograph of a guard with the cutline: "A U.S. Marine points a rifle at a South Vietnamese trying to climb over the wall of the U.S. Embassy Wednesday in desperate attempt to get aboard the evacuation flights." That authorized military publication, not exactly unbiased in its coverage of the U.S. armed forces, added, "The Vietnamese panicked and tried to throw themselves over the walls and wire fences." No wonder Ford and Kissinger, sitting in Washington watching televised images of such disorder, felt a need to halt the evacuation. It must be stressed, however, that gradually the crowds settled down until only the 420 people Captain Herrington recalls were left. The evacuation, by sea and air, was a Herculean effort and nearly got everyone in line to safety. Ten more flights would have completed the mission, but Ford terminated the evacuation, abandoning the remaining 420 people to the Communists.[1]

Other publications chronicled the last two days of April. The *New York Times*, which had so angered Richard Nixon in 1971 with the publication of the Pentagon Papers, carried a large front-page photograph of a helicopter perched atop a Saigon building, evacuees scrambling up a flight of stairs to be loaded by a crewman.[2] That picture was reproduced across the land and some Americans mistakenly thought the building was the actual embassy; it was a CIA safe house, one of many sprinkled across Saigon.

Time magazine's cover displayed eight Communists, waiving weapons and a North Vietnamese flag, under a headline proclaiming "Hanoi's Triumph." The cover also featured the words "The Economy: Upturn Ahead." While not downplaying the fall of Saigon, *Time* was, in effect, diverting our attention to other matters. In *Newsweek* and *Time*, photographs of Ford, Kissinger, and Vice President Nelson Rockefeller, appeared. Two of these pictures are worth commenting on because of their surreal symbolism. Both showed the administration's leaders, as the evacuation reached its climax, dressed in tuxedos.[3] Apparently, they were all dressed up — with somewhere else to go.

When Chiang Kai-shek fled mainland China in 1949, many of President Harry Truman's opponents asked, "Who lost China?" One of the most vocal of these critics was U.S. Representative Richard Nixon. His career was constructed on anti–communism and to see Mao Zedong come to power in Beijing was shocking. Nixon believed that surely this rout of the pro–western Chiang would not have occurred if Truman had been strong. He thought that those around Truman were weak on the red menace. Secretary of State Dean Acheson presided over an institution where students earned "Ph.D.'s from the Cowardly College of Communist Containment," Richard Nixon shouted. As far as he was concerned, it was no wonder Alger Hiss, former State Department official and aid to Franklin D. Roosevelt, felt no hesitation to lie to Congress about his Communist past. Vigilance and the use of American power must govern our approach to Communist encroachment, Nixon's stressed.[4]

By the 1950s, communists had sought to dominate the Korean peninsula. This Cold War episode was also Acheson's fault, Nixon explained, because the Secretary of State had pronounced an Asian defense perimeter that did not include South Korea. The Communists always probed for weakness and lack of resolve. They must be challenged — even if the battlefield was the frozen hills of Korea.[5]

Dwight Eisenhower spoke of the domino theory. Communists wanted to expand their Asian empire beyond Siberia and China. If Laos and Vietnam were toppled, Thailand and the Philippines would be next. The world of the 1950s and 1960s was bipolar in nature. Communists controlled huge sections of Asia and wished to gain the upper hand over Indochina. That's why the French were supported and that's why, after the 1954 debacle at Dien Bien Phu, the Eisenhower Administration stepped in to prop up South Vietnamese President Diem.[6]

John F. Kennedy and Lyndon Johnson were cold warriors in their defense of our non–communist allies in Asia. As we have seen, by 1967 the war in Southeast Asia had begun to be divisive here in the United States as well as militarily frustrating on the battlefield. The Communists were elusive — fighting, hiding, regrouping, and pouncing time and time again. That strategy would wreck Johnson's presidency and set the stage for Nixon's victory in the 1968 elections.

During the campaign, President Thieu sent Nixon a secret message wishing him success. Thieu, sensing that LBJ wished to end his term with peace, believed that Nixon would be steadfast in his defense of the anti–communist Thieu. As we are aware, Nixon had an impressive track record of consistent support of anti–communist groups in Latin America, Europe, Africa, the Middle East, and Asia. He understood the ways of Communists, Thieu believed. Johnson, desperate for a legacy, would negotiate a peace that would abandon Thieu. Nixon, the ferocious anti–communist, would be reliable.[7]

One can imagine the shock, after Nixon's narrow victory, when Nixon proclaimed his support for LBJ's efforts to extricate America from the Southeast Asian morass. Thus, Nixon came to power wishing to find a way out of Vietnam. Furthermore, he came to power willing to discard the anti–communist doctrine that he had patented two decades earlier. Assisted by Henry Kissinger, Nixon spent much time on détente with the Soviet Union and Mao's China. South Vietnam was an "irritant." From the first months of 1969, Thieu would be wary of the new administration that seemed too eager to achieve "peace with honor." Nixon, it seemed, had changed.

By 1973, Nixon had safely been re-elected. In Paris, Kissinger had negotiated a peace settlement that some would argue could have been achieved in 1969, saving 25,000 American lives. Thieu was forced to endorse the agreement, accept hostile forces in his country, and believe Nixon's promise that, if the Paris Peace Accords were violated, the U.S. would unleash the B-52s on Hanoi.[8]

Watergate and the Middle East occupied much of Nixon's time in 1973 and 1974. The American economy suffered from the Arab oil embargo and the aftereffects of Nixon's wage and price controls. Pursued by Congress and the special prosecutor, Nixon had little time for Saigon even though Thieu had been promised assistance in 1973. With Nixon's resignation and the ascension of a caretaker President, it is obvious that South Vietnam's fate was sealed. The assurances made by Nixon, Kissinger, and Ford meant nothing in the world of 1975.[9]

As we attempt to answer the question "Who lost South Vietnam?" it is wise to examine two other presidents who, under tremendous pressure, performed differently. Faced with civil war, Abraham Lincoln never wavered from his goal of achieving victory. When Congress sought to oversee his conduct of the war, he asserted the power of the commander in chief. He told dissenters in his cabinet to cease their criticism of his policies or resign. Battlefield defeats, press criticism, draft riots could not weaken Lincoln's resolve. Lincoln was unafraid of Congress or the wavering public.

Franklin D. Roosevelt, after nearly a decade restructuring the economy, mobilized the nation for war after Pearl Harbor. He explained the threat posed by the Axis powers in such stark terms that few Americans above the age of five could be confused. World War II became a crusade, costing more lives than Vietnam. FDR enlisted Congress in the front ranks of the crusade — something Nixon, Ford, and even Lincoln did not do. Nixon and Ford could not stroke or cajole the leaders of Congress the way FDR did.

President John F. Kennedy may have been the one to start the build-up of American armed forces in South Vietnam; Lyndon Johnson may have escalated that effort to the point where there were over half a million soldiers, airmen, Marines, and sailors incountry; and Congress may have starved our ally of the funds needed to fight off an aggressive enemy, but South Vietnam was lost — abandoned — by two presidents who lacked a commitment to the cause of preventing a Communist takeover in Southeast Asia. Nixon never saw it as "his war." He had other interests— other problems. Ford believed that the American people did not have the stomach for a resumption of our involvement in Asia. He might have been correct in 1975 — after he had crippled his presidency by pardoning Nixon and destroying his own credibility. If Thieu, with his corrupt entourage, were the problem, they should have been dealt with years earlier and not constantly reassured of American support. We, of course, had been known to do that type of thing before. Coups often had our fingerprints on them. Nixon, as Eisenhower's Vice President, knew about Iran in 1953 and Guatemala in 1954.

Reflecting upon the war ten years after the evacuation of Saigon, Richard Nixon wrote a slim volume entitled *No More Vietnams*. He saw no irony when he observed, "When we abandoned the use of power in Indochina, we also abandoned its people to grim fate." His own use of power had been erratic, ill-conceived, and tainted with abuse. In addition, he missed the opportunity early in his presidency to secure the peace terms that he, in 1973, accepted and forced upon Thieu. His weak successor, Gerald Ford, presided over the fruits of these abuses despite the fact that he had many friends in the Congress. They liked Jerry Ford but they

Secretary of State Henry Kissinger (left), Vice President Nelson Rockefeller (center), and President Gerald Ford (right) confer on the evacuation of Saigon. *Courtesy of Gerald R. Ford Library.*

would not follow him. The two Presidents so eroded America's international credibility that, in 1975, Syria's Hafez Assad could tell Kissinger during negotiations in the Middle East, "You've betrayed Vietnam. Someday you're going to sell out Taiwan. And we're going to be around when you get tired of Israel."[10] It would take other wars, such as the Gulf War, to rebuild America's credibility. Rapid and overwhelming force, in concert with firm unwavering support of allies, would be one of the lessons learned from our country's Vietnam experience. Significantly, some of the key figures in Operation Desert Storm were Vietnam veterans. The chairman of the Joint Chiefs of Staff, General Colin Powell, had been wounded in Vietnam. Allied commander Norman Schwarzkopf had also served in Southeast Asia.

Wars that drift along will always drain our vitality. Presidents must focus sharply on the objective (as President George Bush did in 1991), fight, overwhelm the enemy, win, and exit. That sequence did not occur in the Nixon and Ford administrations. Air Force lieutenant colonel Russ Shaw served in Vietnam in 1964 and returned in 1974. His first thoughts upon his return were, "why are we still fighting this war?" The Vietnam War dragged on until it became ensnarled in domestic politics, and then it became a tunnel without an end in sight. The damage was considerable.

Rebecca Goodman, a secretary for the DAO's procurement office, had married a South Vietnamese captain in 1974. She witnessed cease-fire violations, corruption, duplicity, erosion of support for Thieu, and the disinterest of Washington policymakers. With a five-week-old child, she evacuated South Vietnam on April 9, 1975. Her husband would follow two weeks later. Assessing the painful collapse of the nation, she remarks, "The war taught me to be very cautious, to not trust the American government." [11] The first casualty of war may, indeed, be truth. When politicians fail to lead and act with integrity, serious damage is done to our system. That is what happened repeatedly under Presidents Nixon and Ford as they abandoned an ally. Private assurances vanished when an aggressive enemy that only respected strength tested them. To those people who gathered at the Vietnam Memorial in the chilly early morning hours of April 30, 2000, the twenty-fifth anniversary of the war's end, it all came down to questions of honor and betrayal.

Chronology
of Major Events

1919   Ho Chi Minh attempts to meet with President Woodrow Wilson in Paris to discuss self-determination for Vietnam.

1941   Ho returns to Vietnam after a thirty-year absence and creates the Vietminh to struggle against both Japan and France.

1942   U.S. pilots attached to the Flying Tigers fly combat missions in Vietnam against Japanese military installations.

1944–1945   The OSS funds Vietminh actions against the Japanese in Vietnam. OSS operatives work with the Vietnamese to rescue downed U.S. flyers, and go on espionage and sabotage missions with them.

April 12, 1945   President Franklin Roosevelt dies; succeeded by Harry Truman.

September 1945   America supports the French efforts to reimpose colonialism in Vietnam.

May 8, 1950   The United States signs an agreement with France to provide the French Associated States of Vietnam with military assistance.

August 3, 1950   A U.S. military assistance advisory group (MAAG) of thirty-five men arrives in Vietnam to teach troops receiving U.S. weapons how to use them.

September 7, 1951   The Truman administration signs an agreement with Saigon to provide direct military aid to South Vietnam.

September 30, 1953   President Eisenhower approves $785 million for military aid for South Vietnam.

April 7, 1954   At a news conference, President Eisenhower, stressing the importance of defending Dien Bien Phu, enunciates the domino theory.

July 21, 1954   The American observer at Geneva, General Walter Bedell Smith, issues a unilateral declaration stating that the United States will refrain from threatening to use or using force to prevent implementation of the Geneva Accords.

September 8, 1954   The Manila Treaty is concluded, creating SEATO. A separate protocol extends the SEATO umbrella to include Laos, Cambodia, and "the free territory under the jurisdiction of the State of Vietnam" (South Vietnam).

October 24, 1954   President Eisenhower sends a letter to the new leader of South Vietnam, Ngo Dinh Diem, pledging U.S. support and agreeing to send $100 million to build up Diem's military forces. Eisenhower begins the U.S. commitment to maintaining a non–Communist government in South Vietnam.

April 28, 1955   Under severe pressure from a coalition of political enemies, Diem's fledgling regime almost falls. He is saved by the actions of U.S. Air Force colonel Edwin Landsdale, who is also a CIA operative.

October 26, 1955   Diem, after defeating Bao Dai in a rigged election, declares himself to be the President of the Republic of South Vietnam. His government is instantly recognized by the United States.

July 20, 1956   A deadline for holding reunification elections in accordance with the Geneva Accords passes. America supports Diem's refusal to hold elections.

May 8, 1957   Diem makes a triumphant visit to the United States. Eisenhower praises him lavishly and reaffirms American support for his government.

October 1957   Small-scale civil war begins in South Vietnam between Diem's forces and cadres of Vietminh who have remained in South Vietnam after the partition of Vietnam into two parts at the 17th parallel by the Geneva Accords.

April 4, 1959   Eisenhower delivers a speech in which he links American vital interests to the survival of a non–Communist state in South Vietnam.

November 8, 1960   John F. Kennedy defeats Richard Nixon in a close election for the American presidency.

December 20, 1960   The National Liberation Front is formed. It is the Vietminh reborn. The Communist-controlled NLF takes charge of the growing insurgency against the Diem regime. Diem dubs the NLF the "Vietcong," meaning Vietnamese who are Communists.

January 6, 1961   Soviet Premier Khrushchev announces support for all "wars of national liberation" around the world. His speech influences the incoming Kennedy administration's decision to support counterinsurgency in Vietnam.

April 1961   The Kennedy administration confronts a crisis in Laos. Kennedy considers military intervention, then decides to seek a political solution.

May 1961   Kennedy approves sending U.S. Special Forces to South Vietnam. He also authorizes clandestine warfare against North Vietnam and a secret war in Laos.

June 1961   Kennedy and Khrushchev, meeting in Vienna, agree to support a neutral and independent Laos. Kennedy rejects neutrality for Vietnam.

November 1961   The *New York Times* reports that some 3,200 U.S. advisers are operating in battle areas and are authorized to fire back if fired upon.

January 1962   The Air Force launches Operation RANCH HAND, the aerial spraying of defoliating herbicides to deny cover to the Vietcong and to destroy their crops.

February 8, 1962   MACV established in Saigon; its first commander is General Paul D. Harkins.

December 1962   There are now about 9,000 advisory and support personnel in South Vietnam; 109 Americans have been killed or wounded in 1962.

January 2, 1963   At Ap Bac in the Mekong River delta, the ARVN 7th Division, equipped with American weapons and accompanied by U.S. advisers, cannot defeat a lightly armed Vietcong battalion of 300 soldiers. The battle demonstrates that government troops cannot match the tactics or fighting spirit of the insurgents.

May 8, 1963   In Hue, 20,000 Buddhists celebrating the birthday of Gautama Siddhartha Buddha are fired on by government forces. This action begins a series of events that will bring the downfall of the Diem regime.

June 11, 1963   Thich Quang Duc, an elderly monk, immolates himself at a busy Saigon intersection to protest Diem's suppression of the Buddhists.

August 1963   Martin Luther King plans the march on Washington.

August 21, 1963   Military forces loyal to Diem and his brother Nhu attack Buddhist temples. President Kennedy denounces these actions. Meanwhile, a coup to overthrow Diem is being planned by dissident ARVN generals.

September 2, 1963   President Kennedy strongly reaffirms American commitment to Vietnam. He also criticizes Diem's attacks on the Buddhists and calls for reform.

November 1, 1963   A coup, led by General Tran Van Don and General Duong Van Minh, with foreknowledge and encouragement of American officials, leads to the murder of President Diem and his brother and the overthrow of his regime. A military directorate, led by General Minh, succeeds Diem.

November 22, 1963   President Kennedy is assassinated in Dallas, Texas, and Lyndon B. Johnson becomes President of the United States.

November 24, 1963   President Johnson affirms American support for the South Vietnamese government.

December 31, 1963   There are about 16,500 American soldiers in South Vietnam at the year's end; 489 have been killed or wounded during 1963.

January 2, 1964   President Johnson approves covert military operations against North Vietnam to be carried out by South Vietnamese and Asian mercenaries. Called OPLAN 34-A, they include espionage, sabotage, psychological warfare, and intelligence gathering.

January 30, 1964   Minh's government is overthrown in a bloodless coup by General Nguyen Khanh.

March 8–12, 1964   Secretary of Defense Robert McNamara visits South Vietnam. He affirms that America will remain in South Vietnam for as long as it takes to win the war.

April 1964   North Vietnam decides to infiltrate units of the NVA into South Vietnam.

June 20, 1964   General Harkins is succeeded by General William C. Westmoreland as COMUSMACV. Three days later, Henry Cabot Lodge resigns as ambassador to the GVN, and is replaced by General Maxwell Taylor.

July 1964   Both sides are engaged in covert warfare in violation of the 1964 Geneva Accords. North Vietnam is using the Ho Chi Minh Trail to infiltrate NVA troops into the south and to supply the Vietcong. America implements OPLAN 34-A operations. One OPLAN 34-A operation uses U.S. destroyers to conduct surveillance operations off of the North Vietnamese coast. These operations are called DESOTO Missions.

August 2, 1964   North Vietnamese patrol boats attack the USS *Maddox*, which is on a DESOTO mission in waters near the North Vietnamese coast.

August 3, 1964   South Vietnamese PT boats carry out OPLAN 34-A raids, attacking North Vietnamese radar installations in the same area.

August 4–5, 1964   Both USS *Maddox* and another destroyer, the USS *Turner Joy*, which had joined the *Maddox*, report that they are under attack at sea. Carrier-based U.S. naval aircraft fly reprisal raids, ordered by President Johnson, against North Vietnamese targets.

August 7, 1964   At Johnson's request, Congress enacts the Gulf of Tonkin Resolution granting the President the power "to take all necessary measures to repel any armed attack against the forces of the United States and to prevent further aggression ... including the use of armed force...." Johnson will later use this resolution as a postdated declaration of war.

October 1964   General Khanh resigns and is replaced by a civilian, Tran Van Huong.

December 31, 1964   About 23,000 Americans are now serving in South Vietnam. There is now a full-scale undeclared war raging in South Vietnam, and there is also fighting in Laos and Cambodia. There have been 1,278 Americans casualties in 1964.

January 4, 1965   In his State of the Union address, President Johnson reaffirms the American commitment to South Vietnam. He states that American security is tied to peace in Southeast Asia.

January 27–28, 1965   Tran Van Huong is ousted and General Khanh returns to power.

February 7, 1965   The Vietcong attack a U.S. helicopter base and other installations near Pleiku in the Central Highlands. Eight Americans are killed and 126 wounded. Johnson orders retaliatory air strikes on targets in North Vietnam.

February 3, 1965 Johnson orders a sustained bombing campaign against North Vietnam that has long been planned by his advisers. Called ROLLING THUNDER, it will continue, with occasional pauses, until October 31, 1968. The American air war against North Vietnam begins on March 2.

February 25, 1965 General Khanh is forced out by Air Martial Nguyen Cao Ky.

March 8, 1965 The first U.S. combat troops arrive in Vietnam.

April 6, 1965 President Johnson authorizes U.S. forces to take the offensive in order to support ARVN forces.

June 19, 1965 Air Martial Ky becomes premier of the eighth South Vietnamese government since Diem was overthrown.

June 28–30, 1965 U.S. forces undertake the first major American offensive against the Vietcong in War Zone D, twenty miles northeast of Saigon.

July 21–28, 1965 President Johnson makes a series of decisions that amount to committing the United States to a major war in Vietnam. Among the decisions that he makes: draft calls will be raised to 35,000 per month, 50,000 additional troops will be sent to Vietnam with additional increases as the situation demands, and the air war against North Vietnam is extended. Johnson also makes it clear that he wants these decisions implemented in low-key fashion so as to not excite or alarm either the Congress or the American people.

August 7, 1965 The Chinese government warns the United States that it will send men to fight in Vietnam if necessary.

October 23–November 20, 1965 In the largest battle of the war to date, the U.S. 1st Air Cavalry defeats NVA forces in the Drang Valley, in a remote corner of Pleiku province.

December 31, 1965 The year 1965 is a pivotal year of the war. America begins a sustained air war against North Vietnam. It also commits large numbers of forces to ground combat operations in South Vietnam. At year's end, there are 184,000 U.S. troops in South Vietnam. U.S. casualties for the year are 1,369 KIA and 5,300 WIA. 1965 is "Year One" of the American war in Vietnam.

March 9, 1966 The U.S. Department of State issues a White Paper claiming that American intervention in Vietnam is legal under the U.N. Charter, and the U.S. Constitution.

June 9, 1966 U.S. aircraft strike North Vietnamese petroleum storage facilities near Haiphong and Hanoi.

October 19–November 26, 1966 U.S. forces are involved in one of the biggest operations of the war in Tay Ninh province near the Cambodian border, fifty miles northwest of Saigon.

December 31, 1966 The Vietnamese War has become the dominant event in world affairs. During the year the United States has increased its forces in Vietnam from 184,000 to 385,000. The air war against North Vietnam has been expanded significantly, and 5,008 Americans have been killed and 30,093 wounded during the year.

January 8–26, 1967   American troops are involved in the largest offensive of the war. About 16,000 American troops participate in Operation CEDAR FALLS to disrupt Vietcong operations in the Iron Triangle region northeast of Saigon.

February 22–April 1, 1967   The largest allied operation of the war takes place, Operation JUNCTION CITY, involving thirty-four U.S. battalions. Its goal is to smash the V.C. stronghold in War Zone C near the Cambodian border and ease pressure on Saigon.

March 10–11, 1967   U.S. aircraft bomb the Thainguyen steel works near Hanoi; they are the first bombing raids on a major industrial target.

May 14–16, 1967   A U.S. newspaper reports that Chinese Premier Zhou En-lai has threatened to send Chinese troops into North Vietnam if the United States invades that country.

May 19–24, 1967   Secretary McNamara sends a memo to President Johnson arguing against widening the war and proposing curtailing the air war against North Vietnam. Responding to McNamara's dovish memo, the Joint Chiefs of Staff call for expanding the air war against North Vietnam and sending 2000,000 additional troops to South Vietnam.

June 1967   Tensions in the Middle East erupt into the Six-Day War.

July 7–12, 1967   A compromise is worked out between Johnson's dovish and hawkish advisers. McNamara recommends a troop increase of 55,000. The president accepts it.

July 1967   Martin Luther King begins his public criticism of the war.

July 30, 1967   A Gallup poll shows that 52 percent of Americans disapprove of Johnson's Vietnam War policy; 56 percent believe that the U.S. is in a stalemated war.

September 3, 1967   Lieutenant General Nguyen Van Thieu is elected President of South Vietnam and Air Martial Nguyen Cao Ky is elected Vice President.

October 16–21, 1967   Antiwar activists hold antidraft demonstration throughout the United States. The largest occurs at the Army induction center in Oakland, California.

October 21–23, 1967   Fifty thousand demonstrate against the Vietnam War in Washington, D.C.

October 25–30, 1967   The air war against North Vietnam intensifies. Sustained attacks are carried out on targets near Haiphong and Hanoi.

November 2, 1967   President Johnson meets privately with a group of distinguished policymakers. Dubbed the "wise men," they generally support his war policy.

November 3–22, 1967   One of the bloodiest and fiercest battles of the war between American and North Vietnamese troops occurs at Dak To in the Central Highlands.

November 22, 1967   President Johnson brings General Westmoreland home to rally support for the war. Westmoreland tells his audiences that the United States is winning the war.

November 30, 1967   Senator Eugene McCarthy announces that he will challenge Johnson for the Democratic presidential nomination in 1968. He will run on a platform calling for a negotiated settlement of the Vietnam War.

December 31, 1967   At year's end there are about 500,000 U.S. troops in South Vietnam. For the year, the war cost taxpayers about $21 billion. Casualties 9,353 KIA and 99,742 WIA.

January 20–April 14, 1968   One of the most famous battles of the war takes place at Khe Sanh, an American marine base located just south of the DMZ. It is feared that Khe Sanh will become an American Dien Bien Phu. But U.S. airpower eventually breaks the siege, and the Communists are forced to withdraw.

January 30–February 10, 1968   On the first day of the Tet truce, Vietcong forces, supported by NVA troopers, launch the largest offensive of the war. Simultaneous attacks are launched in South Vietnam's largest cities and many provincial capitals. The offensive is crushed by American and GVN forces. Tet is a decisive military victory for the allies, but it turns out to be a psychological and political disaster for them.

February 28, 1968   General Earle Wheeler, chairman of the Joint Chiefs, tells Johnson that General Westmoreland needs an additional 206,000 troops. A crucial point in the war has been reached. If Johnson does not send the troops, he will be conceding that the United States cannot win a military victory. But if he sends the troops, it will require a reserve call-up, and significantly raise the costs and casualties of the war. Johnson delays a decision and asks his new secretary of defense, Clark Clifford, to conduct a through reappraisal of U.S. Vietnam policy.

March 12, 1968   Senator Eugene McCarthy, in the New Hampshire primary, makes a strong showing in a hawkish state. Four days later, Senator Robert Kennedy announces that he too will seek the Democratic nomination and run on an antiwar platform.

March 16, 1968   In what will become the most notorious atrocity committed by American soldiers during the Vietnam War, a platoon of troopers slaughter hundreds of unarmed villagers in the hamlet of My Lai.

March 25–26, 1968   Johnson convenes the "wise men." Most advise against any more troop increases and recommend that the United States seek a negotiated peace in Vietnam.

March 31, 1968   Johnson announces that there will be a unilateral halt to all U.S. bombing north of the 20th parallel and that he will seek to get negotiations started with North Vietnam. He also stuns the nation with an announcement that he will not seek re-election.

April 4, 1968   Civil rights leader King is assassinated in Memphis, Tennessee.

April 22, 1968   Clifford announces that the GVN is going to take responsibility for more and more of the fighting. This is the first announcement of a policy that under Richard Nixon will come to be called Vietnamization.

May 3, 1968   America and North Vietnam agree to begin formal negotiations in Paris on May 10.

June 5, 1968   Robert Kennedy, Democratic presidential aspirant, is assassinated in Los Angeles.

June 10, 1968   General Creighton Abrams succeeds General Westmoreland as COMUSMACV.

August 5–8, 1968   The Republican National Convention, meeting in Miami, Florida, nominates Richard M. Nixon for president. The Republican platform calls for an honorable negotiated peace in Vietnam and for the progressive "de–Americanization" of the war.

August 26–29, 1968   The Democratic National Convention meets in Chicago. Democrats adopt a platform endorsing the administration's policy and nominate Vice President Hubert H. Humphrey for president. On the evening of August 28, there is a full-scale riot in the streets between the Chicago police and antiwar radicals.

October 31, 1968   In a televised address to the nation, President Johnson announces a complete halt to the bombing of North Vietnam.

November 5, 1968   Richard Nixon is elected President of the United States.

December 31, 1968   The major turning point of the American Vietnam War has occurred in 1968. After Tet, Johnson has to abandon his policy of measured escalation in search of military victory and replace it with an early version of Vietnamization looking toward a negotiated settlement. Richard Nixon has been elected president and the general sense at this time is that he has a plan for bringing the war to an early end. The year 1968 is the most intense of the American war: 14,314 KIA and 150,000 WIA and a cost of about $30 billion.

January 25, 1969   The first plenary session of the four-way Paris peace talks among the Americans, the North Vietnamese, the South Vietnamese, and the National Liberation Front occurs.

March 18, 1969   Nixon orders the secret bombing of Communist base camps and supply depots in Cambodia to commence.

May 10–20, 1969   The battle for Hamburger Hill takes place near the A Shau Valley. In ten days of intense fighting and heavy casualties, allied forces take the hill. The hill is abandoned soon thereafter.

June 8, 1969   President Nixon announces that 25,000 U.S. troops will be withdrawn by the end of August and that they will be replaced by South Vietnamese forces. The gradual U.S. phasing out of the war in Vietnam has begun.

June 10, 1969   The NLF announces the formation of a provisional revolutionary government (PRG) to rule in South Vietnam. It amounts to a formal challenge to the Thieu regime for the political control of South Vietnam.

August 4, 1969   Secret negotiations begin in Paris between special envoy Henry Kissinger and North Vietnam's Xuan Thuy.

August 17–26, 1969   During a major battle between U.S. and NVA forces in the Queson Valley about thirty miles south of Danang, the first combat refusal by American troops occurs.

September 23, 1969   Eight antiwar leaders go on trial in Chicago for their part in organizing the antiwar demonstrations occurring in Chicago at the time of the Democratic convention, August 26–29, 1968.

October 15, 1969   The largest antiwar demonstrations in American history take place at many sites across the country.

November 3, 1969   President Nixon makes his most successful speech in defense of his Vietnam War policies. Congress and public opinion overwhelmingly support Vietnamization as he successfully blunts the efforts of the antiwar movement.

November 15, 1969   More than 250,000 people come to Washington, D.C., to protest the Vietnam War. It is the largest single antiwar demonstration to date.

December 31, 1969   At year's end, there are 479,000 U.S. troops in South Vietnam. GVN forces have increased and now number over 900,000. Fighting has continued during the year on a large scale. American KIAs total 9,914 for the year.

February 19–20, 1970   All the defendants in the Chicago trial are convicted of conspiracy to incite rioting and receive maximum sentences of five years in jail and $5,000 fines. All will be acquitted on appeal.

March 18, 1970   In a bloodless coup in Cambodia, pro–Western General Lon Nol ousts Prince Norodom Sihanouk as head of state.

April 11, 1970   Polls show that only 48 percent of Americans support Vietnamization, down from 70 percent in November 1969.

April 20, 1970   President Nixon promises to withdraw 150,000 more troops over the next year if Vietnamization continues to make progress.

May 1, 1970   American forces numbering about 30,000 join with more than 45,000 South Vietnamese troops to invade the Fishhook region of Cambodia. The Cambodian "incursion" is the last major offensive of the Indochina war involving U.S. ground combat forces.

May 4, 1970   National Guard soldiers fire into a group of demonstrators on the campus of Kent State University, killing four and wounding eleven.

May 6, 1970   More than a hundred colleges and universities across the nation shut down because of student protests and riots in response to the Cambodian invasion and the killings at Kent State.

May 8–20, 1970   In New York City, construction workers attack antiwar demonstrators on Wall Street. An estimated 80,000 young people, mostly college students, demonstrate peacefully in the nation's capital. They protest the "Kent State Massacre" and call for the immediate withdrawal of all U.S. troops from Indochina. In New York City, more than 100,000 workers march in support of Nixon's war policies.

June 24, 1970   The Senate, by a vote of eighty-one to ten, repeals the Gulf of Tonkin Resolution. President Nixon states that the legal basis for the American war in Vietnam is not the Gulf of Tonkin Resolution, but the constitutional authority of the president as commander in chief to protect the lives of U.S. military forces in Vietnam.

August 19, 1970   America signs a pact with Cambodia to provide Lon Nol's government with military aid.

November 9, 1970   The Supreme Court refuses to hear a case brought by the Commonwealth of Massachusetts challenging the constitutionality of the Vietnam War.

November 11, 1970   On this day, for the first time in years, no American soldier is killed in Vietnam.

December 31, 1970   The U.S. war in Vietnam is winding down. At year's end there are about 335,000 U.S. troops in South Vietnam. U.S. KIAs for the year number 4,221. However, the war has spread to Cambodia and no progress is reported at the Paris peace talks.

January 1, 1971   Congress forbids the use of American ground troops in either Laos or Cambodia.

March 6–24, 1971   ARVN forces invade Laos to interdict enemy supply routes down the Ho Chi Minh Trail complex. Communist counterattacks drive the invaders out of Laos and inflict heavy casualties. It is a major defeat for the GVN.

April 19–23, 1971   Vietnam Veterans Against the War stage a demonstration in Washington, D.C. It ends with veterans throwing combat ribbons and medals at the Capitol steps.

April 20, 1971   The Pentagon reports that Fragging incidents are increasing. There were ninety-six incidents in 1969 and 209 in 1970.

June 13, 1971   The *New York Times* begins publication of the leaked portion of the Pentagon analysis of the U.S. involvement in Vietnam through 1967. This forty-seven-volume document became known as the "Pentagon Papers."

July 1, 1971   The Twenty-sixth Amendment to the Constitution, granting the vote to eighteen to twenty-one year olds, is ratified.

July 15, 1971   In a surprise announcement, President Nixon tells the American people that he will be visiting China before May 1972.

December 31, 1971   The American war in Vietnam is ending; 156,800 U.S. troops remain. There have been 1,380 KIAs in 1971. As the Americans withdraw, the Communists intensify their attacks in Laos, Cambodia, and parts of South Vietnam. U.S. morale continues to deteriorate. Vietnamization is not working and the Paris talks remained stalled.

February 21–27, 1972   President Nixon makes his historic visit to China. The North Vietnamese fear that China and the United States will make a deal behind their backs (i.e., the U.S. abandoning Taiwan in exchange for peace in Vietnam).

March 30–April 8, 1972   A major NVA offensive begins as Communist forces attack South Vietnamese towns and bases just south of the DMZ. The Communists open a second front with a drive into Binh Long province about seventy miles north of Saigon. Communist forces open a third front with drives into the Central Highlands. The fighting in South Vietnam between GVN and Communist forces is the most intense of the entire war.

April 10, 1972   America responds with air attacks. B-52s strike targets in North Vietnam for the first time since November 1967. B-52s and tactical bombers also strike targets in South Vietnam. America is waging an air war over all of Vietnam.

May 8, 1972   Nixon announces that he has ordered the mining of all North Vietnamese ports.

May 20, 1972   The summit conference between President Nixon and Leonid Brezhnev takes place on schedule in Moscow. Both sides are unwilling to risk détente over the Vietnam War. Nixon's Soviet visit is the first ever by a U.S. president.

June 17, 1972   Five men linked to Nixon's re-election campaign are arrested in the Democratic Party headquarters.

June 28, 1972   President Nixon announces that no more draftees will be sent to Vietnam unless they volunteer.

August 11, 1972   The last U.S. combat unit is withdrawn from South Vietnam. There are now 44,000 American servicemen in South Vietnam.

August 16, 1972   U.S. aircraft fly a record 370 sorties against North Vietnam. Most American aircraft fly from carriers in the Gulf of Tonkin or from bases in Thailand.

September 15, 1972   ARVN forces recapture Quang Tri City. The fighting destroys most of the city, which formerly had a population of 300,000. Most of these people now reside in squalid refugee camps.

October 8–11, 1972   Lengthy secret meetings in Paris between Henry Kissinger and Le Duc Tho produce a tentative settlement of the war. The substance of the agreement is a cease-fire, to be followed by both sides working out a political settlement.

October 22, 1972   President Thieu rejects the proposed settlement.

November 7, 1972   Richard Nixon is re-elected president by a landslide margin. He promises that he will achieve "peace with honor" in Vietnam.

November 11, 1972   The U.S. Army turns over its giant headquarters base at Long Binh to the South Vietnamese, symbolizing the end of the direct American participation in the war after more than seven years.

December 14, 1972   The U.S. breaks off the peace talks with the North Vietnamese that have been going on since Nixon's re-election.

December 18–29, 1972   President Nixon announces the resumption of the bombing and mining of North Vietnam. The most concentrated air offensive of the war begins, aimed mostly at targets in the vicinity of Hanoi and Haiphong.

December 28, 1972   Hanoi announces that it is willing to resume negotiations if the United States will stop bombing above the 20th parallel. The bombing ends on December 29.

December 31, 1972   At year's end there are about 24,000 U.S. troops remaining in South Vietnam. 312 Americans have been killed in action in 1972.

January 8–18, 1973   Henry Kissinger and Le Duc Tho resume negotiations in Paris, and they reach an agreement that is similar to the one that had been rejected by General Thieu.

January 19–26, 1973   There is heavy fighting in South Vietnam between GVN and Communist forces as both sides try to gain as much territory as they can before the ceasefire.

January 21, 1973   Under great pressure form President Nixon, President Thieu reluctantly agrees to the Paris Peace Accords.

January 23, 1973   Nixon announces that the Paris Peace Accords will go into effect at 7:00 P.M. EST. He says that "peace with honor" has been achieved.

January 27, 1973   The draft ends. For the first time since 1949, America has no conscription.

February 12–27, 1973   American POWs begin to come home.

February 21, 1973   A cease-fire formally ends the twenty-year war in Laos.

March 29, 1973   The last U.S. troops leave South Vietnam. Only a Defense Attaché Office (DAO) contingent and Marine embassy guards remain. About 8,500 U.S. civilian officials stay on.

June 4–August 15, 1973   The Senate blocks all funds for any U.S. military activities in Indochina. The House concurs. The Nixon administration works out a compromise agreement with the Congress to permit continued U.S. bombing in Cambodia until August 15. The cessation marks the end of twelve years of American military action in Indochina.

September 12–15, 1973   Chile's Salvadore Allende is overthrown in an American-backed coup.

October 1973   Middle East again erupts in war. Oil embargo begins because of United States support for Israel.

October 10, 1973   Gerald Ford replaces Spiro Agnew as Nixon's Vice President.

November 7, 1973   Congress enacts the War Powers Act over President Nixon's veto. It requires the president to report to Congress within forty-eight hours after committing American forces to combat on foreign soil. It also limits to sixty days the time that the president can commit soldiers to foreign combat without congressional approval.

December 31, 1973   The war in Vietnam continues without U.S. involvement. Most of the provisions of the Paris Peace Accords are not observed by either side. During the year, there have been 13,788 RVNAF KIAs and 45,050 Communist KIAs.

August 5, 1974 Congress makes sharp cuts in the amount of military aid going to the South Vietnamese government.

August 9, 1974 Nixon resigns the presidency under pressure from Watergate scandal; succeeded by Ford.

December 31, 1974 During 1974, 80,000 people, both civilians and soldiers, have been killed in the war. This is the highest total for any year since the war began in 1945.

January 6, 1975 NVA forces overrun Phuoc Long Province. When the Americans do not react, Hanoi concludes that America will not reintroduce its military forces to save the GVN.

January 7, 1975 Phuoc Long Province falls.

January 7–24, 1975 NVA pressure on Tay Ninh Province; refugee exodus follows. NVA convoy traffic up in MR II. Airborne and Marines begin shift to reserve status in MR I.

January 20, 1975 Sappers destroy Pleiku ammo dump.

January 29, 1975 GVN disarms Hoa Hao Militia in MR IV.

February 5, 1975 Lieutenant General Toan becomes MR III commander.

February 14–28, 1975 RVNAF pre-emptive operations against NVA buildups in MRs I, II and III.

March 1–7, 1975 Communist spring-summer campaign opens in MR I and MR II.

March 4–5, 1975 Interdiction of QL-19 east of Pleiku.

March 6, 1975 Interdiction of QL-14 south of Pleiku.

March 7, 1975 Overrun of Thanh Man District Town (Phu Bon).

March 9, 1975 Overrun of Duc Lap District Town (Quang Duc); assault on Ban Me Thuot begins.

March 10, 1975 Overrun of Hau Duc and Tien Phuoc Districts (Quang Tin Province).

March 12, 1975 Contact lost with Ban Me Thuot City.

March 13, 1975 Overrun of Tri Tam District Town (Binh Duong).

March 15, 1975 Evacuation of Northern Highlands begins.

March 16, 1975 Evacuation of Son Ha and Tra Bong districts (Quang Ngai Province).

March 17, 1975 Overrun of Phuoc An District (Darlac Province). Order given to evacuate Pleiku and Kontum.

March 19, 1975 Overrun of Cheo Reo City (Phu Bon). Airborne redeployed from MR I to Saigon. Quang Tri City occupied by NVA.

March 20, 1975 Evacuation of Quang Tri City. Overrun of Hoai Duc District Town (Binh Tuy Province).

March 22, 1975   Evacuation of Quang Duc Province. Overrun of Khanh Duong District (Khanh Hoa Province).

March 23, 1975   Overrun of An Tuc District Town (Binh Dinh Province) and Dinh Quan District Town (Long Khanh Province).

March 24, 1975   Quang Ngai Province abandoned. Contact lost with Hue City. Overrun of Tam Ky City. Decision made to abandon the northern part of MR I entirely.

March 25, 1975   Evacuation of Quang Ngai Province.

March 27, 1975   Overrun of Chu Lai airfield. Evacuation of Tam Quan District (Binh Dinh Province).

March 28, 1975   Evacuation of Lam Dong Province.

March 30, 1975   Contact lost with Danang City. The city falls, completing the collapse of MR I.

March 31, 1975   Overrun of Phu Cat air base.

April 1, 1975   Second Corps headquarters in Nha Trang evacuated. Contact lost with Qui Nhon and Tuy Hoa cities. Central Highlands fall to Communist control.

April 2, 1975   Second Corps moves from Nha Trang.

April 3, 1975   Contact lost with Nha Trang and Dalat cities.

April 4, 1975   U.S. Air Force C5-A "Babylift" aircraft crashes near Saigon. Contact lost with Phan Rang air base, and Cam Ranh City abandoned.

April 9, 1975   Xuan Loc comes under attack.

April 16, 1975   Phan Rang falls to NVA forces.

April 18, 1975   Phan Thiet City, capital of Binh Thuan Province, falls. Conquest of MR II complete. Binh Thuan falls.

April 21, 1975   President Thieu resigns and is succeeded by Vice President Tran Van Huong.

April 22, 1975   Xuan Loc falls after a ferocious defense which has resulted in over 5,000 NVA KIA.

April 23, 1975   President Gerald Ford gives a speech at Tulane University in which he states that the war in Vietnam "is finished as far as America is concerned."

April 27, 1975   Vice President Huong succeeded by Dong Van "Big" Minh. Ba Ria falls.

April 28, 1975   Tan Son Nhut bombed by former VNAF pilots. At Bien Hoa, III Corps staff ceases operations.

April 29, 1975   Cu Chi overrun. Bien Hoa lost. Vung Tau occupied. Major rocket attack on Tan Son Nhut airfield. All remaining U.S. personnel evacuated in "Operation Frequent Wind."

April 30, 1975 President Minh surrenders unconditionally and orders all resistance to cease. Communists quickly occupy and control Saigon. No further combat.

July 11, 1995 Full diplomatic relations are established between the United States and Vietnam.

Glossary

AID	Agency for International Development (also USAID).
AK-47	A Russian and Chinese assault rifle used extensively by the Vietcong and the North Vietnamese Army.
Annam	Central section of Vietnam, a French protectorate from 1883 to 1954.
APC	Armored personnel carrier.
ARVN	Army of the Republic of Vietnam. The regular South Vietnamese national armed forces.
A Teams	Twelve-man Special Forces units.
Attrition warfare	A strategy with the objective of destroying personnel and material faster than they can be replenished until the enemy's ability to wage war is exhausted.
Can Lao	The Can Lao Nhan Vi Cach Mang Dang, or Personalist Labor Revolutionary Party. Ngo Dinh Nhu's secret political party and police force.
Cao Dai	A religious sect formed in 1925 in southern Vietnam.
CAP	Combined action program.
Charlie	GI slang for the Vietcong, a short version of Victor Charlie, from the U.S. military phonetic alphabet for V.C.
Chieu Hoi	Literally "Open Arms," a program set up to encourage Vietcong and NVA soldiers to defect to the South Vietnamese side.

Chinook   CH-47 transport helicopter.

CIA   Central Intelligence Agency.

CIDG   Civilian irregular defense groups, teams devised by CIA operatives that combined defense functions with social and economic development programs designed to win the allegiance of the Montagnards.

CINCPAC   Commander in chief, United States Pacific Command.

Cobra   Bell AH-1G fast attack helicopter, armed with machine guns, grenade launchers, and rockets.

Cochin China   The southern section of Vietnam, a French colony from 1863 to 1954.

COMUSMACV   Commander, United States Military Assistance Command, Vietnam.

CONUS   Military acronym for the continental United States.

CORDS   Civil operations and revolutionary development support.

Corps   Two divisions assigned to defend a military region.

COSVN   Central Office, South Vietnam, the headquarters controlling all Vietcong political and military operations in southern Vietnam.

Counterinsurgency The guiding doctrine of U.S. military forces in Vietnam during early 1960s; its fundamental purpose was to win the allegiance of the people, not destroy the enemy's armed forces. Inspiration for the phrase "winning hearts and minds."

CTZ   Corps tactical zone.

DAO   Defense Attaché Office, an agency that was part of the U.S. mission sent to South Vietnam following the January 1973 Paris Peace Accords that ended the American war; was a replacement for MACV, DAO administered the U.S. military assistance program to the GVN, 1973–1975.

DEROS   Date eligible for return from overseas. The date a soldier's tour of duty in Vietnam ended, usually one year after arriving in the country.

Dien Bien Phu   Site in northwestern Vietnam next to the Laotian border where the French suffered a major defeat in 1954 that led to the end of their power in Vietnam.

DMZ	Demilitarized zone. An area ten kilometers wide that separated North Vietnam and South Vietnam.
DOD	Department of Defense.
DRV	Democratic Republic of Vietnam (North Vietnam), created by Ho Chi Minh, September 2, 1945.
Eagle Pull	Code name of the U.S. evacuation of Phnom Penh in April 1975.
FAC	Forward air controller, a forward spotter who coordinated air strikes, usually airborne.
FMFPAC	Fleet Marine Force, Pacific Command.
Fragging	The murder of a commissioned officer or noncommissioned officer by one of his own enlisted men of lower rank, usually with a fragmentation grenade.
Free-fire zones	Territory considered completely under enemy control. South Vietnamese officials authorized the use of unlimited firepower in such zones.
Frequent Wind	Code name of the U.S. evacuation of Saigon in April 1975.
FSB	Fire support base, a protected forward artillery base.
Green Berets	Famed nickname of soldiers serving in the U.S. Army Special Forces who are trained for counterinsurgency operations. The name is derived form the green berets worn by these elite forces.
Grunt	The most frequent nickname given troops in the U.S. Army and Marine ground combat forces.
GVN	The Government of South Vietnam.
HES	Hamlet evaluation system. A monthly statistical report that provided CORD with information on rural security.
Hoa Hao	A religious sect formed in 1939 in southern Vietnam by Huynh Phu So.
Huey	Nickname given the UH-1 series helicopter.
ICC	International Control Commission, created by the Geneva Accords (1954) to supervise the implementation of the agreements.

ICCS International Commission of Control and Supervision. Agency responsible for administering the January 1973 Paris Peace Accords.

JCS Joint Chiefs of Staff.

JGS Joint General Staff, the South Vietnamese equivalent of the U.S. Joint Chiefs.

JMC Joint Military Commission, consisting of members from North Vietnam, South Vietnam, the Provisional Revolutionary Government (Vietcong), and the United States, responsible for implementing the military provisions of the Paris Peace Accords.

JMT Joint Military Team, consisting of members from North Vietnam, South Vietnam, the Provisional Revolutionary Government (Vietcong), and the United States, responsible for accounting for all prisoners of war and MIAs.

Kampuchea The name given Cambodia in 1975 by the victorious Khmer Rouge.

Khmer Rouge Members of the Pracheachon, a left-wing revolutionary movement that came to power in Cambodia in April 1975.

KIA Killed in action.

Lao Dong The Vietnamese Workers' Party, the North Vietnamese Communist party, founded in 1951. The ruling party in North Vietnam until 1975; thereafter, it ruled the entire country of the reunited Vietnam.

LINEBACKER 1 Code name for U.S. bombing of North Vietnam, resumed in April 1972 in response to the Nguyen Hue offensive.

LINEBACKER II Code name for the U.S. bombing of North Vietnam during December 1972, the so-called Christmas bombing.

LST Landing ship tank, a large, shallow-draft cargo-hauling and landing craft.

LZ Landing zone, for helicopters.

MAAG Military Assistance Advisory Group, the forerunner of MACV, 1955 to 1964.

MACV Military Assistance Command, Vietnam, formed in 1962, lasted until 1973.

Main force	Regular army forces of the North Vietnamese and Vietcong.
MAP	Military assistance program.
MARS	Military affiliate radio station.
Medevac	Helicopters with the mission of transporting wounded soldiers quickly from the battlefield to forward hospitals.
MENU	Code name for the secret B-52 bombing missions in Cambodia.
MIA	Missing in action.
Montagnards	"Mountain dwellers," the indigenous tribal populations of Vietnam, who generally inhabited hilly and mountainous terrain.
MR	Military region, formerly a CTZ, a corps tactical zone.
Napalm	A jellied incendiary weapon used by the French and the Americans during the Indochina wars. It could be dropped from aircraft in canisters or fired from flamethrowers. Used as both a defoliant and antipersonnel weapon.
NCO	Noncommissioned officer.
Neutralize	Word used by Pheonix-Phung Hoang operatives to define putting the V.C. infrastructure out of action. Neutralize could mean killing, capturing, or forcing the infrastructure to go into the Chieu Hoa program.
NLF	National Liberation Front, formed December 20, 1960.
NSAM	National security action memorandum.
NSC	National Security Council.
NVA	North Vietnamese Army.
NVN	North Vietnam or North Vietnamese.
OB	Order of battle, a comprehensive arrangement and disposition of military units deployed in battle.
OCS	Officer candidate school.
OPLAN	Operation plan.

OSS	Office of Strategic Services, World War II intelligence organization, forerunner of the CIA.
PACAF	United States Pacific Air Force.
PACFLT	United States Pacific Fleet.
Pacification	South Vietnamese and U.S. programs designed to win the allegiance of the South Vietnamese people and eliminate the influence of the Vietcong.
Pathet Lao	Laotian Communist insurgents who came to power in 1974–1975.
PAVN	People's Army of Vietnam. The North Vietnamese army.
Pentagon Papers	Secret Department of Defense studies of U.S. involvement in Vietnam, 1945–1967. The papers were stolen by Daniel Ellsberg and Anthony Russo in 1971 and given to the *New York Times*, which published them that same year.
PF	Popular forces, South Vietnamese militia.
PHOENIX	A joint U.S.-South Vietnamese program to detect and to neutralize the Vietcong infrastructure.
Phung Hoang	The South Vietnamese–run program to destroy the V.C. infrastructure; it paralleled the PHOENIX program.
PLA	People's Liberation Army of South Vietnam, the military wing of the Vietcong.
Politburo	The executive committee of the Lao Dong; members were responsible for making all government policies in North Vietnam.
POW	Prisoner of war.
PRG	People's Revolutionary Government/South Vietnam (Vietcong).
PRP	People's Revolutionary Party; founded in 1962, the Communist Party apparatus that controlled the National Liberation Front.
PSYOP	Psychological operations, a form of psychological warfare.
PTSD	Posttraumatic stress disorder.
Ranch Hand	Code name for the Air Force aerial defoliation program to deny ground cover and food crops to the Vietcong.

RDC	Revolutionary development cadres, teams of South Vietnamese pacification workers trained to carry out various missions.
RF	Regional forces.
ROTC	Reserve Officers Training Corps.
RVN	Republic of South Vietnam.
RVAF	Republic of Vietnam Armed Forces, all South Vietnamese military forces including the ARVN, regional forces, and popular forces.
SAC	Strategic Air Command.
SAM	Surface-to-air missile.
SAM-2	Medium-range Communist surface-to-air missile, effective up to 60,000 feet, speed about Mach 2.5.
SANE	Committee for a Sane Nuclear Policy, an organization opposed to the nuclear arms race; active in the late 1950s and early 1960s.
SDS	Students for a Democratic Society, the largest radical student organization in the country during the 1960s; led antiwar activities on many college campuses.
SEATO	Southeast Asia Treaty Organization.
17th parallel	Temporary dividing line separating northern and southern Vietnam, created by the Geneva Accords of 1954, pending unification elections scheduled for July 1956, which were never held. The accords provided for a demilitarized zone (DMZ) five kilometers in depth on each side of this line.
Sortie	An operational flight by one aircraft.
Special Forces	U.S. Army personnel trained to carry out counterinsurgency operations, often covert and unconventional. They also trained Montagnards and South Vietnamese special force units.
Strategic Hamlets	A South Vietnamese program begun in 1962 that concentrated rural populations into fortified villages to gain their allegiance and to both separate and protect them from Vietcong guerrillas.

SVN	South Vietnam.
Tet	The Vietnamese lunar New Year and Vietnam's most important holiday.
Third countries	U.S. allies that furnished military forces for the Vietnam War South Korea, Thailand, the Philippines, Australia, and New Zealand.
Tonkin	The northern section of Vietnam, a French protectorate from 1883 to 1954.
USAID	United States Agency for International Development.
V.C.	Vietcong, a derogatory contraction meaning a Vietnamese who is a Communist.
VCI	Vietcong infrastructure, the political leaders of the Vietcong, also responsible for logistic support of the military forces.
Vietminh	A coalition political party formed by Ho Chi Minh in 1941 dominated by Vietnamese Communist leaders; it came to power in Hanoi on September 2, 1945.
Vietnamization	The word was coined by Secretary of Defense Melvin Laird to describe Nixon's policy, inherited from Johnson, of withdrawing U.S. forces from Vietnam and transferring their responsibilities to the RVN forces.
VNAF	South Vietnamese Air Force.
VNN	South Vietnamese Navy.
WIA	Wounded in action.

Notes

Introduction

1. The literature on American presidents' use of military power is extensive. John S.D. Eisenhower, son of the D-Day commander and later commander in chief Dwight Eisenhower, has ably analyzed James K. Polk's foray into the disputed territory between the Nueces and Rio Grande Rivers (see *So Far from God*, New York, 1989); similarly, Eric Larrabee's *Commander-in-Chief* (New York, 1987) documents Franklin D. Roosevelt's enthusiastic exercise of military might throughout World War II; Abraham Lincoln's entire term was overshadowed by war strategy (see, for example, T. Harry Williams' *Lincoln and His Generals* [Baton Rouge, 1952]; as Thomas Bailey argues in his *Woodrow Wilson and the Great Betrayal* (New York, 1945), however, defeat can often arise from what looks to be military triumph when presidents fall victim to self-serving politics.

2. Contrasted with the shattered presidencies of Lyndon Johnson, Richard Nixon, and Gerald Ford, who were stained by Vietnam's carnage, is the success of Lincoln in developing and tenaciously pursuing a clear strategy which ultimately led to victory and emancipation (see James McPherson, *Battle Cry of Freedom*, New York, 1988, and Garry Wills, *Lincoln at Gettysburg*, New York, 1992).

3. James Flexner's *George Washington in the American Revolution* (New York, 1968) Marcus Cunliff's *Washington: Man and Monument* (New York, 1969) are two of the many studies that offer vivid portraits of George Washington's conduct of war and peace during the critical period from 1776 to 1797.

4. See Joseph Ellis' *Jefferson: America's Sphinx* (New York, 1996) and his Pulitzer Prize–winning *Founding Brothers* (New York, 2000), a book that reveals the factors that created cooperation — and arguments— among the heroes of the American Revolution. Jefferson outwitted — or outlived — rivals like Alexander Hamilton and Aaron Burr.

5. Larry Berman's recently published *No Peace, No Honor* (New York, 2001) and Christopher Hitchen's literary indictment *The Trial of Henry Kissinger* (New York, 2001), added to the earlier works by Berman (*Lyndon Johnson's War*, New

York, 1989), David Halberstam (*The Best and the Brightest*, New York, 1971), Nguyen Tien Hung (*The Palace Files*, New York, 1986), Seymour Hersh (*The Price of Power*, New York, 1983), and William Shawcross (*Sideshow*, New York, 1979), are unflattering glimpses of duplicity at the highest levels of our government during the Vietnam War.

Chapter 1

1. See Edward Lee and Toby Haynsworth's *White Christmas in April: The Collapse of South Vietnam* (New York, 1999) for a description of Smith's predicament as he coordinated America's last days in Vietnam.

2. Anthony Summers (*Richard Nixon: The Arrogance of Power*, New York, 2000), Anthony Lukas (*Nightmare*, Athens, Georgia, 1999), and Nguyen Tien Hung (*The Palace Files*, New York, 1986) provide three views of the political and economic climate that produced the abandonment of South Vietnam and crippled General Smith's efforts to bolster South Vietnam's defenses.

3. From 1994 to 2000, the authors conducted nearly 100 interviews with the last Americans to be evacuated from South Vietnam in 1975. Some of these interviewees are members of the Saigon Mission Association, an organization founded by the civilian and military personnel who witnessed at close range the conclusion of America's longest war.

4. Remarks by General Smith, April 30, 2000, Washington, D.C.; interview with Rosalie Redmond, Washington, D.C., May 27, 2000; Redmond, a civilian Air Force employee, was scheduled to evacuate Saigon on the C-5 aircraft but, at the last minute, chose to remain at her post, perhaps saving her own life.

5. Interview with James Piner, Salisbury, N.C., May 23, 1995; the ill-fated flight was extensively covered in the *New York Times*, April 7, 1975, and the *Washington Post* of that date, as it was in *Time* (April 16, 1975) and *Newsweek* (April 16, 1975).

6. Interview with Piner; interview with Redmond.

7. Interview with Linda Clark, Washington, D.C., April 29, 2000.

8. Smith's remarks, April 30, 2000; interview with Homer Smith, Washington, D.C., April 28, 2000.

Chapter 2

1. See David Garrow's *Bearing the Cross* (New York, 1986) and Adam Faircloth's *To Redeem the Soul of America* (New York, 1987).

2. The pressure exerted by King on Kennedy and, later, Lyndon Johnson helped spark surveillance by J. Edgar Hoover who was convinced that King's civil rights crusade was linked to Communism; see Garrow's *The F.B.I. and Martin Luther King* (New York, 1981).

3. While Johnson aided King's cause, when the minister parted ways with the President over the war in Southeast Asia, LBJ allowed Hoover to increase FBI

harassment of the civil rights leader; see the aforementioned *The F.B.I. and Martin Luther King*.

4. See Doris Kearns Goodwin's *Lyndon Johnson and the American Dream* (New York, 1976).

5. *New York Times*, April 6, 1975; *ibid*. April 7, 1975.

6. *Ibid*.

7. See Lewis Sorley's outstanding biography of Creighton Abrams, *A Better War* (New York, 1999) for a fresh assessment of Abrams in Vietnam.

8. Tet's effect on American public opinion has been thoroughly analyzed; suddenly, it seemed, support for the war began to evaporate — despite the Communist failure during the offensive; see Ronald Spector's *After Tet* (New York, 1993) and James Wirtz's *The Tet Offensive* (Ithaca, 1991).

9. Sorley, 10–11.

Chapter 3

1. In addition to Nixon's own memoirs, *RN* (New York, 1990), we suggest that his earlier *Six Crises* (New York, 1964) and Theodore White's *The Making of a President, 1960* (New York, 1961), *The Making of a President, 1968* (New York, 1969), *The Making of a President, 1972* (New York, 1973), be consulted as well as the sympathetic reassessment by Irwin Gellman (*The Contender*, New York, 1999).

2. Johnson's *The Vantage Point* (New York, 1971), former Defense Secretary Robert McNamara's troubling *In Retrospect* (New York, 1995), and Larry Berman's *Planning a Tragedy* (New York, 1982) document the quagmire into which Nixon stepped in 1969.

3. *Foreign Affairs* (January 1969), 26–42; Anthony Summers' *The Arrogance of Power* (New York, 2000), A. J. Langguth's *Our Vietnam* (New York, 2000), and Larry Berman's *No Peace, No Honor* (New York, 2001) build a compelling case against candidate Nixon and Kissinger in the 1968 campaign; Kissinger (*Years of Upheaval*, Boston, 1982, and *Years of Renewal*, New York, 1999) and Nixon in *RN* have a different recollection of their conduct in 1968 and later.

4. *Foreign Affairs*, 36; *Washington Post*, November 1967; *Washington Post*, January 25, 1968; *Foreign Affairs*, 38.

5. *Foreign Affairs*, 34; Sorley, 5–6.

6. *Foreign Affairs*, 31.

7. *Ibid*., 42.

8. *Ibid*., 37.

9. Sorley, 163.

Chapter 4

1. Sorley, 112–113, 115–116, and 281–82.

2. *Ibid*., 83, 116–20; A.J. Langguth, *Our Vietnam* (New York, 2000), 542–43, 545; Stanley Karnow, *Vietnam: A History* (New York, 1983), 591.

3. Langguth, 515–19.

4. *Ibid.*, 397; Karnow, 591–95.

5. Karnow, 601; Sorley, 139–41; an excellent examination of the battle is Samuel Zaffiri's *Hamburger Hill* (Novato, 1988).

6. Karnow, 601; Sorley, 139–41.

7. *Ibid.*, *Life*, June 27, 1969.

8. *New York Times*, June 25, 1969.

9. Sorley, 139–41.

10. *Ibid.*, 128; Karnow, 593, 596, and 629–31.

11. *Washington Post*, May 15, 1969; Henry Kissinger, *White House Years* (Boston, 1979), 270–74.

12. Karnow, 593; Langguth, 536–42; Kissinger, *White House Years*, 1480–1382.

13. Sorley, 179; Kissinger, *White House Years*, 1480–82.

14. *New York Times*, June 9, 1969; in *RN*, Nixon applauds the formal announcement of Vietnamization, while ignoring Thieu's sense of the commencement of America's abandonment of its commitment to South Vietnam — see *RN*, 642.

15. *Washington Post*, June 21, 1969; Kissinger, *White House Years*, 274.

16. *Foreign Affairs*, 610; Nixon, *Public Papers*, 169, 472; Kissinger, *White House Years*, 275.

17. Kissinger, *White House Years*, 276.

18. *Ibid.*; Nixon, *Public Papers*, 901–09; *Washington Post*, November 4, 1969.

19. Samuel Lipsman and Edward Doyle, *The Vietnam Experience* (Boston, 1983), 53; Sorley, 17–21 and 222–23.

20. JCS-MACV Combined Campaign Plan 1969, September, 1968, Southeast Asia Branch Files, U.S. Army Center of Military History.

21. Nixon, *Public Papers*, 1969, 910; Nixon, *RN*, 393–94.

22. George Herring, *America's Longest War* (New York), 1986, 249; Nixon, *RN*, 393; Kissinger, *White House Years*, 284–85; Seymour Hersh, *The Prince of Power* (New York), 1983, 125–130.

23. Nixon, *RN*, 396; Kissinger, *White House Years*, 280–82.

24. Kissinger, *White House Years*, 282.

25. Kissinger, *White House Years*, 280–82; *Washington Post*, August 24, 1969.

26. Nixon, *RN*, 397; Kissinger, *White House Years*, 262–63.

27. *New York Times*, September 6, 1969, and September 8, 1969.

28. Memorandum, Laird to Nixon, September 4, 1969, White House files, Nixon Presidential Materials, National Archives and Records Administration; *New York Times*, September 14, 1969.

29. Nixon, *RN*, 397; Nixon, *Public Papers, 1969*, 718.

30. Stephen Ambrose, *Triumph of a Politician* (New York, 1988), 302.

31. Nixon, *Public Papers, 1969*, 749; *Washington Post*, September 17, 1969.

32. Nixon, *RN*, 400; *Washington Post*, October 1, 1969.

33. Nixon, *RN*, 400; Memorandum, Nixon to Kissinger, October 1, 1969, White House Central Files, Nixon Presidential Materials, National Archives and Records Administration.

34. *New York Times*, October 5, 1969; *Washington Post*, October 5, 1969.

35. Nixon, *Public Papers, 1969,* 798–800; Nixon, *RN,* 403; *Wall Street Journal,* October 14, 1969.

36. Nixon, *RN,* 285.

37. Langguth, 525.

Chapter 5

1. One of the best accounts of John Kennedy's presidency remains Arthur Schlesinger, Jr.'s *A Thousand Days* (New York, 1965); temper this positive analysis with the more critical Nigel Hamilton's *JFK: Reckless Youth* (New York, 1992), Thomas C. Reeves' *A Question of Character* (Rocklin, 1992), and Richard Reeves' *President Kennedy* (New York, 1993); by 1963, there would be irony in Kennedy's inaugural pledge and there would be assassinations—here and in South Vietnam — see Ellen J. Hammer's *A Death in November* (New York, 1987); see Theodore White's *The Making of a President, 1964* (New York, 1965) for the attempt by Lyndon Johnson to win the presidency as a "peace" candidate, portraying the GOP's Barry Goldwater as reckless—but there was no escape from Southeast Asia (see David Kaiser, *American Tragedy* Cambridge, 2000).

2. Richard Goodwin, a former aid to LBJ and Robert Kennedy, explains America's descent from Camelot into dissension in the streets (*Remembering America,* Boston, 1988); Johnson's assistant Joseph Califano also attempts to analyze the wreckage of Johnson's presidency in *The Triumph and Tragedy of Lyndon Johnson* (New York, 1991).

3. The tumultuous year of 1969 is superbly chronicled in an anniversary edition of *Newsweek,* July 1989.

4. Hoac Ngoc Lung, *Indochina Monographs* (Washington, 1978), 126–28; message Saigon to State, January 24, 1970, Subject: Estimate of Enemy Strategy in NSC Files, Nixon Presidential Materials, National Archives and Records Administration; Kissinger, *White House Years,* 435; Memorandum, Laird for the President, April 4, 1970, Subject: Vietnam, White House Central Files, Nixon Presidential Materials, National Archives and Records Administration; *Newsweek,* February 9, 1970.

5. Nixon, *RN,* 448; Nixon, *Public Papers, 1970,* 373–77.

6. Kissinger, *White House Years,* 478–79; Sorley, 173–74.

7. Nixon, *RN,* 445.

8. *Ibid.,* 467.

9. *New York Times,* March 19, 1970; *Washington Post,* March 20, 1970.

10. U.S. Congress, House of Representatives, Committee on Armed Services, Special Subcommittee on National Defense Posture, *Report of the Vietnam Conflict and Its Impact on U.S. Military Commitments Abroad* (Washington, 1968), 17.

11. Dave Richard Palmer, *Summons of the Trumpet* (Novato, 1978), 229.

12. Kissinger, *White House Years,* 460; *ibid.,* 228.

13. Sorley, 203–210; *Washington Post,* February 23, 1970.

14. Message McCain to Wheeler, February 14, 1970, Subject: Reduction in NVA Sanctuary In Cambodia, Abrams Papers, U.S. Army center of Military History.

15. Historical Division, Joint Secretariat, *U.S. Joint Chiefs of Staff and the War in Vietnam, 1969–1970* (Washington, 1976), 232–33; for a critical assessment of the Joint Chiefs see H.R. McMaster's *Dereliction of Duty* (New York, 1997); message Abrams to McCain, March 30, 1970, Abrams Papers, U.S. Army Center of Military History.

16. James S. Olson and Randy Roberts, *Where the Last Domino Fell* (New York, 1991), 234.

17. Kissinger, *White House Years*, 489–90.

18. *Ibid.*

19. *Ibid.*

20. *Ibid.*

21. *Ibid.*

22. *Ibid.*; Nixon, *RN*, 449; message, Moorer JCS 5623 to McCain, Abrams, April 23, 1970, Subject: Operations in Cambodia, Abrams Papers, U.S. Army Center for Military History.

23. Kissinger, *White House Years*, 490–95; Nixon, *RN*, 449–53.

24. *Washington Post*, April 30, 1970 and May 1, 1970.

25. Nixon, *RN*, 450; Nixon, *Public Papers, 1970*, 405–10; *New York Times*, April 30, 1970; *Wall Street Journal*, May 1, 1970; *Time*, May 18, 1970.

26. *New York Times*, May 1, 1970; *State*, May 1, 1970; *Washington Post*, May 5, 1970; *Newsweek*, May 10, 1970.

27. *New York Times*, May 10, 1970; *Washington Post*, May 10, 1970.

28. *Time*, May 24, 1970; *Newsweek*, June 8, 1970; Palmer, 236.

Chapter 6

1. The march toward racial equality has been eloquently recorded in the works of Richard Kluger (*Simple Justice*, New York, 1987), David J. Garrow (*Bearing the Cross*, New York, 1987), and Juan Williams (*Eyes on the Prize*, New York, 1989).

2. See Theodore White's *The Making of the President, 1968* (New York, 1969) and Joe McGinnes' *The Selling of the President* (New York, 1969) for insightful analyses of the Nixon strategy; in one South Carolina school district that had resisted the *Brown* mandate for more than fifteen years, integration finally arrived in August 1970 — with a Confederate banner hoisted to greet African-American students (*Chester Reporter*, August, 1970).

3. The seeds of Watergate were planted in the soil of Cambodia; Nixon was outraged at criticism of his incursion and lashed out at his foes in the media and the antiwar movement; see, for example, Stanley Kutler's *Wars of Watergate* (New York, 1990) for a detailed account of Nixon's battles with his critics after the invasion of Cambodia; consult A.J. Langguth's *Our Vietnam* (New York, 2000) for the link between domestic scandals and the incursion into Cambodia.

4. Kutler, *Wars of Watergate*, 362.

5. Langguth, 569–77.

6. *Washington Post*, July 17, 1970; *Time*, July 20, 1970.

7. Time, November 11, 1970; *Newsweek,* November 16, 1970.

8. See Patrick Tyler's *A Great Wall* (New York, 1999) for an outstanding account of Nixon's transformation from champion of Taiwan to architect of détente with Mao; the Public Broadcasting System's "Nixon and China," broadcast in 1999, is an excellent source for Nixon's obsession in 1971 with opening the door to the People's Republic of China.

9. Kissinger, *White House Years*, 756–66; Nixon, *RN*, 527.

10. Tyler, 37, 90–92, and 132–33.

11. *Ibid.*, 107–14.

12. *New York Times*, July 11, 1971.

Chapter 7

1. The testimony of Kerry and other veterans was front page news; see *The New York Times*, February 1, 1971; *Washington Post*, February 1, 1971; and the magazines *Time* (February 8, 1971) and *Newsweek* (February 8, 1971).

2. After the failure of Lam Son 719, participants blamed each other; ARVN colonel Hoang Ngoc Lung (*Indochina Monographs*, Washington, 1980) argues on page 93 "the Cambodian foray in 1970 and the Laos operation ... came into being because MACV originated them, promoted them and supported them"; Nixon, characteristically, heralded the invasion as a triumph of Vietnamization — see *New York Times*, April 8, 1971; *Public Papers, 1971*, 524–26.

3. Message, Sutherland to Abrams, 021420Z March, 1971, Abrams Papers, U.S Army Center of Military History; message Abrams to Moorer, March 11, 1971, Abrams Papers, U.S. Army Center of Military History; see Sorley, *A Better War*, 243–260, for a sense of Abrams' disgust with what he labeled "a fucking disaster," 260.

4. *Philadelphia Inquirer*, March 18, 1971.

5. *Philadelphia Bulletin*, March 23, 1971.

6. *Washington Post*, April, 24, 1971.

7. The actions of Ellsberg and the sharp reactions of the Nixon Administration reveal the battle in this country among partisans on all sides to tell — or cover-up — the story of America's involvement in Southeast Asia; see Daniel Ellsberg's *Papers on the War*, (New York, 1972), Mike Gravel's edition of the *Pentagon Papers* (Boston, 1971), and David Rudestine's *The Day the Presses Stopped* (Berkeley, 1996); Langguth, in *Our Vietnam* (New York, 2000), says that Nixon aide H.R. Haldeman recalled "the scene Kissinger staged over the Pentagon Papers was his premier performance," 588; Nixon wanted Ellsberg prosecuted, see Langguth, 588–590, and the newspapers barred from reporting the information found in the Pentagon Papers.

8. Langguth, 455–57; Thieu's corruption is addressed in Langguth, 637–38; as Americans withdrew, Thieu "turned to the security of money," Langguth, 638.

9. Langguth, 600–623; Le Duc Tho seems to have had a similar opinion of Kissinger, telling him in early 1973, "you and no one else stained the honor of the United States," Langguth, 619, while Kissinger writes in *The White House Years*, 1463, "relations on the inside, out of sight of the press, were rather warm."

10. H.R. Haldeman, *The Haldeman Diaries* (New York, 1994), 435; *ibid.*, 512; Kissinger, *White House Years*, 1114–15; Seymour Hersh, *Prince of Power* (New York, 1983), 516.

11. Ngo Quang Truong, *The Easter Offensive of 1972* (Washington, 1980), 9; Luu Van Loi, *Le Duc Tho — Kissinger Negotiations in Paris* (Hanoi, 1996), 216–219 offers a glimpse of North Vietnam's resolve; *New York Times*, May 3, 1972.

12. Hersh, 436; Sorley, 330–331.

13. Langguth, 602–603.

Chapter 8

1. The first volume of Stephen Ambrose's study of Richard Nixon is an excellent chronicle of the President's early career — see *The Education of a Politician* (New York, 1984).

2. See Irwin Gellman's *The Contender* (New York, 1999) for the no-holds-barred rise of Nixon.

3. As Stephen Ambrose notes, the relationship between Eisenhower and Nixon was strained, despite public proclamations to the contrary — see Ambrose's *Eisenhower: Soldier and President* (New York, 1990).

4. Ambrose, *Education of a Politician*, 5.

5. See Stanley Kutler's edition of *Abuse of Power: The New Nixon Tapes* (New York).

6. See Theodore White's *The Making of the President, 1972* (New York, 1973) for the story of the campaign before the waves of Watergate engulfed Nixon's White House.

7. Lincoln was besieged by enemies— in his cabinet and on battlefields. He did, nonetheless, outwit, them as biographers like James McPherson and Richard Current write; FDR also was unafraid to use harsh methods to quiet critics— see Frank Freidel's *Franklin D. Roosevelt* (Boston, 1990) and David Stafford's *Roosevelt and Churchill* (London, 1999).

8. See Hammer's *A Death in November* and *Foreign Relations United States, Vietnam, 1964*, August–December 1963, 511–27.

9. *Foreign Relations United States, Vietnam, 1964*, 352–58; Langguth, 350.

10. See Robert Dallek's *Flawed Giant: Lyndon Johnson and His Times* (New York, 1998) and Doris Kearns Goodwin's *Lyndon Johnson and the American Dream* (New York, 1976); understandably, LBJ was sensitive about the "landslide" label and spends most of *The Vantage Point* (New York, 1971) on his Senate and presidential years, agonizing over his actions in Vietnam; see Garrow's *The F.B.I. and Martin Luther King*.

11. Haldeman, *Diaries*, 475; see Kutler's *Wars of Watergate* for a detailed treatment of the Ellsberg burglary.

12. Kutler, 340.

13. See Carl Bernstein and Bob Woodward's *All the President's Men* (New York, 1973) in which the two reporters recount their dogged pursuit of the "third-rate burglary."

14. These two famous photographs serve as permanent images that brought out the sheer brutality of the conflict.

15. *New York Times*, August 12, 1972.

16. Langguth 613–16; Walter Isaacson, *Kissinger* (New York, 1992), 471 documents the zeal with which Nixon pursued the Christmas bombing as does Nixon himself in *RN*, 741–43.

17. Nixon, *RN*, 741; *New York Times*, December 20, 1972; *Washington Post*, December 27, 1972.

Chapter 10

1. The literature on the women's movement is voluminous; see Betty Friedan's *The Feminine Mystique* (New York, 1963), Rosalind Rosenberg's *Divided Lives* (New York, 1992) and Susan Hartmann's *From Margin to Mainstream* (New York, 1989).

2. *New York Times*, January 21, 1973.

3. *New York Times*, August 16, 1971; Kissinger, *White House Years*, 1563.

4. The two reporters, their editor, Benjamin Bradlee, and their publisher, Katherine Graham, doggedly pursued those in the break-in and the cover-up — see Bernstein and Woodward's *All The President's Men* (New York, 1973).

5. Stanley Kutler, *Watergate* (St. James, New York, 77–79); also see Kutler's *The Wars of Watergate* (New York, 1990).

6. Numerous participants in the investigation published memoirs; see, for instance, John Sirica's *To Set the Record Straight* (New York, 1979), Sam Ervin's *The Whole Truth* (New York, 1980), John Dean's *Blind Ambition* (New York, 1976), and H.R. Haldeman's *Ends of Power* (New York, 1984); *New York Times*, March 31, 1973.

7. The nation sat, entranced, before television sets during the summer of 1973 as the senators dug deeply into the scandal; see Kutler's *The Wars of Watergate* and the committee's records in the National Archives.

8. Dean testified before the Ervin Committee early that summer and later wrote *Blind Ambition* about his fall from grace; for the effect of the former White House counsel's testimony, see Kissinger's *Years of Upheaval* (Boston, 1982), 113 and Nixon's *RN*, 336–40.

9. *New York Times*, April 30, 1973; the White House attempted to smear Dean — see Kutler's *Wars of Watergate*, 358–60; the resignations of Haldeman and Ehrlichman recorded in the former's *End of Power* (New York, 1984) and the latter's *Witness to Power* (New York, 1982).

10. Kutler, *Watergate*, 118–123, 131–33; *New York Times*, July 24, 1973.

11. *Washington Post*, June 17, 1973.

Chapter 11

1. Hersh, *Prince of Power*, 260–74; *New York Times*, September 12–15, 1973; *Washington Post*, September 12–15, 1973; allegations that Americans had helped

"murder" Allende surfaced quickly — see *New York Times*, September 20, 1973; for a good analysis of Allende's regime, consult Nathaniel Davis' *The Last Years of Salvador Allende* (Ithaca, New York, 1985).

2. Kissinger, *Years of Upheaval*, 495; *New York Times*, October 7–25, 1973; clearly reports the Yom Kippur War and Nixon's brinkmanship.

3. *Washington Post*, August 8, 1973, and August 30, 1973; for a documentary treatment of the duties and responsibilities of the special prosecutor and Nixon's view, see Kutler's *Watergate*, 112–18; *Washington Post*, October 13, 1973.

4. Interestingly, Agnew asserts in his memoirs (*Go Quietly*, New York, 1985, 189) that he feared being killed if he failed to resign the vice presidency.

5. *Washington Post*, October 20, 1973; Kissinger, *Years of Upheaval*, 535; Kutler, *Watergate*, 150–59 and Kutler, *Wars of Watergate*, 495–10; additionally, consider Archibald Cox's memoir *The Court and the Constitution* (Boston, 1987).

Chapter 12

1. The ferocious debate over the commander in chief's war-making powers, circa 1973, is recorded in *RN*, 742; Kissinger, *Years of Upheaval*; the *Congressional Record*, October 1–31, 1973; and in the *Washington Post* during the autumn of that year.

2. Kutler, *Wars of Watergate*, 619–20, 496–300, 433.

3. *New York Times*, April 30, 1974; Nixon, *RN*, 994; see the *Times'* edition of *The White House Transcripts* (New York, 1974); *Washington Post*, May 2, 1974.

4. *New York Times*, June 12-July 3, 1974.

5. Kissinger, *Years of Upheaval*, 1151–63; Nixon, *RN*, 1023–33.

6. Kutler, *Wars of Watergate*, 495–96; Kutler, *Watergate*, 173–96 includes an important assortment of documents.

7. Kutler, *Wars of Watergate*, 496–97; while Nixon fought his war against Congress, some members of that body held hearings in July with Ambassador Martin, expressing their criticism of Thieu's government — see *Report of the Situation in the Republic of Vietnam* (Washington, 1974).

8. Kutler, *Wars of Watergate*, 498–505; Kutler, *Watergate*, 197–204; Kissinger, *Years of Upheaval*, 1196–97; Nixon, *RN*, 1053.

9. Kutler, *Wars of Watergate*, 538.

10. Kissinger, *Years of Upheaval*, 1196; *Washington Post*, August 8, 1974.

11. See Theodore White's *Breach of Trust* (London, 1975), 10, and Woodward and Bernstein's *The Final Days* (New York, 1976), 269; Nixon, *RN*, 1978; *Washington Post*, August 9–10, 1974. -

Chapter 13

1. An early biography of Ford is Clark Mollenhoff's *The Man Who Pardoned Nixon* (New York, 1976); for Ford's appointment in the aftermath of Vice President

Agnew's resignation, see Kutler, *Wars of Watergate*, 418–31; Ford's own *A Time To Heal* (New York, 1979) is useful.

2. *Washington Post*, August 11, 1974; Ford, 178–82; even his plan to offer amnesty to draft dodgers and deserters did little to blunt the criticism of Ford's pardon of Nixon — see Langguth 639–40.

3. Langguth, 626–32; Karnow, 660–61; William LeGro, *Vietnam from Cease Fire to Capitulation* (Washington, 1981), 136–46; Van Tien Dung, *Our Great Spring Victory* (New York, 1977), 24–27, is a valuable North Vietnamese account.

4. *Washington Post*, September 13, 1974; interestingly, Ford had, upon assuming the presidency, reassured Thieu of the United States' continued support — see Hung, 240–51; Kissinger, *Years of Upheaval*, 1540.

5. Dung, *Our Great Spring Victory*, 7.

6. Cao Vin Vien, *The Final Collapse* (Washington, 1983), 45–54, offers a bleak analysis of the U.S. Congress' appropriations to South Vietnam; interview with John Murray, August 15, 1996, Fairfax, Virginia; LeGro, 84–87.

7. Stephen Hosmer, *The Fall of South Vietnam* (New York, 1980), 32, 148–62; interview with William LeGro, January 8, 1996, Washington, D.C.; Dung, 24.

8. Interview with John Guffey, July 23, 1996, Shawnee, Oklahoma; interview with Guffey, April 29, 2000, Washington, D.C.

9. Hosmer, 32; interview with LeGro; LeGro, 122–33.

10. Interview with Guffey.

11. Interview with Rosalie Redmond, May 27, 2000, Washington, D.C.

Chapter 14

1. Interviews with Guffey; see also Lee and Haynsworth, *White Christmas in April* (New York, 1999), 87–92.

2. Interview with Murray; interview with Wolfgang Lehman, August 13, 1996, Washington, D.C.

3. Dung, 18–20.

4. *Ibid.*, 21; LeGro, 135–36; Dung, 22.

5. Dung, 27.

6. *Ibid.*, 23–25.

7. *Ibid.*, 11; LeGro, 145; interviews with Guffey.

8. Dung, 24; interviews with Homer Smith, January 2, 1997 and April 29, 2000; interview with Murray; interview with Tran Trong Khanh, August 12, 1996, Washington, D.C.; The last interview, with a Vietnamese diplomat, confirms that the Communists, in early 1975, were testing America's resolve.

9. Grant — and Lincoln — masterfully split the Confederacy in half, emphasizing its weaknesses; see Ulysses S. Grant, *Memoirs* (Boston, 1881); LeGro, 139–40.

10. Interviews with Smith.

11. LeGro, 149.

12. Interview with Lehman.

13. LeGro, 149.

14. Dung, 39–40.

15. *Ibid.*, 44.
16. *Ibid.*, 47–53.
17. Larry Engelmann, *Tears Before the Rain* (New York), 236–45.
18. Dung, 42–51; David Butler, *The Fall of Saigon* (New York), 35.
19. Dung, 63.
20. Butler, 56–57; *ibid.*, 483.
21. Dung, 65.
22. Interviews with Smith; Hosmer, 84.
23. Harry Summers, *Historical Atlas of the Vietnam War* (New York, 1995), 194.
24. Hosmer, 38–39; *ibid.*, 86; LeGro, 152.
25. Hosmer, 85–89; interviews with Smith; interview with Lehman.
26. Frank Snepp, *Decent Interval* (New York, 1979), 193; LeGro, 152.
27. Hosmer, 90; Butler, 76; Hosmer, 90; interviews with Smith.
28. Hosmer, 92–94.
29. Summers, *Historical Atlas*, 196.
30. Dung, 93–94.
31. Hosmer, 94; LeGro, 153.
32. Hosmer, 95.
33. Hosmer, 95–96.
34. Butler, 105–06.
35. *Ibid.*, 106–07.
36. *Ibid.*, 120–21.
37. Hosmer, 96.
38. Cao Van Vien, *The Final Collapse* (Washington, 1983), 95.
39. Dung, 45.
40. *Ibid.*, 55–56.
41. *Ibid.*, 57–59; LeGro, 162; interviews with Smith.
42. LeGro, 163; Hosmer, 98.
43. LeGro, 151–52.
44. Engelmann, 236.
45. Hosmer, 85.
46. *Ibid.*, 99.
47. *Ibid.*, 100.
48. Engelmann, 238.
49. Interview with Jack Brady, January 10, 1996, Washington, D.C.; interview with Piner; interview with Richard Armitage, August 14, 1998, Arlington, Virginia.

Chapter 15

1. Nguyen Cao Ky, *Twenty Years and Twenty Days* (New York, 1976), 101–05; Tran Van Don, *Our Endless War* (San Rafael, California, 1978), 236–38; Langguth, 633–40 chronicles the deterioration of Thieu's presidency as the United states, in 1974, diverted its attention elsewhere.

2. Hosmer, 102.
3. LeGro, 155; Hosmer, 103.
4. LeGro, 155.
5. Hosmer, 87.
6. Vien, 78; interview with Murray; Snepp, 156.
7. Vien, 99.
8. LeGro, 156.
9. *Ibid.*, 157.
10. Hosmer, 104.
11. LeGro, 158.
12. Dung, 102.
13. Vien, 100–02.
14. Interview with LeGro.
15. Interview with Brady; interview with Haney Howell, June 6, 1995, and July 27,1999, Rock Hill, S.C.— Howell, a CBS journalist in Saigon, shared a common alma mater with the ambassador.
16. Interview with Edwin Pelosky, January 9, 1996, Denton, Maryland; interview with Pelosky, April 29, 2000, Washington, D.C.
17. Dung, 103–110.
18. Interviews with Donald Berney, April 29, 2000, Washington, D.C. and July 30, 1996, San Diego, California.
19. Hung, 269–70, 279; Snepp, 649.
20. Hung, 273–90; Snepp, 296–302; Dung, 125–42.
21. Interview with Alexander Haig, March 6, 1997, New York, N.Y.
22. *Washington Post*, March 22, 1975.

Chapter 16

1. Dung, 8, 24–27, 135–42.
2. Interview with Stuart Herrington, August 13 and 14, 1996, Carlisle, Pennsylvania; interview with Haig; interview with Redmond; Snepp, 298.
3. Interview with Smith; interview with Russ Shaw, June 4, 2000, Denver, Colorado; interview with Thomas Polgar, November 25, 1996, Orlando, Florida; Dung, 205.
4. Interview with Smith; interview with Piner; interview with Berney; interview with Willam Ryder, August 27, 1996, Indian Harbor Beach, Florida.
5. Interview with Polgar; Snepp, 386–89; interview with Armitage.
6. Interviews with Sally Vinyard July 28, 1996, Fallbrook, California and April 29, 2000, Washington, D.C.; interview with Redmond; interviews with Smith; interview with Piner; Snepp, 304; interview with Benjamin Register, April 29, 2000, Washington, D.C.; interviews with John Guffey.
7. Interviews with Smith; Dung, 179–81, 209–10.
8. *New York Times*, April 13, 1975.
9. Hung, 333–44; Snepp, 490; interviews with Smith.

Chapter 17

1. Hersh, 632; *Washington Post*, May 21, 1973.
2. Hung, 333; *Washington Post*, April 17, 1975; Langguth, 652–56.
3. Hung, 321–30; *Washington Post*, April 19, 1975.
4. Hung, 328–30, 331; Snepp, 339; Dung, 199.
5. *New York Times*, April 26, 1975; Hung, 333.
6. *Washington Post*, April 25, 1975; Hung, 334–42.
7. *New York Times*, April 24, 1975; interview with Armitage.

Chapter 18

1. Interview with William Estep, July 23, 1996, Oklahoma City, Oklahoma; interviews with Smith.
2. Interviews with Smith.
3. *Ibid.*
4. Interview with Pelosky.
5. Interviews with Berney; Berney shared with the authors his private files that contain detailed lists of the numbers of passengers evacuated in Military Sealift Command chartered vessels; interview with Ryder.
6. *Ibid.*
7. Interview with Arthur Laehr, July 22, 1996, Pensacola, Florida; an excellent study of the air evacuation is a monograph prepared by Laehr, John Hilgenberg, and Joseph Tobin (*Last Flight from Saigon*, Washington, D.C., 1976).
8. Interviews with Vinyard.
9. *New York Times*, April 20, 1975, April 22, 1975, April 24, 1975.
10. Interview with Ann Hazard, July 26, 1996, Las Cruces, New Mexico; the authors obtained through a Freedom of Information Act request the results of the investigation that exonerated Hazard of responsibility for supervising the incomplete destruction of the funds.
11. See ex–CIA operative Frank Snepp's controversial *Decent Interval* (New York, 1977), David Butler's *Fall of Saigon* (New York, 1985); interview with Tran Trong Khanh; interview with Polgar.
12. Interview with Laehr.
13. See Hilgenberg et al., *Last Flight Out*, 72–80.
14. *Ibid.*, 86.
15. Interview with John Hilgenberg, July 14, 1995, Orlando, Florida.
16. Interview with Smith, January 2, 1997.
17. See Terry McNamara's *Escape with Honor* (Dulles, 1997); interview with Terry McNamara, August 6, 1996, Herndon, Virginia; interview with Glenn Rounsevell, August 12, 1995, Falls Church, Virginia.
18. *New York Times*, April 25, 1975; interview with Rounsevell.
19. Interview with Rounsevell.
20. Parker, James E., Jr., *Last Man Out* (Camden, S.C, 1996), 425–27; interview with McNamara.

21. Interview with Lehman; interviews with Smith.

22. Interview with Richard Carey, July 9, 1996, Plano Texas.

23. *Ibid.*

24. Interview with Herrington.

25. Interview with Carey.

26. Interview with Herrington.

27. *Ibid.*; Kissinger, *White House Years*, 1141.

28. Numerous sources exist concerning the ambassador's last moments in Saigon (see for instance, Snepp's *Decent Interval* and Butler's *The Fall of Saigon*); our research on this scene was enhanced by interviews with Wolfgang Lehman, Homer Smith, and James Piner.

29. Interview with Terry Bennington, July 2, 1996, Quantico, Virginia.

30. Interview with Herrington; see Stuart Herrington's bitter *Peace with Honor?* (Novato, California, 1983).

31. Interviews with Berney and Ryder.

32. Interview with Leon Nguyen, August 21, 1996, Charlotte, N.C.

33. Interview with Bung Ly, November 30, 1996, Orlando Florida.

34. Interview with Bung Ly; interview with Lawrence Chambers, April 27, 1995; interview with Larry Grimes, May 2, 1995, Pensacola, Florida; see also the Fall 1993 issue of *Foundation* magazine for Chambers' account of the rescue of Bung Ly's family.

Chapter 19

1. *Stars and Stripes*, May 1, 1975; while CNN had not yet been born, the final agonizing days of the war were tailor-made for coverage by the three networks— ABC, CBS, and NBC — all of which carried reports from South Vietnam during the last two weeks of April, 1975; *Time*, May 5, 1975; interview with Herrington.

2. *New York Times*, April 30, 1975.

3. *Time*, May 5, 1975; *Newsweek*, May 5, 1975.

4. While Nixon remains a polarizing figure, his biographers agree on the role he played as a staunch critic of the Truman administration's China policy; see, for example, Gellman's *The Contender*, Ambrose's *The Education of a Politician*, Joan Hoff's *Nixon Reconsidered* (New York, 1994), and Herman Parmet's *Richard Nixon and His America* (New York, 1990).

5. *Ibid.*

6. See Ambrose's *Eisenhower* for a balanced account of the President's anti–communism — which was tempered by Eisenhower's reluctance to see American ground troops used in Southeast Asia.

7. Langguth, 522–23; Hung, 23–29; these are two sources that document Nixon's intrigue during the 1968 election campaign.

8. Hung's *The Palace File* contains an impressive appendix that includes correspondence between Thieu, Nixon and Ford; obviously, both American Presidents assured Thieu repeatedly that the United States would honor its commitment to South Vietnam after the 1973 Paris Peace Accords; for example, Nixon

wrote a worried Thieu on February 22 "From here on the emphasis must be on our close cooperation,..." 398.

9. Upon assuming the presidency in August 1974, Ford wrote Thieu on August 10 "...the existing commitments this nation has made in the past are still valid and will be fully honored in my administration." Hung's *Palace File*, 434.

10. Richard Nixon, *No More Vietnams* (New York, 1985), 6; *Newsweek*, July 24, 1999.

11. Interview with Rebecca Goodman, August 4, 2000, San Diego, California.

Bibliography

Our book *Nixon, Ford and the Abandonment of South Vietnam* is a fresh look at the time period stretching from the 1968 election of Richard Nixon to the 1975 collapse of South Vietnam. Coming more than 25 years after the last helicopter left Saigon with the handful of U.S. Marines who had hid on the embassy's rooftop, this book is part of a movement to reappraise America's longest war. Essential to our efforts have been numerous interviews we conducted from 1996 to 2000. We have also pored over government documents, newspapers, and secondary sources, attempting to tell of the tragedy that was fueled by events far from the battlefields of Southeast Asia. Here are some of the sources that helped us tell the story:

Interviews

Armitage, Richard. Interview. August 14, 1998. Arlington, Virginia.
Bennington, Terry. Interview. July 2, 1996. Quantico, Virginia.
Berney, Donald. Interview. July 30, 1996. San Diego, California.
_____. April 29, 2000. Washington, D.C.
Brady, Jack. Interview. January 10, 1996. Washington, D.C.
Bung Ly. Interview. April 8, 1995. Orlando, Florida.
Carey, Richard. Interview. July 9, 1996. Plano, Texas.
Chambers, Lawrence. Interview. April 27, 1995. Reston, Virginia.
Esper, George. Interview. July 1, 1996. New York, N.Y.
Estep, John. Interview. July 23, 1996. Oklahoma City, Oklahoma.
Gildea, Joseph. Interview. July 29, 1996. Hollidaysburg, Pennsylvania.
Goodman, Rebecca. Interview. August 4, 2000. San Diego, California.
Grimes, Larry. Interview. May 2, 1995. Pensacola, Florida.
Guffey, John. Interview. July 23, 1996. Shawnee, Oklahoma.

Haig, Alexander. Interview. March 6, 1997. New York, N.Y.
Hazard, Ann. Interview. July 26, 1996. Las Cruces, New Mexico.
Herrington, Stuart. Interview, August 13–14, 1996. Carlisle, Pennsylvania.
Hilgenberg, John. Interview. July 14, 1995. Orlando, Florida.
Howell, Haney. Interview. April 10, 1995. Rock Hill, S.C.
_____. July 27, 1999. Rock Hill, S.C.
Komisarcik, Adam. Interview. April 17, 1995. Reston, Virginia.
Laehr, Arthur. Interview, July 22, 1996. Pensacola, Florida.
LeGro, William. Interview. January 8, 1996. Washington, D.C.
Lehman, Wolfgang. Interview. August 13, 1996. Washington, D.C.
McNamara, Terry. Interview. August 6, 1996. Herndon, Virginia.
Murray, John. Interview. August 13, 1996. Fairfax, Virginia.
Nguyen, Leon. Interview. August 21, 1996. Charlotte, N.C.
Pelosky, Edwin. Interview. January 9, 1996. Denton, Maryland.
Polgar, Thomas. Interview. November 25, 1996. Orlando, Florida.
Redmond, Rosalie. Interview. May 27, 2000. Washington, D.C.
Register, Benjamin. Interview. April 29, 2000. Washington, D.C.
Rounsevell, Glenn. Interview. August 12, 1996. Falls Church, Virginia.
Ryder, William. Interview. August 27, 1996. Indian Harbor Beach, Florida.
Shaw, Russ. Interview. June 4, 2000. Denver, Colorado.
Smith, Homer. Interview. January 2, 1997. San Antonio, Texas.
_____. April 29, 2000. Washington, D.C.
Tran Trong Khanh. Interview. August 12, 1996. Washington, D.C.
Vinyard, Sally. Interview. July 28, 1996. Fallbrook, California.
Vu, Mary. Interview. August 7, 1996. Rock Hill, S.C.

Government Documents

Foreign Relations of the United States, Vietnam. Edited by John P. Glennon. Washington, D.C. 1988.
Public Papers of the Presidents of the United States: John F. Kennedy. Washington, D.C., 1961–1963.
Public Papers of the Presidents of the United States: Richard Nixon. Washington, D.C., 1969–74.
U.S. Department of the Air Force. *The 1972 Invasions of Military Region I: Fall of Quang Tri and Defense of Hue.* Christiansburg, Virginia, n.d.
U.S. Department of the Army. *U.S. Special Forces, 1961–1971.* Washington, D.C., 1972.
U.S. Senate Committee on Foreign Relations. *Vietnam Commitments, 1961.* Washington, D.C., 1972.

Journals

Blight, James G., Joseph S. Nye, Jr., and David A. Welch. "The Cuban Missile Crisis Revisited." *Foreign Affairs*, Fall 1987.

Carey, Richard E. "Frequent Wind Organization and Assembly." *Marine Corps Gazette*, February-May 1976.
Greenstein, Fred, and Richard Emmerman. "What Did Eisenhower Tell Kennedy About Indochina?" *Journal of American History*, September 1992.
Karnow, Stanley. "Spook." *New York Times Magazine*, January 3, 1999, 34.
Wicker, Tom. "The Wrong Rubicon." *Atlantic Monthly*, May 1968.
Thompson, James. "How Could Vietnam Happen?" *Atlantic Monthly*, April 1968.

Newspapers

Charlotte Observer
Herald
The State
Chester Reporter
New York Times
Washington Post
Wall Street Journal

Books

Albin, David A., and Marlow Hood, eds. *The Cambodian Agony*. Armonk, New York, 1987.
Abramson, Rudy. *Spanning the Century: The Life of W. Averell Harriman*. New York, 1992.
Acheson, Dean. *Present at the Creation*. New York, 1987.
Adler, Renata. *Reckless Disregard*. New York, 1986.
Ambrose, Stephen E. *Eisenhower: Soldier and President*. New York, 1990.
_____. *Nixon: The Triumph of a Politician 1962–72*. New York, 1989.
An, Tai Sung. *The Vietnam War*. Cranbury, N.J., 1998.
Appy, Christian G. *Working-Class War*. Chapel Hill, N.C., 1993.
Archer, Jules. *Mao Tse-Tung*. New York, 1972.
Arnett, Peter. *Live from the Battlefield*. New York, 1994.
Ashmore, Harry S., and William Baggs. *Mission to Hanoi*. New York, 1968.
Ball, George W. *The Past Has Another Pattern*. New York, 1982.
Bao Ninh. *The Sorrow of War*. Translated by Frank Palmos. London, 1994.
Baritz, Loren. *Backfire*. New York, 1985.
Barrett, David M. *Uncertain Warriors: Lyndon Johnson and His Vietnam Advisors*. Lawrence, Kansas, 1993.
_____ (ed.). *Lyndon B. Johnson's Vietnam Papers*. Austin, Texas, 1997.
Bator, Viktor. *Vietnam: A Diplomatic Tragedy*. Dobbs Ferry, New York, 1965.
Bergerud, Eric. *Red Thunder, Tropic Lightning*. Boulder, Colorado, 1993.
Berman, Edgar. *Hubert*. New York, 1979.
Berman, Larry. *Lyndon Johnson's War*. New York, 1989.
_____. *Planning a Tragedy*. New York, 1982.

_____. *No Peace, No Honor: Nixon, Kissinger, and Betrayal in Vietnam*. New York, 2001.

Berval, René de. *Kingdom of Laos*. Saigon, 1959.

Beschloss, Michael R. *Kennedy and Roosevelt*. New York, 1980.

_____. *Taking Charge: The Johnson White House Tapes, 1963–1964*. New York, 1997.

Bigart, Homer. *Forward Positions*. Betsy Wade, ed. Fayetteville, Arkansas, 1992.

Bilton, Michael, and Kevin Sim. *Four Hours in My Lai*. New York, 1992.

Bird, Kai. *The Chairman*. New York, 1992.

_____. *The Color of Truth*. New York, 1998.

Blumenfeld, Ralph, and the Staff and Editors of the *New York Post. Henry Kissinger*. New York, 1974.

Bowden, Tim. *One Crowded Hour*. Sydney, 1987.

Bowles, Chester. *Promises to Keep*. New York, 1971

Bradlee, Benjamin C. *Conversations with Kennedy*. New York, 1975.

Braestrup, Peter. *Big Story*. 2 vols. Boulder, Colorado, 1975.

Brigham, Robert K. *Guerrilla Diplomacy: The NLF's Foreign Relations and the Vietnam War*. Ithaca, New York, 1999.

Brown, Malcolm, *Muddy Boots and Red Socks*. New York, 1993.

_____. *The New Face of War*. New York, 1968.

Brown, Weldon A. *Prelude to Disaster*. Port Washington, New York, 1975.

Buchwald, Art. *Son of the Great Society*. London, 1967.

Bui Diem, with David Charnoff. *In the Jaws of History*. Boston, 1987.

Bui Tin. *Following Ho Chi Minh*. Translated by Judy Stowe and Do Van. Honolulu, 1995.

Bundy, William A. *A Tangled Web*. New York, 1998.

Burchett, Wilfred G. *Vietnam North*. New York, 1966.

Burr, William (ed.). *The Kissinger Transcripts*. New York, 1998.

Butler, David. *The Fall of Saigon*. New York, 1985.

Buttinger, Joseph. *Vietnam: A Dragon Embattled*. 2 vols. New York, 1967.

_____. *Vietnam: A Political History*. New York, 1968.

Caldwell, Dan (ed.). *Henry Kissinger*. Durham, N.C. 1983.

Califano, Joseph A., Jr. *The Triumph and Tragedy of Lyndon Johnson*. New York, 1991.

Capps, Walter H. *The Unfinished War*. Boston, 1990.

Castle, Timothy N. *One Day Too Long*. New York, 1999.

Chaffard, Georges. *Les Carnets secrets de la décolonisation*. Paris, 1965.

Chandler, David P. *Brother Number One*. Boulder, Colorado, 1992.

Chang, Pao-Min. *Kampuchea Between China and Vietnam*. Singapore, 1985.

Chanoff, David, and Doan Van Toai. *Vietnam*. London, 1996.

Chapuis, Oscar. *A History of Vietnam*. Westport, Connecticut, 1995.

Chi, Hoang Van. *From Colonialism to Communism: A Case History of North Vietnam*. New York, 1964.

Clavir, Judy, and John Spitzer (eds.). *The Conspiracy Trial*. Indianapolis, 1970.

Clifford, Clark, with Richard Holbrooke. *Counsel to the President*. New York, 1991.

Colby, William, and Peter Forbath. *Honorable Men: My Life in the CIA*. New York, 1978.

Collier, Peter, and David Horowitz. *The Kennedys: An American Drama*. New York, 1984.

Cooper, Chester L. *The Last Crusade*. New York, 1970.

Corn, David. *Blond Ghost*. New York, 1994.

Craig, Gordon A., and Francis L. Lowenheim. *The Diplomats 1939–1979*. Princeton, N.J., 1994.

Cray, Ed. *General of the Army*. New York, 1990.

Critchfield, Richard. *The Long Charade*. New York, 1968.

Curry, Cecil B. *Edward Lansdale*. Boston, 1988.

_____. *Victory at Any Cost*. Washington, D.C, 1997.

Dallek, Robert. *Flawed Giant: Lyndon Johnson and His Times 1961–1973*. New York, 1998.

Davidson, Phillip B. *Vietnam at War*. Oxford, 1988.

Davis, James Kirkpatrick. *Assault on the Left*. Westport, Connecticut, 1997.

Dawson, Allan. *55 Days: The Fall of Saigon*. Englewood Cliffs, N.J., 1997.

DeGaulle, Charles. *War Memoirs*. New York, 1967.

Dellums, Ronald V. *The Committee Hearings on War Crimes in Vietnam*. Edited by The Citizens Commission of Inquiry. New York, 1972.

Dictionary of the Vietnam War. Edited by James Olson. New York, 1987.

Dictionary of the Vietnam War. Edited by Marc Leepson, with Helen Hannaford. New York, 1999.

DiLeo, David L. *George Ball, Vietnam, and the Rethinking of Containment*. Chapel Hill, N.C., 1991.

Dobrynin, Anatoly. *In Confidence*. New York, 1995.

Dommen, Arthur J. *Laos*. Boulder, Colorado, 1985.

Don, Tran Van. *Our Endless War*. San Rafael, California, 1978.

Dong, Pham Van. *Selected Writings*. Hanoi, 1977.

Doyle, Edward, and Samuel Lipsman (eds.). *Setting the Stage*. Boston, 1981.

Duiker, William J. *The Communist Road to Power in Vietnam*. New York, 1996.

_____. *Ho Chi Minh*. New York, 2000.

_____. *U.S. Containment Policy and the Conflict in Indochina*. Stanford, California, 1994.

Dung, Van Tien. *Our Great Spring Victory*. Translated by John Spragens, Jr. New York, 1977.

Eisenhower, Dwight D. *At Ease: Stories I Tell to Friends*. New York, 1988.

Elliot, David W. P. *Political Integration in North Vietnam: The Cooperativization Period*. New York, 1974.

Ellsberg, Daniel. *Papers on the War*. New York, 1972.

Emerson, Gloria. *Winners and Losers*. New York, 1976.

Engelmann, Larry. *Tears Before the Rain: An Oral History of the Fall of Saigon*. New York, 1990.

Epstein, Jason. *The Great Conspiracy Trial*. New York, 1970.

Fairbank, John King. *The Chinese Revolution 1800–1985*. New York, 1986.

Fairlee, Henry. *The Kennedy Promise*. Garden City, New York, 1973.

Falk, Richard. *Appropriating Tet*. Princeton, N.J., 1988.

_____. *What's Wrong with Henry Kissinger's Foreign Policy*. Princeton, N.J., 1974.

Fall, Bernard B. *Street Without Joy*. 1961. Reprint, Mechanicsburg, Pennsylvania, 1989.

_____. *The Two Vietnams*. New York, 1964.

Fang, Percy Jucheng, and Lucy Guinong J. Fang. *Zhou Enlai: A Profile.* Beijing, 1986.

Farrell, James J. *The Spirit of the Sixties.* New York, 1997.

Fay, Paul B. *The Pleasure of His Company.* New York, 1966.

Fenn, Charles. *Ho Chi Minh.* New York, 1973.

Fifield, Russell H. *The Diplomacy of Southeast Asia: 1945–1958.* New York, 1958.

Fishel, Wesley R. (ed.). *Vietnam: Anatomy of a Conflict.* Itasca, Illinois, 1968.

FitzGerald, Frances. *Fire in the Lake.* New York, 1972.

Ford, Gerald R. *A Time to Heal.* New York, 1979.

Ford, Harold P. *CIA and the Vietnam Policymakers: Three Episodes, 1962–1968.* Washington, D.C., 1998.

Ford, Ronnie E. *Tet 1968: Understanding the Surprise.* London, 1995.

Frankel, Max. *The Times of My Life.* New York, 1999.

Freidel, Frank. *Franklin D. Roosevelt.* Boston, 1990.

Gaiduk, Ilya V. *The Soviet Union and the Vietnam War.* Chicago, 1996.

Galbraith, John Kenneth. *Name-Dropping.* Boston, 1999.

Gardner, Lloyd C. *Approaching Vietnam.* New York, 1988.

_____. *Pay Any Price.* Chicago, 1995.

Garrettson, Charles Lloyd, III. *Hubert H. Humphrey.* New Brunswick, N.J., 1993.

Gelb, Leslie H., with Richard K. Betts. *The Irony of Vietnam: the System Worked.* Washington, D.C., 1979.

Gettleman, Marvin E., et al. (eds.). *Vietnam and America.* New York, 1995.

Giap, Vo Nguyen. *The Military Art of People's War.* Edited by Russell Stetler. New York, 1970.

_____. *Unforgettable Days.* Hanoi, 1975.

Gibbons, William Conrad. *The U.S. Government and the Vietnam War.* 4 vols. Princeton, N.J., 1986–95.

Gilbert, Marc Jason, and William Head (eds.). *The Tet Offensive.* Westport, Connecticut, 1996.

Gitlin, Todd. *The Sixties.* New York, 1987.

Goldstein, Joseph, Burk Marshall and Jack Schwartz. *The My Lai Massacre and Its Cover-up: Beyond the Reach of the Law?* New York, 1976.

Goodwin, Doris Kearns. *Lyndon Johnson and the American Dream.* New York, 1976.

Goodwin, Richard. *Remembering America.* Boston, 1976.

Grant, Zalin. *Facing the Phoenix.* New York, 1991.

Gravel, Mike (ed.). *Pentagon Papers: The Defense Department History of United States Decision Making on Vietnam.* Senator Gravel Edition. Boston, 1971.

Greene, Graham. *The Quiet American.* London, 1955.

Greene, John Robert. *The Presidency of Gerald R. Ford.* Lawrence, Kansas, 1995.

Gruening, Ernest, and Herbert Wilson Beaser. *Vietnam Folly.* Washington, D.C., 1968.

Gunn, Geoffrey C. *Rebellion in Laos.* Boulder, Colorado, 1990.

Guthman, Edwin. *We Band of Brothers.* New York, 1972.

Halberstam, David. *The Best and the Brightest.* New York, 1971.

_____. *Ho.* New York, 1971.

_____. *The Making of a Quagmire.* 1964. Reprint, edited with an introduction by Daniel J. Singal. New York, 1988.

_____. *The Powers That Be.* New York, 1979.

_____. *The Reckoning.* New York, 1986.

Haldeman, H. R. *The Haldeman Diaries.* New York, 1994.

_____. *The Ends of Power.* New York, 1978.

Hallin, Daniel C. *The "Uncensored War."* Berkeley, California, 1989.

Hamilton, Nigel. *JFK: Reckless Youth.* New York, 1992.

Hammer, Ellen J. *A Death in November.* New York, 1987.

Hammond, William M. *The Military and the Media, 1962–1968.* Washington, D.C., 1988.

Han Suyin. *The Morning Deluge: Mao Tsetung and the Chinese Revolution.* Boston, 1972.

Hayden, Tom. *Reunion.* New York, 1988.

Hendrickson, Paul. *The Living and the Dead.* New York, 1996.

Herr, Michael. *Dispatches.* New York, 1977.

Herring, George. *LBJ and Vietnam.* Austin, Texas, 1994.

_____. *America's Longest War.* Austin, Texas, 1985.

_____. *The Secret Diplomacy of the Vietnam War: The Negotiating Volumes of the Pentagon Papers.* Austin, Texas, 1983.

Herrington, Stuart. *Peace with Honor? An American Report on Vietnam, 1973–1975.* Novato, California, 1983.

Hersh, Burton. *The Old Boys: The American Elite and the Origins of the CIA.* New York, 1992.

Hersh, Seymour M. *The Dark Side of Camelot.* New York, 1997.

_____. *The Price of Power.* New York, 1983.

Herz, Martin F. *The Prestige Press and the Christmas Bombing, 1972.* Washington, D.C., 1980.

Higgins, Marguerite. *Our Vietnam Nightmare.* New York, 1965.

Hilsman, Roger. *To Move a Nation.* New York, 1967.

Hitchens, Christopher. *The Trial of Henry Kissinger.* New York, 2001.

Hoan, Hoang Van. *A Drop in the Ocean.* Beijing, 1988.

Ho Chi Minh. *Prison Diary.* Translated by Dang The Binh. Hanoi, 1994.

_____. *Selected Articles and Speeches, 1920–1967.* Edited by Jack Woddis. London, 1969.

_____. *Selected Writings (1920–1969).* Hanoi, 1973.

Hoff, Joan. *Nixon Reconsidered.* New York, 1994.

Honey, P. J. *Communism in North Vietnam.* Westport, Connecticut, 1963.

Hoopes, Townsend. *The Limits of Intervention.* New York, 1987.

Hosmer, Stephen T., Konrad Kellen and Brian M. Jenkins. *The Fall of South Vietnam.* New York, 1980.

Howes, Craig. *Voices of the Vietnam POWs.* New York, 1993.

Humphrey, Hubert H. *The Education of a Public Man.* Edited by Norman Sherman. Garden City, New York, 1976.

Hung Nguyen Tien, and Jerrold L. Schecter. *The Palace File.* New York, 1986.

Huyen, N. Khac. *Vision Accomplished? The Enigma of Ho Chi Minh.* New York, 1971.

Isaacs, Arnold. *Without Honor: Defeat in Vietnam and Cambodia.* Baltimore, Maryland, 1983.

Isaacson, Walter. *Kissinger*. New York, 1992.

Isaacson, Walter, and Evan Thomas. *The Wise Men*. New York, 1986.

Jenson-Stevenson, Monika, and William Stevenson. *Kiss the Boys Goodbye*. New York, 1990.

Johnson, Lyndon B. *Lyndon B. Johnson's Vietnam Papers*. Edited by David M. Barrett. College Station, Texas, 1997.

_____. *The Vantage Point*. New York, 1971.

Kahin, George M. *Intervention*. New York, 1986.

Kaiser, David. *American Tragedy*. Cambridge, Massachusetts, 2000.

Kalb, Marvin, and Bernard Kalb. *Kissinger*. Boston, 1974.

Kaplan, Morton A., et al. *Vietnam Settlement: Why 1973, Not 1969*. Washington, D.C., 1973.

Karnow, Stanley. *Vietnam: A History*. New York, 1983.

Kasiaficas, George (ed.). *Vietnam Documents: American and Vietnamese Views of the War*. Armonk, New York, 1992.

Kattenburg, Paul M. *The Vietnam Trauma in American Foreign Policy, 1945–75*. New Brunswick, Connecticut, 1980.

Kelly, Francis J. *The Green Berets in Vietnam, 1961–71*. McLean, Virginia, 1991.

_____. *U.S. Army Special Forces, 1961–71*. Washington, D.C., 1973.

Kennedy, John F. *The Kennedy Presidential Press Conferences*. New York, 1978.

_____. *The Kennedy Wit*. Edited by Bill Adler. New York, 1991.

Kennedy, Robert. *Thirteen Days*. New York, 1969.

Khrushchev, Nikita. *The Glasnost Tapes*. Edited and translated by Jerrold L. Schecter, with Vyacheslav V. Luchkov. Boston, 1990.

_____. *Khrushchev Remembers*. Edited and translated by Strobe Talbott. Boston, 1970.

Kiernan, Frances. *Seeing Mary Plain: A Life of Mary McCarthy*. New York, 2000.

Kimball, Jeffrey. *Nixon's Vietnam War*. Lawrence, Kansas, 1998.

King, Russell. *Land Reform*. Boulder, Colorado, 1977.

Kinnard, Douglas. *The Certain Trumpet*. McLean, Virginia, 1991.

Kissinger, Henry. *The White House Years*. Boston, 1979.

_____. *Does America Need a Foreign Policy?* New York, 2001.

_____. *Years of Renewal*. New York, 1999.

_____. *Years of Upheaval*. New York, 1982.

Komer, Robert W. *Bureaucracy at War*. Boulder, Colorado, 1986.

Krohn, Charles A. *The Lost Battalion*. Westport, Connecticut, 1993.

Kutler, Stanley I. (ed.). *Abuse of Power: The New Nixon Tapes*. New York, 1997.

_____. *Encyclopedia of the Vietnam War*. New York, 1996.

_____. *Ways of Watergate*. New York, 1995.

_____. *Watergate*. New York, 1991.

Ky, Nguyen Cao. *Twenty Years and Twenty Days*. New York, 1976.

Lacouture, Jean. *Ho Chi Minh*. Translated by Peter Wiles. New York, 1968.

Lasky, Victor. *JFK: The Man and the Myth*. New York, 1963.

Le Duan. *On Some Present International Problems*. Hanoi, 1964.

_____. *Selected Writings*. Hanoi, 1977.

_____. *This Nation and Socialism Are One*. Edited by Tran Van Dinh. Chicago, 1976.

Leckie, Robert. *The Wars Of America*. Vol. 2. New York, 1992.

Lederer, William J. and Eugene Burdick. *The Ugly American*. New York, 1958.

Lee, J. Edward, and Toby Haynsworth. *White Christmas in April: The Collapse of South Vietnam*. New York, 1999.

Leepson, Marc, with Helen Hannaford (eds.). *Dictionary of the Vietnam War*. New York, 1999.

LeGro, William E. *Vietnam From Cease Fire to Capitulation*. Washington, D.C., 1981.

Lewy, Guenter. *America in Vietnam*. Oxford, 1978.

Li Jui. *The Early Revolutionary Activities of Comrade Mao Tse-Tung*. Translated by Anthony W. Sariti. White Plains, New York, 1977.

Li, Tana, and Anthony Reid (eds.). *Southern Vietnam Under Nguyen*. Canberra, Australia, 1993.

Li, Zhisui. *The Private Life of Chairman Mao*. Translated by Tai Hung-Chao. New York, 1994.

Liebchen, Peter A. *Kontum: Battle for the Central Highlands, 30 March–10 June, 1972*. San Francisco, 1972.

Lincoln, Evelyn. *Kennedy and Johnson*. New York, 1968.

Lind, Michael. *Vietnam: The Necessary War*. New York, 1999.

Linh, Nguyen Van. *Vietnam: Urgent Problems*. Hanoi, 1988.

Lodge, Henry Cabot. *As It Was*. New York, 1976.

Logevall, Fredrik. *Choosing War*. Berkeley, California, 1999.

Loi, Luu Van, and Nguyen Anh Vu. *Le Duc Tho — Kissinger Negotiations in Paris*. Hanoi, 1996.

Lowenheim, Frances L., Harold D. Langley and Manfred Jonas (eds.). *Roosevelt and Churchill: Their Secret Wartime Correspondence*. New York, 1975.

Loye, J. F., Jr., et al. *Lam Son 719*. Christiansburg, Virginia, n.d.

Macdonald, Peter. *Giap*. New York, 1993.

MacGarrigle, George. *Taking the Offensive: October 1966 to October 1967*. Washington, D.C, 1998.

Mahony, Phillip. *From Both Sides Now*. New York, 1998.

Maneli, Mieczyslaw. *War of the Vanquished*. Translated by Maria de Gorgey. New York, 1971.

Marr, David G. *Vietnamese Tradition on Trial, 1920–1945*. Berkley, California, 1981.

Marrin, Albert. *Mao Tse-Tung and His China*. New York, 1989.

May, Ernest R., and Philip D. Seiko (eds.). *The Kennedy Tapes*. Cambridge, Massachusetts, 1997.

McAlister, John T., Jr. *Vietnam: The Origins of Revolution*. New York, 1969.

McConnell, Malcolm. *Inside Hanoi's Secret Archives*. New York, 1995.

McMaster, H. R. *Dereliction of Duty*. New York, 1997.

McNamara, Francis Terry, with Adrian Hill. *Escape with Honor: My Last Hours in Vietnam*. Washington, D.C., 1997.

McNamara, Robert, with James Blight, Thomas Biersteker and Col. Herbert Schandler. *Argument Without End*. New York, 1999.

_____. *In Retrospect*. New York, 1995.

McPherson, Harry. *A Political Education*. Boston, 1972.

Mecklin, John. *Mission in Torment*. Garden City, N.J., 1965.

Meshad, Shad. *Captain for Dark Mornings*. Playa del Rey, California, 1982.

Meyerson, Harvey. *Vinh Long*. Boston, 1970.

Miller, Merle. *Lyndon*. New York, 1980.

Miller, William J. *Henry Cabot Lodge*. New York, 1967.

Milton, David, and Nancy Dall Milton. *The Wind Will Not Subside: Years in Revolutionary China, 1964–1969*. New York, 1976.

Moore, Harold G., and Joseph Galloway. *We Were Soldiers Once— and Young*. New York, 1992.

Morris, Roger. *Haig: The General's Progress*. New York, 1982.

_____. *Richard Milhous Nixon*. New York, 1990.

Moss, George Donelson (ed.). *A Vietnam Reader*. New York, 1991.

Moyar, Mark. *Phoenix and the Birds of Prey*. Annapolis, Maryland, 1997.

Murphy, Edward F. *Dak To*. Novato, California, 1993.

Nessen, Ron. *It Sure Looks Different from the Inside*. New York, 1978.

Newman, John M. *JFK and Vietnam*. New York, 1992.

Nixon, Richard. *RN: The Memoirs of Richard Nixon*. New York, 1990.

Oberdorfer, Don. *Tet*. New York, 1984.

O'Donnell, Kenneth P., and David F. Powers, with Joseph McCarthy. *Johnny, We Hardly Knew Ye*. New York, 1972.

Olson, Gregory A. *Mansfield and Vietnam*. East Lansing Michigan, 1995.

O'Nan, Stewart (ed.) *The Vietnam Reader*. New York, 1998.

O'Neill, Robert J. *General Giap*. New York, 1969.

Osborne, Milton. *Before Kampuchea*. London, 1979.

_____. *Sihanouk*. Honolulu, 1994.

O'Toole, G. J. A. *Honorable Treachery*. New York, 1991.

Oudes, Bruce (ed.). *From the President: Richard Nixon's Secret Files*. New York, 1988.

Page, Tim. *Page After Page*. New York, 1989.

Page, Tim and John Pimlott (eds.). *Nam: The Vietnam Experience, 1965–75*. New York, 1990.

Palmer, David Richard. *Summons of the Trumpet*. San Rafael, California, 1978.

Parker, F. Charles, IV. *Vietnam: Strategy for a Stalemate*. New York, 1989.

Parker, James E., Jr. *Last Man Out*. Camden, South Carolina, 1996.

Parmet, Herbert S. *Jack: The Struggles of John F. Kennedy*. New York, 1980.

Patti, Archimedes L. *Why Vietnam?* Berkeley, California, 1980.

The Pentagon Papers as Published by the New York Times. Based upon investigative reporting by Neil Sheehan et al. New York, 1971.

Pentagon Papers Case Collection. Edited by Ann Fagan Ginger. Berkeley, California, 1975.

Perry, Mark. *Four Stars*. Boston, 1989.

Phathanothai, Sirin. *The Dragon's Pearl*. New York, 1994.

Pike, Douglas. *History of Vietnamese Communism, 1925–1976*. Stanford, California, 1978.

_____. *PAVN: People's Army of Vietnam*. Novato, California, 1986.

_____. *Viet Cong*. Cambridge, Massachusetts, 1967.

_____. *War, Peace and the Viet Cong*. Cambridge, Massachusetts, 1969.

Pilger, John, and Anthony Barnett. *Aftermath: The Struggle of Cambodia and Vietnam*. London, 1982.

Pimlott, John. *Vietnam: The Decisive Battles.* New York, 1990.

Porter, Gareth. *A Peace Denied.* Bloomington, Indiana, 1975.

_____. *Vietnam: The Politics of Bureaucratic Socialism.* Ithaca, New York, 1993.

Powers, Thomas. *The Man Who Kept the Secrets.* New York, 1979.

_____. *The War at Home.* New York, 1973.

Prados, John. *The Hidden History of the Vietnam War.* Chicago, 1995.

Pratt, John Clark (ed.). *Vietnam Voices.* New York, 1984.

Price, Raymond. *With Nixon.* New York, 1977.

Prochnau, William. *Once Upon a Distant War.* New York, 1975.

Raskin, Marcus G., and Bernard B. Fall. *The Vietnam Reader.* New York, 1965.

Reeves, Richard. *President Kennedy.* New York, 1993.

Reeves, Thomas C. *A Question of Character.* Rocklin, California, 1992.

Risner, Robinson. *The Passing of the Night.* New York, 1973.

Roosevelt, Elliott. *As He Saw It.* New York, 1946.

Roosevelt, James, and Sidney Shalett. *Affectionately, FDR.* New York, 1959.

Rostow, W. W. *The Diffusion of Power.* New York, 1972.

_____. *Getting from Here to There.* New York, 1978.

Roy, Jules. *The Battle of Dien Bien Phu.* Translated by Robert Baldick. New York, 1965.

Rudenstine, David. *The Day the Presses Stopped.* Berkeley, California, 1996.

Rusk, Dean. *As I Saw It.* As told to Richard Rusk. Daniel S. Papp (ed.). New York, 1990.

Safer, Morley. *Flashbacks.* New York, 1990.

Safire, William. *Before the Fall.* Garden City, New York, 1975.

Sainteny, Jean. *Ho Chi Minh and His Vietnam.* Translated by Herma Briffault. Chicago, 1972.

Salisbury, Harrison E. *Behind the Lines—Hanoi.* New York, 1967.

_____. *The Long March.* 1985.

_____. *Without Fear and Favor.* New York, 1980.

_____. *Vietnam Reconsidered.* New York, 1984.

Santoli, Al. *Everything We Had.* New York, 1981.

Schaffer, Howard B. *Chester Bowles: New Dealer in the Cold War.* Cambridge, Massachusetts, 1993.

Schalk, David L. *War and the Ivory Tower.* New York, 1991.

Schlesinger, Arthur, Jr. *Robert Kennedy and His Times.* 2 vols. Boston, 1978.

_____. *A Thousand Days.* New York, 1965.

Schultz, John. *Motion Will Be Denied.* New York, 1972.

Schulzinger, Robert D. *A Time for War.* New York, 1997.

Shaplen, Robert. *The Lost Revolution.* New York, 1965.

Shapley, Deborah. *Promise and Power.* Boston, 1993.

Sharp, U.S. Grant. *Strategy for Defeat.* Novato, California, 1978.

Sharp, U.S. Grant, and William Westmoreland. *Report on the War in Vietnam.* Washington, D.C., 1969.

Shawcross, William. *Sideshow.* New York, 1979.

Sheehan, Neil. *After the War Was Over.* New York, 1992.

_____. *A Bright Shinning Lie.* New York, 1988.

Shesol, Jeff. *Mutual Contempt.* New York, 1997.

Short, Philip. *Mao*. New York, 1999.

Siao-Yu. *Mao Tse-Tung and I Were Beggars*. Syracuse, New York, 1956.

Simpson, Howard R. *Dien Bien Phu*. Washington, D.C., 1994.

Sinke, Ralph E. G., Jr. *Don't Cry for Us*. Dale City, Virginia, 1984

Smith, George E. *P.O.W.: Two Years With the Vietcong*. Berkeley, California, 1971.

Smith, R. B. *An International History of the Vietnam War*. London, 1983.

Snepp, Frank. *Decent Interval*. New York, 1977.

_____. *Irreparable Harm*. New York, 1999.

Snow, Edgar. *The Lost Revolution*. New York, 1971.

_____. *Red Star Over China*. 1937. Reprint, New York, 1968.

Solberg, Carl. *Hubert Humphrey*. New York, 1984.

Sontag, Susan. *Trip to Hanoi*. New York, 1968.

Sorensen, Theodore C. *Decision Making in the White House*. New York, 1963.

_____. *Kennedy*. New York, 1965.

Sorley, Lewis. *A Better War*. New York, 1999.

Spector, Ronald H. *After Tet*. New York, 1993.

Spence, Jonathan. *Mao Zedong*. New York, 1999.

Stavis, Ralph, Richard J. Barnet and Marcus G. Raskin. *Washington Plans an Aggressive War*. New York, 1971.

Steel, Ronald. *Walter Lippmann and the American Century*. New York, 1980.

Stone, I. F. *In a Time of Torment*. New York, 1968.

_____. *Polemics and Prophecies*. Boston, 1970.

Summers, Harry G. *On Strategy*. Novato, California, 1984.

_____. *Historical Atlas of the Vietnam War*. New York, 1995.

_____. *Vietnam War Almanac*. New York, 1985.

Tang, Truong Nhu, with David Chanoff and Doan Van Toai. *A Vietnam Memoir*. San Diego, 1985.

Taylor, John M. *General Maxwell Taylor*. New York, 1989.

Taylor, Maxwell D. *Responsibility and Response*. New York, 1967.

terHorst, Jerald F. *Gerald Ford and the Future of the Presidency*. New York, 1974.

Terrill, Ross. *Mao*. New York, 1980.

Terzani, Tiziano. *Gia Phong!* New York, 1976.

Thai, Hoang Van. *How South Vietnam Was Liberated*. Hanoi, 1996.

Thao, Hoang Minh. *The Victorious Tay Nguyen Campaign*. Hanoi, 1979.

Thompson, James, with Peter Stanley and John Curtis Perry. *Sentimental Imperialists*. New York, 1981.

_____. *While China Faced West*. Cambridge, Massachusetts, 1969.

Tobin, Allen et al. *Last Flight Out*. Washington, D.C., 1997.

Tonnesson, Stein. *The Vietnamese Revolution of 1945*. London, 1991.

Topping, Seymour. *Journey Between Two Chinas*. New York, 1972.

Tornquist, David. *Vietnam Then and Now*. London, 1991.

Truong, Chinh. *The Resistance Will Win*. Hanoi, 1966.

Truong, Ngo Quang. *The Easter Offensive of 1972*. Washington, D.C., 1980.

Tuohy, William. *Dangerous Company*. New York, 1987.

Turley, G. H. *The Easter Offensive*. Annapolis, Maryland, 1985.

Ungar, Sanford J. *The Papers & The Papers*. New York, 1972.

Valenti, Jack. *A Very Human President*. New York, 1975.

Valentine, Douglas. *The Phoenix Program.* New York, 1990.
Vandiver, Frank. *Shadows of Vietnam.* College Station, Texas, 1997.
Vien, Nguyen Khac, and Phong Hien. *American Neo-Colonialism in South Vietnam (1954–1975) Socio-Cultural Aspects.* Hanoi, n.d.
_____. *Tradition and Revolution in Vietnam.* Berkeley, California, 1974.
Vogelgesang, Sandy. *Long Dark Night of the Soul.* New York, 1974.
Walters, Vernon A. *Silent Missions.* New York, 1978.
Warbey, Williams. *Ho Chi Minh.* London, 1972.
Warner, Denis. *Certain Victory: How Hanoi Won the War.* Kansas City, 1977.
Werner, Jayne S., and Luu Doan Huynh (eds.). *The Vietnam War: Vietnamese and American Perspectives.* Armonk, New York, 1993.
Westad, Odd Arne, et al. (ed.). *77 Conversations Between Chinese and Foreign Leaders on the Wars in Indochina, 1964–1977.* Washington, D.C., 1998.
Westmoreland, William. *A Soldier Reports.* New York, 1989.
White, Theodore. *The Making of the President, 1960.* New York, 1961.
_____. *The Making of the President, 1964.* New York, 1965.
_____. *The Making of the President, 1968.* New York, 1969.
_____. *The Making of the President, 1972.* New York, 1973.
Wicker, Tom. *One of Us: Richard Nixon and the American Dream.* New York, 1991.
Willbanks, James H. *Neither Peace nor Honor: Vietnamization, U.S. Withdrawal, and the Fall of South Vietnam.* Ph.D. dissertation, History, University of Kansas, 1998.
Wilson, Dick. *Zhou Enlai.* New York, 1984.
_____ (ed.). *Mao Tse-Tung in the Scales of History.* Cambridge, 1977.
Wirtz, James J. *The Tet Offensive.* Ithaca, New York, 1991.
Wyatt, Clarence R. *Paper Soldiers.* New York, 1993.
Yarborough, Colonel Tom. *Danang Diary.* New York, 1990.
Young, A. L., and G. M. Reggiani (eds.). *Agent Orange.* Amsterdam, 1988.
Young, Marilyn. *The Vietnam Wars, 1945–1990.* New York, 1991.
Zaroulis, Nancy, and Gerald Sullivan. *Who Spoke Up?* Garden City, New York, 1984.
Zasloff, Joseph J. *The Pathet Lao.* Lexington, Massachusetts, 1973.

Index

LEE COUNTY LIBRARY SYSTEM

DISCARD

3 3262 00231 5684

959.704
L
Lee
Nixon, Ford and the abondonment
   of South Vietnam

DISCARD
LEE COUNTY LIBRARY
107 Hawkins Ave.
Sanford, NC 27330   GAYLORD S